HOLD ON WORLD

HOLD ON WORLD

The Lasting Impact of

John Lennon and Yoko Ono's Plastic Ono Band,

Fifty Years On

John Kruth

Backbeat Books

Guilford, Connecticut

Backbeat Books
An imprint of The Rowman & Littlefield Publishing Group, Inc.
4501 Forbes Blvd., Ste. 200
Lanham, MD 20706
www.rowman.com

Distributed by NATIONAL BOOK NETWORK

Library of Congress Cataloging-in-Publication Data available

ISBN 978-1-4930-5235-6 (paperback)
ISBN 978-1-4930-5236-3 (e-book)

♾™ The paper used in this publication meets the minimum requirements of American
National Standard for Information Sciences—Permanence of Paper for Printed Library
Materials, ANSI/NISO Z39.48-1992

For Hal Willner, whose passion for the original in music, poetry, and comedy helped bring it to a broader audience.

Those Plastic Ono Band songs . . . they stand up to any songs that were written when I was a Beatle. Now, it may take you twenty or thirty years to appreciate that; but the fact is, these songs are as good as any fucking stuff that was ever done.

—John Lennon, 1980

People can listen to the music and make their own judgement.

—Yoko Ono, 1992

CONTENTS

INTRODUCTION
BY BILL FRISELL

So Much Happened . . . FAST

JFK was killed.
A few months later we saw
The Beatles on the Ed Sullivan Show.
1964.
So much happened . . . FAST
The Civil Rights Act was signed.
Cassius Clay beat Sonny Liston.
"A Love Supreme."
Life changing.
1968.
The world was changing every day.
MLK was killed.
Wes Montgomery died.
I heard Hendrix.
1969.
I heard Charles Lloyd.
Graduated high school.
My grandfather died.
We landed on the moon.
Woodstock.
Coming apart at the seams.
Vietnam and everything else.
So much beauty at the same time.
The music . . .
John Lennon and Yoko Ono.
"Cambridge 1969"
Wow . . . hearing this now for the first time!
Sounds like it could be today.
There was hope. A voice.
Thankful for them.

So Much Happened . . . FAST
COME TOGETHER and apart at same time.
I can't help but wish—IMAGINE where John would be . . .
Or what we would be hearing now . . .
Or where they might have taken things.
Pulling apart and putting back together.
Imagination.
He opened doors in ours and hers.
She opened doors in his and ours.
But that's just selfish.
There's SO much to be thankful for.

1

SHOCK

John Lennon was looking for a way out. He'd languished in the London suburbs long enough, bored and unfulfilled, when he suddenly found inspiration in the Zen pranks and whimsical poetry of a petite Japanese conceptual artist. Despite a razor-sharp wit and cynical streak that bordered on the sinister, John Lennon, at heart, was an incurable romantic. He fell hard for Yoko Ono, instantly turning his back on his wife, Cynthia, and six-year-old son, Julian, along with old friends and bandmates. As John later explained, meeting Yoko was like "when you first meet your first woman and leave the guys at the bar and you don't go play football anymore."

Lennon crossed paths with Ono on November 7, 1966, at the Indica Gallery in London, where she'd just finished installing a one-woman show with the vague but intriguing title of *Unfinished Paintings*. Yoko, along with her then-husband Tony Cox, had flown to London to attend a symposium titled "Destruction in Art," and she soon convinced gallery owner and first husband of Marianne Faithfull, John Dunbar, to exhibit her work.

Although it's difficult to believe, Ono, as an avant-garde artist who inhabited different spheres of consciousness, claimed to never have heard of John Lennon or the Beatles. "I didn't know who he was. And when I found out, I didn't care," she told *Look* magazine in March 1969.

Fond of puns and intellectual shenanigans of all sorts, Lennon was happy to play along with Ono's captivating mind games. "I decided that people should pay five shillings to hammer each nail [into one of the wall installations]," Yoko recalled. "But when the gallery owner told John he had to pay, he stopped for a moment and asked if he could just hammer an imaginary nail. It was fantastic. That is what my art is about. It was my game. The two of us were playing the same game."

A moment later, Lennon climbed atop a white, painted ladder and peered through a small magnifying glass, where he discovered the word *Yes* printed in tiny black letters on a panel above his head. In that instant, the all-encompassing, illogical lightning bolt of love zapped him "right between the eyes," as he later sang in his big-game hunting farce, "The Continuing Story of Bungalow Bill." The ever-impulsive John Lennon immediately threw all concern to the changing winds and took the plunge, head first, into a new life.

John would later claim he was happy Ono's work was not the typical "smash the piano with [a] hammer, break the sculpture, boring negative crap" that was in vogue at the time. "That *Yes* made me stay," he emphasized.

Whether he'd known it or not, John Lennon had been searching for Yoko Ono (whom he affectionately dubbed "Mother") ever since the night of July 15, 1958, when his troubled mum, Julia, was tragically run down by a car while crossing Menlove Avenue in Liverpool. Having already been abandoned by his ne'er-do-well father, Alf (later known as "Freddie"), John was raised by his prim and proper Aunt Mimi, who tried her best, but (thankfully) failed to instill in him the notion that playing guitar was a fine hobby but no way to make a proper living. Interestingly, Aunt Mimi gave an interview in 1981, one year after John's assassination, in which she confessed to having "battled against it for a long time" before claiming to have bought the aspiring rocker his first guitar.

The "savage genius," as author Tom Wolfe once dubbed John Lennon, grew up an angry young man, frustrated and impatient, with a propensity toward cruelty and committing occasional acts of violence. Clever as he was, Lennon apparently possessed a nasty streak that often got the best of him and anyone he deemed deserving of a tongue lashing or fist thrashing. Many of his early songs reveal an alarming harshness towards women. He openly stalked them in "I'll Get You in the End," "No Reply," and the disturbing "Run for Your Life," in which he threatened to murder his girlfriend if she dared step out of line for a moment. Lennon routinely sought revenge on his exes, bitterly warning "I'll be back again someday" in "I'll Cry Instead," while confessing to beating his woman and keeping "her apart from the things that she loved" in the bridge to his partner Paul McCartney's chipper Summer-of-Love anthem "Getting Better."

As John confided at the height of Beatlemania, he was "never cute," he was "just Lennon." Antiauthoritarian to the core, Lennon fought his way through elementary school (much of his anger and frustration was later chalked up to dyslexia), only to become an art school dropout with a hazy future. As a visual artist, Lennon was a whimsical doodler at best. His James Thurber-esque ink sketches, which amused his fellow students and teachers alike, would eventually illustrate his books of absurdist short stories and poems, published after the Beatles' popularity skyrocketed. "The

Writing Beatle," as John was dubbed, was portrayed hugging and kissing his first book, *In His Own Write* (1964), in an amusing scene from the Beatles' second film, *Help!*

In rock 'n' roll, John Lennon had finally found the perfect release for his pent-up emotions and unresolved life issues. Although a highly articulate lyricist, John often expressed himself best when screaming his lungs out on full-tilt rockers like Larry Williams's "Dizzy Miss Lizzy."

Lennon's art school pal Stu Sutcliffe was admittedly not much of a musician. But the Beatles' original bassist would play a major role in John's life, inadvertently planting the seed for what an ideal relationship with a woman could be. After Sutcliffe met the alluring photographer Astrid Kircherr in 1960 at the Kaiserkeller, a seedy dive bar in the red-light district of Hamburg, John was inspired to find a muse of his own. Astrid and a gang of friends, which included artist/bassist Klaus Voormann (best known for his cover illustration on the Beatles' 1966 release *Revolver*, as well as his simple, solid bass-playing for Manfred Mann and, later, the Plastic Ono Band), became obsessed with the Beatles, returning night after night to catch the band's wild stage show during their six-week residency at the club.

An aspiring existentialist (whom John nicknamed "The Exis"), Astrid Kircherr religiously dressed in black and constantly chain-smoked. Mesmerized by her exotic bohemian beauty, Sutcliffe was undoubtedly intrigued by the taboo of dating a German fräulein just fifteen years after the end of World War II.

Although she loved their music and energy, Astrid found the Beatles' 1950s rockabilly style dreadfully passé and soon gave Stu a radical makeover, combing his slicked-back chestnut hair down over his ears and eyes and dressing him, like herself, in a black turtleneck. Not surprisingly, the band fell over laughing at the sight of Sutcliffe coolly strolling into the club that night, resembling his German girlfriend. For Kircherr, Stu's change of style was no big deal. Klaus and a number of German boys were already wearing their hair down in what soon became the world-famous "Beatle mop top." It wasn't long before the rest of the group followed suit, except for their soon-to-be ousted drummer, Pete Best, who wanted no part of their daft neobohemian look.

Lennon (along with George and particularly Paul) mocked Stu's neophyte thumping on the bass and taunted him over his lack of commitment to the band. But painting was Sutcliffe's true passion. He and his cool German girlfriend left such an indelible impression on John that he wrote to his future wife, Cynthia Powell, raving so unabashedly about Astrid that she roiled with jealousy.

Even as the Beatles skyrocketed to "the toppermost of the poppermost," Lennon began having doubts about his steady girlfriend back in Liverpool. Like Stu—who would soon quit the group and remain in Hamburg, where he became engaged to Astrid—John yearned for a woman who was in every way his equal, someone he could artistically collaborate with and make passionate love to.

"I was hoping for a woman who would give me what I got from a man intellectually," John later said. "I wanted someone I could be meself with." That dream would have to wait a few more years—until November 1966 when he met Yoko Ono.

Whether Stu and Astrid ever had any clue how deeply they impacted the course of Lennon's life, they set the template for John and Yoko's future relationship, starting with the unthinkable notion of a Beatle dating a daughter of the much-reviled Axis Powers.

While the London *Times* initially portrayed Yoko Ono as "an attractive young woman, with long black hair and a soft shy voice," the media changed their tune once they realized John was serious. Judging her "unfit" for a Beatle, they branded her as "ugly," a judgment most likely stoked by the racist attitudes that many Brits (and Americans) still harbored toward the Japanese. While hardly frightful, Yoko's frizzy mane, drooping breasts, and naked body—which the world ogled on the alarming cover to their 1968 album, *Unfinished Music No.1: Two Virgins*—did little to dissuade the newspaper's disparaging claim. Yoko had a womanly physique in an age when the ultra-skinny British supermodel Twiggy defined feminine beauty.

Ono initially loved London, finding the English "poetic and sensitive," while the press had been "extremely kind" to her. But that was, as she pointed out, "until one of their boys got together with me."

In his *Rolling Stone* review of Yoko's *Plastic Ono Band,* the astute and brutally honest rock critic Lester Bangs nailed the dynamic that continually dogged her throughout her public life: "Not only do most people have no taste for the kind of far-out warbling Yoko specializes in; they probably wouldn't give her the time of day if she looked like [actor] Paula Prentiss and sang like Aretha [Franklin]."

Deeply hurt by both the media and his bandmates' harsh rejection of his ideal woman, Lennon confided to his old Liverpool pal Pete Shotton after he and Ono spent first their night together, "Fuck everything! Fuck the Beatles! Fuck money! I'll go live in a tent [with her] if I have to."

"The media might be ranting that Yoko was breaking up the Beatles, but the fact was they had fallen in love," their trusted assistant/personal photographer Dan Richter reckoned. "John hung on Yoko's every word. He wanted to be a conceptual artist and Yoko wanted to be a rock star. This, of course, presented a lot of problems."

Seeking sanctuary from the mounting backlash against the couple's sudden union, Paul McCartney temporarily offered Lennon and Ono his London apartment, until, feeling jilted, he left a nasty typewritten note where they were certain to find it. "You and your Jap tart think you're hot shit," the malicious message read. Although McCartney claimed he was only having "a lark," he had clearly crossed a line. Shocked and further estranged from Paul, John and Yoko moved into Ringo's flat at 34 Montagu Square.

"What power does she have over him?" Cynthia Lennon wondered, having discovered Yoko, barefoot in her bathrobe with John, casually lounging about in their kitchen after "Cyn" unexpectedly returned from a brief vacation in Greece.

While John sought an equal partner in creativity and love, he soon discovered that Yoko, most likely due to her aristocratic upbringing, thought of men as her assistants. This was a sentiment her two ex-husbands, the Japanese avant-garde pianist/composer Toshi Ichiyanagi and the American artist Tony Cox, could both attest to. John was not exaggerating when he explained his wife's attitude toward the men in her life. "I was getting very famous," Yoko told Betty Rollin of *Look* magazine. "My career was going well, but my husband [Tony Cox] and I were fighting about who would answer the phone. . . . I always thought of him as my assistant."

For Paul McCartney, George Harrison, and Ringo Starr, Yoko Ono's effect on their friend and one-time leader was both alienating and aggravating, particularly as John had flagrantly broken the band's unspoken rule of never bringing wives or girlfriends into the sanctuary of the recording studio. Lennon first invited Ono to Abbey Road during the recording of Paul's whimsical "Fool on the Hill" in September 1967. By the following year, Yoko had become a permanent fixture in the studio, glued to John's side throughout the fractious sessions for *The Beatles* (better known as the *White Album*).

"John had discovered that Yoko was willing to be his foil: his lover, attendant, teacher, and prime minister," Dan Richter explained. "Imagine how effective it was for his purpose of breaking up the *Beatles* to always have her present at recordings and meetings. This, of course, increased the howls of derision directed at her."

Cynthia Lennon once described the band as a bunch of "typical northern male chauvinists." Beatle women, she revealed, were "to be on constant call," yet simultaneously "not get in the way of their husbands." Although John first met Cyn while they both attended Liverpool Art School, he never encouraged or supported any of her creative endeavors. Once she became pregnant with their son, Julian, John felt trapped but nonetheless did "the noble thing."

As Lennon later told *Look* magazine: "The way it was with Cyn was she got pregnant. We got married. We never had much to say to each other." With a ten-pound note begrudgingly shelled out by his ever-disapproving Aunt Mimi, John purchased a plain gold band. He wed Cynthia Powell on a rainy morning on August 23, 1962, in a civil ceremony at the Mount Pleasant register office in Liverpool (the same dreary government bureau where his parents had previously tied the knot twenty-six years before). Following the service, there was a chicken dinner before the evening's gig, courtesy of Brian Epstein, John's devoted manager and best man.

* * *

Frustrated and tired of not being able to hear themselves onstage over the shrill locust cry of their fans, the Beatles decided to quit performing live, much to their manager's dismay. Lennon claimed he felt like a "performing flea" in a surrealistic circus. There was little possibility for the Beatles to develop musically under such impossible conditions—playing short sets to screaming crowds who came for the spectacle rather than to listen to the band. Although relieved to be done with the road, John quickly became a rudderless ship after the Beatles' final concert at San Francisco's Candlestick Park in August 1966. The leader of the world's most popular band wound up languishing in the London suburbs—getting high, gaining weight, and watching "the telly" day and night with a wife and son he could barely relate to. Finding the self-described "Nowhere Man" in a "large, heavily paneled, heavily carpeted mock Tudor house," journalist Maureen Cleave described Lennon as "probably the laziest person in England," claiming he could "sleep almost indefinitely" (as John confessed in his wistful "I'm Only Sleeping").

While continuing to write and sing brilliant songs that stretched the parameters of popular music with their poetic lyrics and innovative musical motifs, Lennon's growing ambivalence towards his fellow bandmates was becoming more evident. Between his failing marriage, an increasing appetite for pot and acid, and Brian Epstein's death from a barbiturate overdose on August 27, 1967, John seemed lost in a hazy world, where, as Ringo once put it, "Tomorrow Never Knows."

With Brian gone, John desperately began seeking another father figure. In the meantime, George Harrison's budding spiritual quest would led the Beatles to the lotus (though some would say "clay") feet of the Maharishi Mahesh Yogi, who temporarily filled the aching void left by Brian's death with his all-knowing answers to the many questions posed by his naïve but earnest acolytes.

While on retreat in February 1968 at the Maharishi's ashram in Rishikesh, India, John was bombarded by a steady flow of postcards from Yoko Ono, filled with strange, poetic instructions that spoke to him in ways the Hindu holy man's meditation training and philosophy never could. Brimming with sparkling metaphor, Yoko's unique imagination, sense of intuition, and simple approach to language charmed Lennon beyond the work of any of his peers—from the mad, illuminated ramblings of Bob Dylan's song/poetry to the earthy blues grooves the Rolling Stones conjured up.

"Think that snow is falling," Yoko wrote, casting her poetic spell. "Think that snow is falling everywhere all the time. When you talk with a person, think that snow is falling between you and on the person. Stop conversing when you think the person is covered by snow."

"I'm a cloud, watch for me in the sky," another postcard promised. And: "Steal a moon on the water with a bucket. Keep stealing until no moon is seen on the water," Ono coyly instructed. Yoko's poetic fragments and ethereal concepts sparked Lennon's imagination and desire. John soon began thinking of Yoko as "a woman, not just an intellectual woman."

"John was intrigued," Harrison's wife Pattie Boyd concurred in her 2008 memoir, *Wonderful Tonight*. "She was probably everything that Cynthia—and probably every other woman he'd met—was not." Boyd described Ono as "anarchic, original, afraid of nothing—and she didn't fall into the stereotype of the subservient woman that John was used to. John said he'd never known love like it, and she seemed to take the place of everyone else in his life."

Obsessed with Ono, Lennon could barely wait to return to England and fled the Maharishi's sacred sanctuary in a huff after making (what were eventually established as false) accusations that the giggling guru, whom he disparagingly dubbed "Sexy Sadie," was guilty of sexual indiscretion among his female followers.

"There was no substance to those rumors," George Harrison imparted years later in an interview for the Beatles' *Anthology*. "John was just pissed off [when he left the Maharishi's ashram]."

That fall, Lennon bankrolled an exhibition of Ono's art entitled *Yoko Plus Me: Half-a-Wind* from October 11 through November 14, 1967. The show, on view at London's Lisson Gallery, featured various pieces of living room furniture that had been painted white and inexplicably sawed in half. Lisson Gallery had originally agreed that John's patronage was meant to remain anonymous, but they couldn't resist exploiting his name in hopes of promoting the show. When somebody suggested to Yoko that she should include half of a person in the show as well, she replied, "But we are halves already," hinting that her relationship with her famous patron stretched beyond the professional.

"We were just friends. I respected her work," Lennon explained. "She was havin' trouble with her husband. I tried to teach her how to meditate." In another version of their fated meeting, John claimed Yoko had called him while searching for "scores of [his] songs for John Cage, for some book."

Yoko had been hunting down musical texts by various composers and pop musicians for a handmade book that she would bind and give to John Cage as a birthday present. Ono had originally approached Paul McCartney, the most accessible member of the band at the time, but Paul refused, claiming to never part with original scores. In turn, he suggested Yoko try John, who presented her with a colorful lyric sheet for "The Word," the Beatles' funky anthem to universal love that appeared on 1965's *Rubber Soul*. Illustrated with Lennon and McCartney's cosmic (stoned) crayon doodles, the lyrics to "The Word" were later reproduced in Cage's book *Notations*.

A certain obnoxiousness often envelops a couple deep in the initial thrall of love, particularly after they start to mirror each other's mannerisms, whether talking, dressing, or combing their hair alike. Nothing estranges old friends quicker than a clingy new girlfriend whispering in the ear of their constantly distracted pal.

"Everybody was sort of tense around us," Lennon observed while he and Yoko were in the early "glow of love." The mounting tension between John and his bandmates was clear while viewing Michael Lindsay-Hogg's dreary documentary *Let It Be*. As fractious as the recording sessions for the *White Album* had been, the Beatles' brotherhood would finally sour beyond repair during the endless filming sessions in the big, drafty dungeon of Twickenham Studios.

Paul McCartney wasn't fooling anybody with the lyrics to his groovy new swamp-rocker "Get Back," which contained his thinly veiled disdain for Yoko, as he warned "Jojo" to "Get back to where [she] once belonged."

"Yoko only wants to be accepted," Lennon pleaded with his bandmates on her behalf. "She wants to be one of us." When Ringo replied, "She's not a Beatle, John, and she never will be," Lennon dug in his heels, claiming: "Yoko is part of me now. We're John and Yoko—we're together." Starr later confessed to being deeply saddened by the thought.

"The group had problems long before Yoko came along . . . many problems," George Harrison told Dick Cavett on November 23, 1971. "We didn't break up because we weren't friends," Lennon confided to Tom Snyder in his last televised interview on the *Tomorrow* show (on April 28, 1975). "We broke up out of sheer boredom, and boredom creates tension. It got like a marriage that didn't work."

While the Beatles seemed flippant over their acrimonious breakup, it left their devoted followers disillusioned, wondering what had become of the infectious cama-raderie the Fab Four once exuded onstage, in their songs, and in their films. That giddy gush of love they originally inspired, no matter how fleeting or superficial it may have seemed, stretched beyond popular music to ultimately inspire more peaceful relations between countries, cultures, and races around the globe. While the Beatles never played behind the Iron Curtain, as their music was banned in Russia in 1964, McCartney's first performance in the USSR in May 2003 may have had more to do with ending Communism than détente. But along with the Beatles' demise went all sense of the '60s optimism.

Following the back-to-back assassinations of Dr. Martin Luther King Jr. and Bobby Kennedy in the spring of 1968, a heavy malaise began to hang over America. Despite massive protests and the reigning philosophy of peace and love, the Vietnam War continued to escalate year after year, while the nonviolent battle that Black America first waged for civil rights turned militant after the Black Panthers' attempt to feed, educate, and protect their own communities was met with brutality. Frustrated and desperate for justice, the Panthers embraced Malcolm X's philosophy, "By whatever means necessary," as their creed. In the meantime the riots at the 1968 Democratic Convention in Chicago, followed by the tragic shooting of unarmed students protesting the draft at Kent State University in May 1970, proved to middle-class White kids that they were not above the reproach of Nixon's "tin soldiers," as Neil Young dubbed the reckless National Guardsmen in his song "Ohio."

Although much had been achieved, the '60s dream came crashing down on an ominous note as Mick Jagger predicted the approaching "storm threatening [his] very life" in "Gimme Shelter." As the Rolling Stones struggled with their flamboyant founder Brian Jones's recent death, the band suddenly came face to face with the very darkness they'd evoked in songs like "Sympathy for the Devil" at the disastrous Altamont free concert on December 6, 1969.

The Stones' hastily planned free concert at Altamont Speedway, in the words of Jefferson Airplane's lead guitarist Jorma Kaukonen, was "a travesty . . . a perfect storm of incompetence, fate, and unrealistic expectations. The whole thing looked dodgy all along. There were plenty of negative signs but [the Airplane] chose to go anyway. Paul Kantner's mantra was always 'free dope, free love, free music.' It's an interesting utopian dream, but there are always bills to be paid. It's hard for me to really grasp the expectations that people at a free concert might have. As an eighty-year-old man, it occurs to me now that sometimes you really get what you pay for. They paid nothing, and that's what they got."

Meanwhile, Charles Manson and his gang of brainwashed runaways were hauled into court for their horrific murder of actress Sharon Tate, along with four friends. This took place on the very same August weekend that hordes of hippies flocked to the bucolic fields of Bethel, New York, creating an historic moment of peace, love, and music at the Woodstock Festival.

Just days before the Altamont tragedy, Susan Atkins (a.k.a. "Sadie Mae Glutz," or "Sexy Sadie" as she was known among the Manson family) delivered her testimony to the jury. She was followed by Charles Manson—once an aspiring singer/song-writer produced by Beach Boys drummer/vocalist Dennis Wilson—who declared: "The music is telling the youth to rise up against the establishment. . . . Why blame it on me? I didn't write the music." Apparently, Manson had misinterpreted Paul McCartney's hard-rocking "Helter Skelter" (originally inspired by a carnival ride) as his very own personal message from the Fab Four. Manson's twisted mind had convinced him that a race war was imminent, and if he and his "family" hoped to survive, they'd better take up arms and start to kill before being killed. The "mania" the Beatles inspired in Charlie Manson turned out to be something to truly scream about.

Meanwhile, *Let It Be* managed to pull the plug on the last vestiges of what the Clash once dubbed "phony Beatlemania." Watching the depressing film, it quickly became apparent that the lads from Liverpool no longer lived the jolly one-for-all and all-for-one life, all together "in a yellow submarine."

Although the band was officially still intact, Lennon already had one foot out the door. McCartney then announced that he was leaving the Beatles through a glib self-interview found inside the record sleeve to his eponymous new album, released on April 17, 1970. A month later *McCartney* would sell over a million copies and reach No. 1 on the charts. The dream was irrevocably over. John loved Yoko. Paul loved Linda. George loved Krishna, while Ringo loved . . . to boogie.

With the release of each new solo album by the former Beatles, it quickly became obvious how fast and far the band had grown apart. Compared with John and Yoko's avant-garde adventures and George's eclectic film soundtrack, *Wonderwall*, and *Electronic Sound*, a sonic sketchbook based on his new Moog synthesizer, were quite listenable. Much like the caricature of the mopey, loveable, can-kicking, street photographer we were introduced to in *A Hard Day's Night*, Ringo's debut album, *Sentimental Journey*, was quaint and likeable if a bit knuckleheaded.

Produced by the meticulous George Martin, *Sentimental Journey* offered a collection of old favorites once adored by Ringo's mother, Elsie. Released on March 27, 1970, Starr's sappy valentine helped to unwittingly spark a retro trend that inspired a slew of singers to reinterpret the enduring standards of their parent's generation.

Sixth months later, Ringo would return with a schmaltzy C&W tribute entitled *Beaucoups of Blues*. Beyond his gunslinger-inspired stage name, Ringo Starr's passion for country music was first revealed with the Beatles' earnest cover of Buck Owens's "Act Naturally," which they followed with a country rocker of their own: "What Goes On." (Starr received a rare cowriting credit with John and Paul for this, for contributing "about five words" as he later recalled.) Ringo would also write the hapless hoedown "Don't Pass Me By," which would end up on the *White Album*.

Following in the footsteps of the Byrds' surprising foray into country music, *Sweetheart of the Rodeo*, in 1968, and Dylan's much maligned *Nashville Skyline*, Ringo was determined to forge his own country-rock opus. He flew to "Music City" for a three-day session between June 25 and 27, 1970. "I'd learn five songs in the morning and record five songs that night," Starr explained. "It was really good." Produced by Pete Drake, whose lush pedal-steel guitar hugged the verses of Dylan's latest hit single, "Lay Lady Lay," the album featured a who's who of legendary Nashville session pros. They included Charlie Daniels; Junior Huskey; Ben Keith; and Charlie McCoy; as well as Elvis's back-up vocalists, the Jordanaires; and drummer D. J. Fontana (who maintained Ringo possessed "the greatest conception of tempo" he'd ever heard). But beyond the good-time honky-tonk groove of "Loser's Lounge," Starr's woeful vocals sometimes made *Beaucoups of Blues* a chore to listen to.

While the album was initially well received (even John dubbed it "a good record," and was relieved he "didn't feel as embarrassed" by it as he'd been by *Sentimental Journey*), it wasn't until a year later in 1971 that Ringo found his way back to the pop charts with "It Don't Come Easy," cowritten and produced by George Harrison (although he remained uncredited). Another single/collaboration with George, "Back Off Boogaloo," followed a year later in March 1972. Infatuated with diminutive glam rocker Marc Bolan of T. Rex, Starr directed the charming but patchy documentary *Born to Boogie*. In return for his sophomoric cinematic efforts, Ringo, with Harrison's help, scored a Top 10 hit with "Back Off Boogaloo," inspired by a bit of Bolan's jive talk.

Released in 1973, Starr's third album, *Ringo*, was another hit, thanks to a lot of help from his friends. All three of his ex-bandmates not only sang and played on the record but also provided a clutch of catchy new songs to the mix, including John's delightful "I'm the Greatest."

Inspired by watching the national premiere of *A Hard Day's Night* on the BBC on December 28, 1970, Lennon sat down at the piano and quickly knocked off a nostalgic ditty built around the popular catch phrase of loud-mouthed world champion boxer/proto-rapper Muhammad Ali: "I'm the Greatest." The next day John recorded the song at his Ascot home studio along with another tune with the working title "Make Love Not War" (later to become "Mind Games" in October 1973). Driven by a funky keyboard vamp, "I'm the Greatest" was tailor made for Starr's bumbling delivery. If Lennon had dared to release such a conceited sentiment, the world would have been appalled. But coming from Starr, it was nothing less than charming.

While *Ringo* contained the new single "Photograph" (written and originally recorded by George Harrison), Starr's love of country music was well represented with the foot-stompin' fiddle tune "Sunshine Life for Me" (also penned by George), which featured members of the Band.

In December 1969, having sufficiently alienated himself from his bandmates (although his instinctual mistrust of Allen Klein turned out to be on target), Paul McCartney began secretly recording his debut solo album on a four-track Studer tape deck in a makeshift studio at his home in St. John's Wood. Determined to prove he was the undisputable musical genius behind the Beatles, Paul transformed into an indomitable one-man band of the likes rarely seen before in popular music, except for Stevie Wonder. Making a true "solo" album, McCartney did everything himself. He recorded an impressive array of guitar, piano, bass, and drum parts, as well as laying down all lead and harmony vocals except for the occasional wispy vocal from his wife, photographer Linda Eastman. But beyond the emotional jolt of "Maybe I'm Amazed," *McCartney* was, for the most part, a lightweight affair, comprised of rejects from the *White Album* and *Let It Be*, along with a few instrumental sketches that stretched all the way back to the band's gigs on the Reeperbahn.

When queried about Paul's solo efforts, Ringo replied, "I feel sad with Paul's albums." Although Starr considered his former band member "a great artist, incredibly creative [and] clever," he added that ultimately he "disappoints me on his albums."

While McCartney worked alone in secrecy, Harrison's opus, *All Things Must Pass*, was a celebration, bringing together an assortment of musicians he loved and respected. With the release of *Abbey Road*, the Beatles' "Dark Horse" had come in first with a pair of hits. "Something" and "Here Comes the Sun" would at long last prove, if there was still any doubt, that George's songwriting was finally on par with, if not beyond that of, the domineering team of Lennon and McCartney.

All Things Must Pass

Following the madness of Beatlemania, short flings with LSD, and transcendental meditation, George Harrison discovered his bliss at the lotus feet of Lord Krishna. Although Harrison never went so far as to shave his head or don saffron robes, he became what he described as "a plain-clothes devotee." He donated enormous sums of money to buy a hefty piece of real estate known as "The Manor" and restore it as a lavish temple for Krishna devotees on the outskirts of London. Harrison also began composing songs that openly celebrated the blue, flute-playing shepherd boy worshipped by millions of Hindus as the human incarnation of God. Adopting a vegetarian diet and voraciously studying the *Bhagavad Gita*, George practiced japa-yoga (the ritual chanting of Lord Krishna's name on a rosary of 108 knobby wooden beads).

Appearing as a special guest with American-roots rockers Delaney and Bonnie Bramlett on their 1969 European tour, Harrison begged Delaney to show him the finer points of writing a gospel song. Sitting down with a pair of acoustic guitars, they began to strum, getting into a groove with the Edwin Hawkins Singers' rapturous "Oh Happy Day." Joined by Bonnie and Rita Coolidge, George's praise song soon took shape with a repetitive minor-chord vamp reminiscent of the Chiffons' 1963 hit "He's So Fine" as everyone chimed in on the chorus: "Oh my lord, my sweet lord, hallelujah." Inspired by his new-found passion for Krishna, "Hallelujah" quickly morphed into "Hare Krishna."

Gorgeous as the song was, Harrison's valentine to his "Sweet Lord" eventually landed him in court with a hefty plagiarism suit, costing him nearly $600,000 for having allegedly pilfered the melody of "He's So Fine." Although Delaney claimed that Harrison's tune was "completely different," he would later confess he felt guilty for not having pointed out the song's obvious similarities to his friend.

George had already earned a reputation for pinching musical ideas. Originally written as an ode to Lord Krishna but then changed to Pattie to quell any doubt about his sexual orientation, Harrison's chart-topping hit "Something" was initially inspired by James Taylor's "Something in the Way She Moves." George had, in fact, lifted the entire opening line of Taylor's song. But Taylor figured it was a small price to pay in return for the Beatles having launched his career with *James Taylor*, the beautiful self-titled album produced by Peter Asher and released on their prestigious Apple label. (The album also featured Paul McCartney plunking a bouncy bass line on Taylor's "Carolina in My Mind.")

Meanwhile "My Sweet Lord" took the Krishna's Maha (Great) Mantra chant to the top of the charts. "My Sweet Lord" wasn't the only song dedicated to Krishna on Harrison's *All Things Must Pass*. Over a Phil Spector-produced "wall of sound," Harrison ("The Quiet One") assured his faithful fans that peace of mind was within their reach by simply "chanting the name of the Lord," as he sang in "Awaiting on You All."

"It's enough to make me believe in God or something," Lennon quipped, obviously miffed by "My Sweet Lord" receiving heavy radio play as compared to his recently released "Mother." Many of the album's tunes—including the title track, "The Art of Dying," "Hear Me Lord," "Isn't It a Pity," and "Beware of Darkness"—contained insightful (and not overly preachy) musical statements about the dismal failure of the material world.

Yet Harrison was attacked by the press and friends alike for his sanctimonious attitude. Around the Apple offices, George was secretly referred to as "His Lectureship" by those who found his lyrics and conversation too self-righteous and dour for their liking. "I'm sick of all these young people boogying around, wasting their lives," George groused. "Let's face it," he said regarding his spiritual quest. "If you're going to have to stand up and be counted, I'd rather be one of the devotees of God than one of the straight, so-called sane or normal people."

Harrison had released two earlier solo projects before the massive success of *All Things Must Pass*: the deliciously mystical soundtrack to *Wonderwall*, Joe Massot's trippy film about an aging professor who spies on his neighbor—a young, lovely model—through a crack in the wall; and 1969's *Electronic Sound*, a self-indulgent foray into the newly developed and marketed Moog synthesizer. While Beatle fans were curious about *Wonderwall*, *Electronic Sound* (released on the Beatles' new experimental Zapple label, along with Lennon and Ono's controversial *Unfinished Music No. 2: Life with the Lions*) was instantly deemed a throwaway.

To make matters worse, the bulk of *Electronic Sound* had allegedly been pilfered from electronic music pioneer Bernie Krause. In his memoir, *Into a Wild Sanctuary,* Krause wrote that he'd gone to England to teach Harrison how to use the Moog. To help him understand the complex workings of the new instrument, Krause created a smattering of recorded sounds and programs. George guaranteed Bernie that if he used any of his work, both credit and payment would be forthcoming. "Trust me, I'm a Beatle," Harrison assured him. Disillusioned by George's appropriation of his music, Bernie demanded his name be stricken from the album cover credits. He soon quit the pop music world for good, preferring to spend his time in the wild, recording the natural sounds of whales, gorillas, and polar bears.

According to Derek and the Dominoes' Bobby Whitlock, who played keys on much of *All Things Must Pass*, John Lennon had been invited to attend a listening session for Harrison's new album and "was completely blown away. . . . He was beaming from ear to ear." Yet John's appraisal of his former bandmate's work was far less generous when he later groused to *Rolling Stone* that he "wouldn't play that kind of music at home."

Released in England on November 27, 1970, *All Things Must Pass*—a specially priced three-record set—was clearly a milestone for Harrison. Essentially a double album, it included a reprise of the weepy "Isn't It a Pity," along with a curious, listen-once disc of loose rock improvs entitled *Apple*

Jam. All Things Must Pass (along with George's posthumously released album *Brainwashed*) remains among the best solo releases in the Beatles' catalogue.

From a marketing perspective, a three-record set spelled certain disaster. But much to John's chagrin, it quickly eclipsed his much-anticipated *Plastic Ono Band*, which contained little in the way of radio-friendly pop tunes.

Lennon's condescending attitude toward Harrison had been shaped long ago during the band's early days in Liverpool. As Lennon told Jann Wenner in *Rolling Stone*, "George is ten years younger than me . . . or some shit like that [about two and a half years actually]. I couldn't be bothered with him when he first came around. He used to follow me around like a bloody kid."

But "the bloody kid" had clearly arrived . . . and in good company, with Phil Spector producing, Eric Clapton secretly playing guitar on most of the album, and Bob Dylan's touch on a pair of tunes, including "If Not for You" and the cowritten "I'd Have You Anytime." "Behind That Locked Door," a country-flavored number, was written for Bob on the eve of his triumphant return to the stage at the Isle of Wight Festival with the Band in August 1969.

While recording *All Things Must Pass*, George faced a variety of unforeseen challenges, particularly the erratic behavior of his producer, Phil Spector, whose alleged heavy consumption of brandy rendered him useless at times in the studio. Harrison later claimed he "ended up doing about 80 percent of the work" himself.

"Phil stayed in the control room the whole time we were recording the album," Bobby Whitlock recalled. "Phil had this hand-held phaser with big RCA knobs. He wanted to phase everything! The piano . . . the drums . . . everything. . . . He was one funny mofo. But he was really upset that he couldn't bring his gun into England."

Notoriously paranoid, Phil garnered a reputation for being well-armed. On February 3, 2003, Spector's love of gunplay spiraled out of control when he murdered actress Lana Clarkson in his suburban fortress known as "the Pyrenees Castle," which stands surrounded by trees, high on a hill, above the Los Angeles suburb of Alhambra.

But Harrison had the last laugh in January 2001 when he rereleased *All Things Must Pass* after stripping away the superfluous layers of Spector's sonic icing. Coaxed back onstage on April 6, 1992, for his first (and last) performance in England since 1969—to benefit the utopian political collective known as the Natural Law Party—George admitted he "enjoyed playing," although he quickly disparaged the notion of performing before a live audience. "It's unhealthy to be a star," Harrison grumbled, and then bitterly denounced his stint with the Beatles as "a waste of time." Apparently, playing in the world's most popular rock 'n' roll band led him to "getting caught up in this big tangle and creating more and more karma. . . . I wouldn't want to do it again." Undoubtedly, he'd been inspired by the Hare Krishna philosophy that one's true purpose on this earth is to worship Lord Krishna by chanting his holy names, then to move on to eternal life in the Spiritual Sky. While a very high-minded goal, it is quite difficult for most mortals to achieve.

2

YOU BECOME NAKED

No three words better sum up John Lennon's metamorphosis from "charismatic/ smart aleck Beatle" to "dedicated truth seeker/holy fool/peace warrior" than the phrase Yoko Ono whispered toward the end of "Revolution #9": "You become naked." The most bizarre and disturbing track on the Beatles' 1968 double-album opus the *White Album* (if not in their entire oeuvre), "Revolution #9" perfectly reflected the chaos that engulfed the world at the time, with a swirling cacophony of nonsensical sounds and voices that leapt out at the listener like a swarm of malevolent spooks from the funhouse of John Lennon's mind.

Earlier on the *White Album*, John bared his heart and soul on "Julia," a tender ballad written for his mother, while the stark "Yer Blues" and "I'm So Tired" were brutal reflections of his ragged psychological state. While many of John's new songs revealed a fresh, "heavy" feel, he was not to be outdone by Paul, whose proto-metal rocker "Helter Skelter" left us with blisters on our eardrums.

"I identified with the depth of his problems, as expressed in 'Yer Blues.' That song kind of summed it all up for me," LA-based singer/songwriter Peter Case told me. "John was offering companionship to the mad youth of the world when he sang, 'I'm lonely, want to die.'"

***

With the release of *Rubber Soul* in December 1965, the Beatles had suddenly burst out of their "cute" cocoon and begun flapping their new multicolored wings toward a strange, uncharted horizon. Gone were their nicely tailored suits and carefully coiffed mop tops, replaced by casual jeans and suede and a fresh approach to writing and recording their music. Drugs undoubtedly had something to do with it. Bob Dylan had allegedly opened the door after introducing the band to their first taste of pot. Soon after, their hipster dentist (whom John and George feared was a "swinger" attempting to lure them into an orgy) dosed their coffee with lysergic-laced sugar cubes. While LSD (and Tibetan Buddhism) triggered the mystical trance of "Tomorrow

Never Knows" along with the backwards gibberish on the coda of "Rain," the Beatles' hallucinatory daydream, "A Day in the Life" (from their 1967 masterpiece *Sergeant Pepper's Lonely Hearts Club Band*), with its swirling cacophony of trumpets and violins, would singlehandedly throw open the door to a new frontier of sonic possibility. Never before had a piece of pop music so boldly reflected the psychological state of the song's singer, illuminating the lyrics with blaring horns and swooping violins that all spiraled toward a mad climax.

* * *

Aggravated by McCartney's announcement in the press that the world's most popular band was through, John wasted no time moving on with his life. Meanwhile John's bandmates, friends, and peers stood by watching, gobsmacked as he appeared to commit artistic and commercial suicide before their very eyes. It seemed like Lennon, with Ono's help and encouragement, was deliberately out to destroy the Beatles' legacy while redefining pop culture in their own new, peculiar image.

Even Queen Elizabeth noticed something odd about England's favorite pop stars when she confided to EMI's chairman, "Sir Joe" (as John glibly called him) Lockwood: "The Beatles are turning awfully funny, aren't they?"

Although John had yet to officially announce his intentions of quitting the band and leaving his wife, he'd already begun to move on with Yoko. Adopting a defensive attitude from the start, Lennon claimed they were just "two innocents, lost in a world gone mad." Believing everyone was against them was both romantic and naïve. His most devoted fans stoically stood by, but no matter how weird things got, Lennon/Ono failed to realize that their narcissistic projects and performances would trigger such an ugly response.

However outrageous their fragmented "Unfinished" songs and convoluted tape loops got (many of which were reportedly the handiwork of John's old pal, Pete Shotton), their sonic collages paled in comparison to the cover photo for their first collaboration, *Unfinished Music No. 1: Two Virgins*. Portrayed standing nude, side by side, John and Yoko look a bit puffy and terribly unsexy. Some considered the image the grossest photographic crime of the classic rock era. John bluntly described themselves as "two slightly overweight ex-junkies."

While both John and Yoko were married to others at the time, they appeared clueless about how their respective spouses (or younger Beatles fans) might react to their sudden and very public liaison. Of all Lennon's scandalous antics (from the

"Bigger than Jesus" quip to his flippant retort of "two queers" when asked about the inspiration for "Eleanor Rigby"), John posing with his penis brazenly on display for the whole world to see ignited an array of guffaws, disgust, and outrage.

First released in America on November 11, 1968, followed by the UK edition on the 29th, *Unfinished Music No. 1: Two Virgins* was treated like pornography—wrapped and distributed in a brown paper bag after EMI, Apple Records' parent company, refused to touch it. For John, the scandalous photo "just seemed natural for us. . . . We're all naked really," he said nonchalantly. For Yoko, nudity was nothing new or outrageous, as she belonged to an "artistic community where a painter [Yves Klein] did a thing . . . rolling a naked woman with blue paint on her body on a canvas." "That was going on at the time," she explained. "The only difference was [on the *Two Virgins* album cover] we were going to stand together. . . . I liked that concept."

Julia Baird, John's half sister, recalled Aunt Mimi's typically British response, declaring that it would have been better for all concerned had John and Yoko decided to "stay dressed." But as journalist/author Jonathan Cott clarified, "The point [that Aunt Mimi and so many others missed] is that the act of taking off one's clothes is merely a metaphor for uncovering the self."

Lennon's bold leap into the unpredictable and unprofitable realm of the avant-garde disappointed and confounded fans and critics alike. After reaching a modicum of success, most artists tend to repeat the formula that led them there. But Lennon's initial abandonment of popular music went far beyond the stylistic experiments of musical chameleons like Bob Dylan, David Bowie, or Miles Davis, who routinely reinvented themselves following each new milestone they achieved.

After John Coltrane's lilting interpretation of Rodgers and Hammerstein's "My Favorite Things" brought him worldwide fame in 1961, the great jazz saxophonist quickly turned his back on the possibility of any further commercial success and dove headfirst into the uncharted waters of free jazz. Inspired by the radical innovations of Ornette Coleman and Cecil Taylor, Coltrane discarded playing the warm ballads that brought him fame to stretch the limits of his fans' tastes, imaginations, and patience with his spiritually fueled improvisations. Coltrane was a man on a mission, whose violent, screaming tenor sax perfectly reflected the chaos of the world. His passion for free jazz soon led him to gigs at half-empty clubs after having achieved the near-impossible: a jazz musician with a hit song who made the cover of *Time* magazine. Lennon, of course, had a much larger financial cushion, as well as the ability to bounce back at any time by writing and singing the occasional chart-topping hit—from "Imagine" to "Mind Games" (1973) to "Whatever Gets You Through the Night" (1974)—to keep his confused fans from finally deserting him.

3

YEAR 1 AP (AFTER PEACE)

Either you get it, or you don't.

—John Lennon

"After Yoko and I met, I didn't realize I was in love with her. I was still thinking it was an artistic collaboration, as it were—producer and artist," Lennon told David Sheff in one of his final interviews for *Playboy* in 1980. "My ex-wife [Cynthia] was away . . . and Yoko came to visit me [at their suburban Weybridge home in the stockbroker belt of London].

"Instead of making love, we went upstairs and made tapes. I had this room full of different tapes where I would write and make strange loops and things like that for the Beatles' stuff. So, we made a tape all night. She was doing her funny voices and I was pushing all different buttons on my tape recorder and getting sound effects. And then as the sun rose, we made love and that was *Two Virgins*."

On March 20, 1969, John and Yoko flew to Gibraltar for their wedding. "At first, I didn't want to get married . . . we got such a kick out of just bein' in love," John explained. "But then . . . we thought the baby was comin'." (Yoko miscarried John Lennon II, she claimed, due to the "strain of our two divorces.")

Following their hasty nuptials, Lennon/Ono hopped the next plane to Amsterdam, where they stayed in bed for the next week (from March 25 to 31) in room 902 at the Hilton. Their public "honeymoon," as Lennon explained, was essentially "a commercial for news about peace, instead of war. . . . I don't expect the prime ministers or kings and queens of the world to suddenly change their policies just because John and Yoko have said, 'Peace brother!' It's youth we're addressing. Youth is the future! If we can get inside their minds and tell them to think in favor of nonviolence, we'll be satisfied. What's the point of getting fame as a Beatle and not using it?" John begged. Perhaps it was best that Brian Epstein had passed away rather than having a stroke trying to subdue the Lennon/Ono peace campaign.

While camping out in bed in the name of peace, John courted additional controversy after publishing a set of fourteen stone lithograph prints (in limited editions of three hundred) depicting everything from the couple's wedding ceremony to their steamy lovemaking. Most objectionable to the British establishment were John's sketches of the twosome enjoying the delights of oral sex. Dubbed "Bag One," and packaged in a stylish white vinyl briefcase, Lennon's portfolio of fine-line drawings were immediately seized by the authorities and put on trial for obscenity, for which he was ultimately acquitted.

The entire first side of Lennon/Ono's *Wedding Album* (released October 20, 1969, in America and November 7 in the UK) was comprised of John and Yoko repetitively calling each other's names. This sometimes humorous but mostly boring routine was inspired by radio personality/comedian Stan Freberg's *John and Marsha* routine. "It really makes your hair stand on end," Lennon confessed. The album's second side documented their week-long March residency at the Amsterdam Hilton. Constructed from interviews about their peace campaign, fragments of conversations, and various sounds, the album included an early version of Yoko's "John, John, Let's Hope for Peace."

In search of a new home and studio space where they could live and create together, Lennon/Ono purchased a three-hundred-year-old mansion known as Tittenhurst Park for £145,000 on May 4, 1969. It was situated on seventy-two acres. John, unlike George Harrison, had little interest in gardening. Instead, "the Krishna people," as he explained, would "farm some of the land" in return for allowing their itinerant Swami Prabhupada to stay in the couple's boathouse while he was based in London. "We're hoping to grow nonchemical food," John said. "Maybe we can sell it at Harrods." But the arrangement with the swami and his crew of spiritual gardeners did not last long.

While notoriously lazy, Lennon, the author of dream-inspired songs like "I'm Only Sleeping" and "Watching the Wheels," was hardly a homebody. He claimed to "get more pleasure from [his collection of] old 78s than from reveling in the size and glory of [his] home." "It means nothing to me," he said.

On May 9, 1969, the experimental/avant-garde division of Apple Records, dubbed "Zapple," released Lennon/Ono's *Unfinished Music No. 2: Life with the Lions* along with George Harrison's weird and wonky *Electronic Sound.* The label also promised an impressive roster of spoken-word albums by comedian/free-speech activist Lenny Bruce and cream-of-the-crop San Francisco poets including Richard

Brautigan, Michael McClure, and Lawrence Ferlinghetti, which sadly never saw the light of day.

The previous October, Yoko had been admitted to the Queen Charlotte Hospital in Hammersmith, where she suffered another miscarriage. "On the cover [photograph of *Unfinished Music No. 2: Life with the Lions*] we're having my [sic] miscarriage and we were arrested on the other side. . . . We're like a newspaper," John explained. But like the daily tabloids, Lennon/Ono's first three collaborations (except for the collector or hardcore fan) were both disposable and quickly forgotten.

Photographed by Susan Wood, the album's cover portrayed Yoko as a sad-eyed, stormy-haired Madonna, lying in bed with her blue-jeaned husband faithfully camped on an air mattress beside her. Wood remembered Yoko beneath the mound of covers, "trying to stay quiet and calm and prevent the miscarriage," while John was "so amazingly supportive of her."

Recalling the photo shoot for the March 1969 issue of *Look* magazine, Wood described how "they look absolutely delighted with each other. . . . Either that or they're just so stoned, they are thrilled with everything." Journalist Betty Rollin recalled John "as so pale. But he seems tranquil, so settled in a nice way . . . having one of his glassy-eyed daydreams (I think that's what they are)," never considering for a moment that her favorite Beatle might have been high on junk. And while sympathetic to John, Rollin, a former roommate of Ono's at Sarah Lawrence, was rather catty when comparing a pregnant Yoko to the husky, gap-toothed actor Ernest Borgnine.

Yoko would express how shocked and hurt she'd been by Betty Rollin's callous remarks on *The Dick Cavett Show*, claiming the article had been "very important" to her as it "introduced [her] to America." Ono explained how she'd trusted Rollin: "She came, and I thought, well, since we are friends, I should cook for her. So, I made a nice lunch," which Rollin described in her piece with everyone sitting "cross-legged on the floor" wolfing Yoko's macrobiotic vegetable patties.

Ono was on target regarding the influence Rollin's feature in *Look* would have on American youth. As singer/songwriter/guitarist Peter Case recalled, "There was an article about them in *Look* magazine, around the time of the *White Album*, with a photo spread that made a big impression on me. I really admired them . . . John with his girl and guitar in a big house where nobody could tell him what to do. It helped clarify my ideas about life at the time. Of course, my image of him was rubbish. He was mad, painfully insane, destroying his mind with drugs, about to break up his great band. But that flux was part of what was great about him. I would consciously, and unconsciously, imitate all of that before too long myself."

The story of Yoko's miscarriage and the lack of accommodations for her famous husband were chronicled with their dissonant lullaby "No Bed for Beatle John." In a wistful, childlike voice, Ono improvised a lilting melody evocative of traditional Japanese folk songs, with lyrics provided by a recent newspaper article. John responded to Yoko's "call," singing in a somber, monk-like drone words from another newspaper article that detailed his impending divorce from Cynthia.

A four-minute, forty-two-second slice of "life as art," the original "No Bed for Beatle John" was followed by a five-minute recording of the beating heart of Lennon/Ono's doomed baby, John Lennon II.

In 2016 Yoko released *Yes, I'm a Witch Too*, a double album featuring a striking remix of "No Bed for Beatle John" by Ebony Bones, who weaved Yoko's original haunting vocals into a dark sonic tapestry of sweeping keyboards that combined elements of electronica with a punchy afro-beat groove.

Clocking in at twenty-six and a half minutes, *Life with the Lions'* entire first side was comprised of a single track titled "Cambridge 1969," which had been recorded live at Lady Mitchell Hall, Cambridge University, on Sunday, March 2, 1969. Douglas Oliver, who attended the concert, recalled the event as "an extraordinary experience," finding Ono and Lennon's performance "strange and chilling." "At no time did the music become comforting," he observed in his review for the *Cambridge Evening News*.

Lennon/Ono's rough-edged avant-garde collaborations shocked and disoriented many of John's fans who adored the Beatles' warm, gorgeous harmonies. While Ono's tortured screams can be instantly dismissed as strange, horrific noise, the sheer stamina and emotional depth of her vocalizing on "Cambridge 1969" is remarkable. There is something pure and psychically scouring about this music, suggestive of Albert Ayler's scorching saxophone or the "white heat" that the Velvet Underground once unleashed on small crowds in New York and Boston clubs.

Blistering and unnerving, "Cambridge 1969" is demanding stuff to listen to. Like Lou Reed's 1975 release, *Metal Machine Music*, it is a nerve-rattling experiment in the textures and tonalities of raw, unfiltered sound. Yet "Cambridge 1969" remains as startlingly fresh today as the day it was recorded. While this music is clearly not for most folks, it does have its champions. Wayne Coyne of the Flaming Lips once praised Lennon/Ono's first public performance as "uncompromising and confrontational . . . rock's most disturbing performance-art jam."

In 2007 Coyne edited and remixed "Cambridge 1969" for Yoko's *Yes, I'm A Witch*, laying down a hard, grooving rhythm section with undulating keyboards, while keeping Yoko's shrieks and John's feedback at the forefront of the mix to create a new track for a new generation of fearless listeners.

"We had never done anything like it before," John explained. "I was invited [by Yoko] to Cambridge to do . . . a sort of avant-garde number and they didn't realize we were together." Yoko had asked John, "'Well, are you going to bring a band?' I replied, 'Well, *I'm* the band. . . . But don't tell them.'"

"People were looking and saying, 'Is it? Is it?' I just had a guitar and amp and that was the first time I played that style," Lennon said, recalling the scene. "I just turned up my guitar and blew my mind out. She blew hers out and either you get it, or you don't."

With his hollow-body blond Epiphone Casino guitar pointed directly at his amplifier, John knelt with his back to the crowd, conjuring a barrage of haunted feedback, while Yoko screamed and yowled an undecipherable sonic alphabet of nonsense syllables . . . much to the audience's shock and dismay. As a seasoned performance artist, Yoko's source of expression drew heavily from personal experience. She once explained that the inspiration for her bloodcurdling screams was carved into her consciousness as a child, after hearing her family's maid imitating a young mother's screams while giving birth. Unbeknownst to her at the time, Yoko had already mastered the primal scream technique that John would soon discover through Dr. Arthur Janov's primal scream therapy.

"The audience was very weird," John groused. "All these sort of intellectual artsy-fartsies from Cambridge . . . were uptight because the rock 'n' roll guy was there. It's just pure sound . . . because what else can you do when a woman's howling? You just go along with it, right? It's just us expressing ourselves, like a child does," Lennon said, foreshadowing their sessions that would take place a year later with Janov in California.

Scheduled to follow Yoko's performance was the Danish free-jazz saxophonist and composer John Tchicai, who'd played and recorded with fiery improvisors like Archie Shepp, Albert Ayler, and John Coltrane. Tchicai, along with percussionist John Stevens (a founding member of the Spontaneous Music Ensemble) and bassist Barre Phillips, were invited by John and Yoko to join them. Unfortunately, their contribution to the final recording was minimal, as they didn't dive into the sonic fray until its final six minutes. And as they played acoustic instruments, they were barely audible in the mix, drowned out by John's searing guitar and Yoko's hair-raising shriek.

"John had a big alarm clock," Tchicai later recalled in a 2010 interview, "and when they started performing, he set it to ring at a certain time—that was the signal for the end of their part."

"I just hung around and played feedback, and people got very upset because they recognized me [and wondered] 'What's he doing here?'" Lennon said. Inspired by his wild wife, John began fervently stretching the boundaries of the popular music he once defined. But he was both surprised and disappointed to discover that people always expected them to "stay in [their] bag. . . . When she tried to rock, they said, 'What's she doing here?' And when I went with her and tried to be the instrument . . . just be her band, like a sort of Ike Turner to her Tina—only her Tina was a different, avant-garde Tina—well, even some of the jazz guys got upset."

According to British musician/author David Toop, who went backstage after the performance in hopes of meeting John and Yoko, "There was a lot of tension with Lennon feeling like he and Yoko had been disrespected by people who didn't understand what they were trying to do." Toop recalled that the "Natural Music Concert Workshop" (which also featured a set by guitarist John McLaughlin) was far from the "avant-garde lovefest" that many have made it out to be. "It was a weird, fragmented, tense, and chaotic event."

While Ono's name appeared on the poster, no one expected that John Lennon would be joining her. As concert producer Anthony Barnett recalled, "It turned into a big occasion" for the crowd, comprised mostly of college students who'd been encouraged "to bring their own small instruments to play." Barnett felt that "Cambridge, 1969" "was in no way a reflection of the concert as a whole. In my view, Lennon was trying to show off and be more avant-garde than anyone in avant-garde music."

Jamming with Yoko came naturally to John, an expression of his love. And for the time being he was in the privileged position where his fame and fortune allowed for whatever self-indulgent happenings they might dream up. As Lester Bangs observed, Lennon/Ono were "two rich waifs awash in the avant-garde."

"What we're saying is make your own music!" John said, explaining the idea behind the "Unfinished Music" series—as they called the series of three avant-garde recordings released throughout 1969.

While the concept seemed superficial, Yoko has continually maintained that "Everything in the universe is unfinished." "Of course, that's taken from classical music . . . Schubert's 'Unfinished Music,'" Ono told WNYC's *Spinning on Air*'s host David Garland years later in May 2012.

Composed six years before his death in 1828 at age 31, Franz Schubert complet-ed just two movements of his "Unfinished" *Symphony No. 8 in B Minor*. Early drafts reveal that the composer intended to finish all four movements that traditionally comprise a symphonic work, but the "Unfinished" piece continues to remain an enigma, particularly as Schubert managed to write his "Great" *Symphony No. 9 in C Major*, along with a variety of songs and theater pieces, despite his deteriorating health (whether due to typhoid fever or syphilis).

Over one hundred years later, Lennon/Ono were intrigued and inspired enough by the idea to create their own "Unfinished Music" series, although their concept, as Yoko pointed out, "was quite different," as the work was intentionally left incomplete in hopes of inspiring people to "put their own sounds on it too."

As John explained at the time: "We're not giving you a finished product, wrapped up in a bit of paper, saying, 'Here you are. . . . Aren't we clever? Here's a nice, finished box of chocolates for you.' We're giving you a box, maybe, with a few chocolates [so that] you can make your own."

But this seemingly haphazard approach to recording and marketing quickly backfired, alienating the bulk of Lennon's fans who'd been greatly anticipating his "solo" projects. On the other hand, Yoko, an avant-garde artist, was used to being ignored and misunderstood, knowing all too well that rejection just came with the job. And if her work somehow failed to befuddle and aggravate the art world or chase people from the concert hall, then no one from her peers to the press would muster an ounce of respect for her.

And now John Lennon, one of the world's most popular musicians, with mil-lions of fans who hung on each new lyric and melody that spilled from his lips, would soon become guilty by association. John, the Beatles' self-described "dream weaver," watched, perplexed, as each new album he released was routinely outsold by his for-mer bandmates . . . even Ringo.

Yet Lennon relished the experience of playing live music with his wife. Not only was he having fun, but it also threw open a door of new, unexpected musical possibilities. As he recalled, "Yoko and I went to Cambridge and did the show and I discovered more about the guitar than I did for all these years [with the Beatles]. I enjoyed it."

No stranger to the unexpected thrills and rewards of aural experimentation, Lennon first employed elements of "pure sound" as early as 1964 with "I Feel Fine," when he accidentally discovered feedback after absentmindedly propping his guitar against an amplifier. Then came the surreal effect of inadvertently playing a reel-to-reel tape backwards, which led to the mystical babble heard on the coda of the Beatles' 1966 B-side, "Rain." But both of these happy accidents had taken place within the sanctuary of the recording studio, while John had just experienced the exhilaration of sonically assaulting a live audience with Yoko.

Lennon was suddenly overjoyed to find himself "un-Beatled." He was delving into unknown territories beyond the safety net of the carefully constructed three-minute pop song, free of Paul and George's exquisite but constraining harmonies, and he dug it!

Lennon/Ono's first public performance had actually taken place at the chaotic *Rolling Stones' Circus* television special filmed on December 11 and 12, 1968. Following a smoldering version of "Yer Blues" by the Dirty Mac—a one-off supergroup led by John and featuring guitar "God" Eric Clapton, Keith Richards on bass, and Jimi Hendrix's polyrhythmic drummer Mitch Mitchell—Yoko joined the fray for a "heavy" chugging bluesy avant/noise jam later titled "Whole Lotta Yoko." Also invited to participate was the virtuoso Israeli violinist Ivry Gitlis, who played acoustically into a microphone and was sadly drowned out by the group's electric caterwaul. The film and recording of the lost concert (which featured performances by Taj Mahal and the Who that surpassed the Stones' ragged set) finally saw the light of day in October 1996. Whether the audience hooted and hollered for the band or the cameras, their enthusiasm was irrefutable.

Not everyone shared such unbridled passion for Lennon/Ono's strange sonic experiments. A bewildered George Martin apparently could not bring himself to offer anything beyond "No comment," a snub that John and Yoko displayed on the back cover of *Life with the Lions* like a shining badge of rebellion.

Despite the perplexing music within, many Lennon/Ono fans bought *Life with the Lions* for the iconic photo that graced the back of the record jacket, which depicted John boldly cradling Yoko in his arms while engulfed by a mob of menacing bobbies outside the Marylebone courthouse in London. John stands, defiantly protecting his diminutive wife, whose long, black hair had just been yanked by one of her many detractors. Just moments before, Lennon had pled guilty to a slap-on-the-wrist charge of possessing eleven grams of cannabis after the police had raided Ringo's Montagu Square apartment on October 18, 1968. Arrested and released on bail, John was charged a mere fifteen pounds plus court costs. But his decision to accept the court's sentence (which absolved Yoko of any wrongdoing, lest she be deported or branded an unfit mother for Kyoko) would cause Lennon untold trouble years later when applying for American citizenship.

Meanwhile *Disc + Music Echo* magazine branded *Unfinished Music No. 2: Life with the Lions* "a sad album," predicting that "most people's reactions will be either to laugh it off as a bad joke or shake their heads in disbelief."

New York singer/songwriter Larkin Grimm was not among them, however. She fervently disagreed with *Disc + Music Echo*'s assessment: "Listening to *Life with the Lions,* I can't even imagine the strength it took for Yoko to record an album in a hospital bed while having a miscarriage," she pointed out. "I once tended to a friend of my mother's during her miscarriage, and the grief, the horror, and the pain this friend experienced marked my mind forever. She had all the agony of childbirth and none of the reward. . . . 'Yoko the Brave,' we should call her. 'Yoko the Enduring.' She has eggs, that woman. She sang through her pain and expressed the sorrow and ecstasy of women everywhere that was simply *not being heard.*"

"You couldn't even find *Two Virgins* back then," the eclectic record/television producer Hal Willner told me. Distributors were discouraged from handling the album after being threatened with charges for trafficking in pornography. Despite thirty thousand copies of the taboo record being repackaged like smut in a brown paper bag, they were still seized by New Jersey police. As Beatles chronicler Nicholas Schaffner put it ten years later: "Never had an album been so talked about yet so seldom listened to by those lucky enough to find a copy."

"But I did have *Life with the Lions* though," Willner said. "I bought it at E. J. Korvette's [a popular East Coast discount chain store]. *Rolling Stone,* which was still the bible at the time, wrote about it. The mainstream and the avant-garde were meeting in John and Yoko along with [Miles Davis's] *Bitches Brew.* George was makin' *Electronic Sound*! FM radio played old tapes of [the zany British radio program] *The Goon Show* [which starred a then-unknown Peter Sellers], and Al Douglas was releasing Lenny Bruce records, making him a god."

"It was just a strange time. I was fine with it," Willner said, referring to Lennon's searing feedback and Ono's skull-rattling banshee wail. "The sound was just part of it. I didn't think of what they were doing as separate [from the Beatles]. They were like Sonny and Cher . . . only better. It was John and Yoko!"

Presented as a document of Lennon and Ono's tumultuous life together, *Unfinished Music No. 2: Life with the Lions* managed to turn a few of the more open-minded Beatle/Lennon fans on to free jazz, as well as the concept of *musique*

concrète (employing and manipulating prerecorded sound to create new compositions). Inspired by John Cage's *Imaginary Landscape No. 4 for Twelve Radios*, John
and Yoko would record over twelve minutes of random broadcasts for "Radio Play,"
which at best struck people as clever filler and, at worst, a waste of vinyl (and their
money).

Prior to collaborating with Yoko, Lennon had employed elements of *musique
concrète* when he randomly twiddled a radio dial, recording snippets of music and
Shakespeare's *King Lear* (with the voice of Sir John Gielgud), which he mixed into
the swirling surrealist atmosphere of "I Am the Walrus."

The album's title and the concept of "Unfinished Music" also evoked John Cage,
whose sonic explorations often relied on happenstance and were presented in an unfinished state. In 1952, Cage hatched the radical notion of presenting four minutes
and thirty-three seconds of silence as a piece entitled "Silent Composition." While
a minute of silence is routinely requested in commemorating fallen world leaders,
sports figures, and entertainers (including John after he was murdered in December
1980), Lennon/Ono, undoubtedly inspired by Cage, would dedicate two minutes
of blank vinyl as a symbol of peace to the baby Yoko had recently lost. (Cage had
admired Yoko's work as well, publishing Ono's "Beat Piece" years before it appeared
on *Wedding Album* in November 1969.) "Two Minutes Silence" posed an interesting
dilemma for the listener. If they skipped over the track, listeners had to consider if
they were disrespecting John and Yoko's unborn son.

Despite its overall woeful response, *Unfinished Music No. 2: Life with the Lions*,
as John pointed out, still managed to reach No. 174 on the charts and sell 60,000
copies in America. While some undoubtedly assumed the album's title was a play
on "Life with the Lennons," or perhaps a pretentious reference to John and Yoko
being "young" and "great" or at "the top of their game" (emerging jazz stars are often
dubbed "Young Lions"), the poetic title was yet another tongue-in-cheek television
reference (John, a television junkie, had previously worked the title of the popular
British TV show *Meet the Wife* into the lyrics of *Sgt. Pepper's* "Good Morning, Good
Morning"). This time John was referring to *Life with the Lyons*, the popular 1950s
TV sitcom that he once loved about an American family that relocates to London.

Ironically, *Record Mirror's* review dismissed *Life with the Lions* as "a fine example
of how two young people can amuse themselves without television." But one look at
Susan Wood's uncropped portrait of Lennon/Ono in the hospital room that was used
for the album's cover reveals they were doing just that—watching TV.

The 1997 Rykodisc reissue of *Unfinished Music No. 2: Life with the Lions* included two bonus tracks. The hauntingly lovely "Song for John" featured Yoko singing to John's gently fingerpicked guitar (played in a similar style to "Dear Prudence"). "We'll have our wings and the wind will be with us," Ono assured her lover in a soft, breathy voice, evoking the fleeting images and emotions of a bleak, windy afternoon. "Mulberry" (arguably the album's most important track after "Cambridge 1969") unfortunately remained unreleased for twenty-nine years. Had it been included in the album's original playlist, the piece might have helped Lennon/Ono's disillusioned fans gain a greater understanding of their collaborations.

Inspired by her family's days in exile following the evacuation of Tokyo, Ono recalled the experience of being a young girl, alone and cold, picking berries "from the mulberry bush so that I could feed my younger brother and sister and myself." Yoko's pathetic whimpers and cries were meant to evoke her "feeling a bit frightened because [the local farmers] said there were many ghosts in the field." The track features some of John Lennon's most innovative and playful guitar improvisation as he employs a slide while tapping the strings and thumping on the instrument's body, creating a rhythmic foundation for his wife's keening vocals.

"There were guys 'tapping' back in the '30s," avant-garde guitarist/composer Elliott Sharp points out. "Others using that technique included Italian guitarist Vittorio Camardese [who played with jazz violinist Joe Venuti and trumpeter Chet Baker], and Jimi Hendrix, who was doing that in the '60s. So was Keith Rowe, a member of [British avant-garde piainist] Mike Westbrook's band, until he made the unwise career choice to never tune his guitar again."

"'Mulberry' is an incredible piece of music for a variety of reasons," pianist/composer Thollem McDonas concurred. "This duo between Yoko and John is haunting emotionally and equally fascinating musically. John's guitar work is amazing, a total departure from everything before. There's a sense like he is rediscovering music and his relationship to the guitar all over again. It's like a rebirth for him in a way. The recording was made with a simple stereo mic in a room of a house . . . a reinvigorating and cathartic moment, so personal, so raw and simple . . . just pure expression." *Rolling Stone,* which had been a great supporter of Lennon/Ono's projects up to this point (the magazine even featured their naked butts on the cover of their November 23, 1968, issue), trashed the album, dismissing it as "utter bullshit."

"The Plastic Ono Band is free-form," Lennon told journalist Jutta Ney in the May 1970 issue of *Jazz & Pop.* "Once everyone gets adjusted to that and not expecting the Fab Four then they'll dig what's happening."

Marketing rock musicians while trying to control their unpredictable behavior has always been a tricky business, as Brian Epstein knew all too well. Part of John Lennon's broad appeal in *A Hard Day's Night* was his snarky, rebellious image, the bad boy, always cutting up while sticking it to the authority figure. In this case that was "Norm," their flummoxed road manager whom John denigrated as "a swine."

So it wasn't surprising that in the wake of the Beatles' spectacularly successful cartoon series (broadcast Saturday mornings from September 25, 1965, through October 21, 1967) that a pair of enterprising TV producers named Bob Rafelson and Bert Schneider created what became the enormously popular sitcom called *The Monkees*. Davy Jones, Mickey Dolenz, Peter Tork, and Mike Nesmith—a.k.a. the "Pre-Fab Four" were chosen at an audition of over four hundred hopefuls, not for their musical talent but for their irrepressible charisma. Broadcast on Monday nights at 7:30 p.m. (from September 12, 1966, through March 25, 1968), *The Monkees* was delicious fluff with thin plots, each of which predictably led to a new song by the group. While the Monkees sang well, their hits were written by the team of Tommy Boyce and Bobby Hart, and their instruments were handled by seasoned session musicians. But following the release of their first album, the band began to rebel against their cute, made-for-TV image, hoping to prove to the world (and themselves) that they were a real, "honest" rock 'n' roll band. While Nesmith was a competent guitarist, Tork had played piano and twanged banjo back in his Greenwich Village folky days. Hoping to appear credible on the drums, Dolenz took lessons and applied himself until he gained an acceptable level of proficiency on the instrument. The Monkees' mutiny continued when they demanded to play live concerts. Suddenly, music publisher/producer Don Kirshner came face to face with the not-so-cute monster he'd helped create. He wisely let the Monkees have their way and moved on to his next project, *The Archies* (which aired from 1968 to 1973), the adventures of a cute cartoon combo that sang bubblegum hits like "Sugar, Sugar." Kirshner soon discovered that managing two-dimensional pop groups was much easier than flesh-and-blood human beings.

Oddly enough, John and Yoko's original concept for the Plastic Ono Band—four clear polystyrene cubes containing state-of-the-art sound, video, and lighting equipment, which could be set up to perform in lieu of a live band—was not far off from Kirshner's brainstorm. While lacking emotion or sex appeal, robots were more dependable than human musicians, who might show up late or stoned or play too loud or out of tune. In lieu of a group photo, the plastic "Plastic Ono Band" was portrayed on the sleeve of the single "Give Peace a Chance" (released July 4, 1969, in America and backed with Yoko's lilting "Remember Love" on the B-side).

Not only were the original members of the Plastic Ono Band "plastic," they were meant to be interchangeable as well. The initial advertisement announcing Lennon/Ono's musical collaboration declared "You are the Plastic Ono Band." In theory, they didn't even have to be there for the group to exist.

"You're in it. Everybody's in it!" John cheered, while Apple's mastermind press secretary Derek Taylor took their idea one step further, claiming the band "represents freedom. . . . It could be children in a playground screaming their release from the bondage of the classroom or it could be John and Yoko screaming their love for each other. It could be anything!"

That was apparent from the band's repertoire, which, as Lennon explained, comprised everything from old rock 'n' roll favorites from the '50s like "'Blue Suede Shoes' to ancient John Cage." The band's lineup was just as unpredictable. In the wake of the Beatles' breakup, John refused to be tied down to another musical marriage. Initially the Plastic Ono Band was formed by John and Yoko, with Klaus Voormann, Eric Clapton, and either Alan White or Ringo on drums, but the lineup expanded at will to include George Harrison, Nicky Hopkins, and Jim Keltner, along with the Beatles' devoted roadie/friend Mal Evans, who shook a bit of tambourine and was credited with providing "tea and sympathy" in the liner notes of John's *Plastic Ono Band*.

When queried about the band's future plans, Lennon glibly replied—as if he were one of the liberated children in Derek Taylor's playground—"We don't plan it. It either happens or it doesn't."

The Plastic Ono Band's debut at the Toronto Rock 'n' Roll Revival (better known as the Toronto Peace Festival after John and Yoko released *Live Peace in Toronto,* their recording of the band's premier gig) was a perfect example of Lennon's love of operating in the moment. The concert was scheduled for September 13, 1969. With only two days to go, the organizers, Kenny Walker and John Brower, called Lennon/Ono in London to see if they'd consider appearing as the "King and Queen" of the festival. Lennon shocked Brower when he unexpectedly replied he much preferred to play rather than simply make a cameo and asked for a day to throw a band together.

Having just returned from the States after a disappointing tour as part of the new supergroup Blind Faith, Eric Clapton received a surprising telegram from John inviting him to play the impromptu gig. Apparently Eric's gardener awoke him with the urgent message. Clapton later recalled being "really excited and very pleased. . . . It sounded like such a good idea, even though none of us had played together onstage before." (In fact, Lennon, Ono, and Clapton had performed together the previous December at the Rolling Stones' Circus.)

The Beatles' old friend bassist Klaus Voormann was free and willing, as was drummer Alan White, who would soon join Yes. White had been making dinner when the telephone rang. At the time, the twenty-year-old musician had been "living with a bunch of guys . . . we had our own band and we were [playing] all over London," he recalled in a 2019 interview with *The Aquarian*. It was John Lennon on the line, calling "out of nowhere." Lennon had recently seen White play in a London club and invited him to perform with him at the festival in Toronto. Naturally, White thought it was a prank call, "a friend of mine putting me on, so I put the phone down on him. . . . And then he called again and said, 'No, this is John Lennon and we're doing this gig. Would you play with us?' And I kind of dropped the phone. Then I said, 'Sure, I'll do it.'"

The following morning a limo arrived, promptly delivering White to the airport, where John and Yoko were waiting. "He hadn't told me on the phone, but then he said, 'Oh, by the way, Eric Clapton is playing guitar at this show.' So, we got on the plane . . . and went straight from the plane to the gig and played *Live Peace in Toronto* . . . It was a little bit dreamlike."

Despite George Harrison's arrogance towards Yoko, John felt compelled to invite his old bandmate along to join in the musical fray. But Harrison, never famous for spontaneity, chose to remain sequestered within the serene and fragrant gardens of his Friar Park home rather than risk the slightest possible flashback of Beatlemania.

With little time to rehearse, Lennon and company pulled a set together consisting of old Cavern Club standards "Blue Suede Shoes," "Money," and "Johnny B. Goode"—"numbers that we know 'cause we never played together before," John explained as he anxiously stepped up to the mike for his first public performance since the Beatles' farewell concert at Candlestick Park four years before.

"Everything was very last minute," Klaus Voormann recalled. "They reserved some seats in the last row of the plane, and [we] rehearsed on the flight over." Before flying to Canada, Klaus had never met Yoko or Alan White.

"We formed on the plane coming over here, and now we're gonna play in front of twenty thousand people," John confided to journalist Ritchie Yorke. Jet-lagged and nervous about performing live again, Lennon allegedly ran to the toilet and vomited repeatedly before taking the stage. But according to Eric Clapton, it wasn't merely a case of nerves that caused John a terrible bout of nausea.

In an interview with journalist/author Robert Palmer, Clapton recalled first hearing about the gig just a couple of hours before gathering his equipment and rushing to the airport. A moment of comic relief ensued when the band, in the thick of learning the repertoire on the plane, was interrupted by a Gillette salesman who, as Eric recalled, "was trying to give us free razors 'cause we all had beards." But Clapton confessed to being "slightly disillusioned" after the plane landed in Toronto, and watching perplexed as John and Yoko were "whisked off in a limousine" while the rest of the group were left standing in the rain like second-class citizens. After arriving at the stadium, Eric claimed he snorted "so much coke that I actually threw up and passed out. They had to take me and lay me on the ground." Roused by the news that it was time to play, Clapton admitted he was "terrified . . . shaking . . . having to go on between Jerry Lee Lewis and Chuck Berry." But in the end, as he recalled, "it turned out to be a great experience."

Plastic Ono Band's ragged yet inspired forty-minute set included Lennon's existential "Yer Blues," a perfect vehicle for Clapton's smoldering blues riffs, along with a spirited rave-up of "Give Peace a Chance" and the live debut of "Cold Turkey," John's chilling ode to heroin withdrawal.

"When the Plastic Ono Band 45 of 'Cold Turkey' came out in 1969, my brother Alex bought it, and we were totally blown away by its intensity, its feverish catharsis," Wilco guitarist Nels Cline recalled.

> At age fourteen, we knew nothing about heroin withdrawal, and terms such as *cold turkey, addicted, jonesing,* and the like had yet to be popularly applied outside of the drug world. We just thought it was 'tough.' And one of the toughest things about that track is John Lennon's slashing guitar riff as it repeats and repeats, mingling with his howls of withdrawal. Thinking back on this song and its sound, it seems to me that the power and directness of the guitar on 'Cold Turkey' has been profoundly influential on me. The guitar *sounds* like pain. And the transmission of pure feeling in music is a real achievement.

Much to the audience's dismay, after just six songs Lennon handed the stage over to Yoko, who preceded to shriek and scream while the band jammed on a repetitive, swampy blues vamp that soon morphed into something totally uncategorizable. This was no longer just a bunch of long-haired blokes playing heavy boogie riffs for a happy, stoned audience. Although diminutive in stature and seemingly shy, often speaking in a whisper for interviews while hiding beneath her thick mane of black hair, Yoko's Kabuki caterwaul instantly sliced through the band's electric instruments, shattering the crowd's understanding of everything from rock to art . . . to life itself.

And that is precisely why John (ever the instigator) took such enormous pleasure in presenting his much-maligned wife on the same stage as himself, Eric Clapton, and a host of 1950s rock 'n' roll legends that included Bo Diddley, Jerry Lee Lewis, Little Richard, and Chuck Berry. (Berry's eyes would nearly pop out of his skull when Ono yowled over his classic hit "Memphis, Tennessee" as they played together on *The Mike Douglas Show* in 1972.)

"Now Yoko's gonna do her thing . . . all over you," John said, taunting the crowd as Ono stepped out of a large white bag and the band broke into a lurching blues groove. Clapton drilled a searing slide-guitar riff, propelling Yoko's ululating vocals on "Don't Worry Kyoko (Mummy's Only Looking for Her Hand in the Snow)." Ono began chanting repeatedly: "Don't worry, don't worry, don't worry " in a relentless, brokenhearted mantra. With a feeling of existential despair similar to Robert Johnson's "Walking Blues," the Plastic Ono Band conjured their own version of the Delta blues, harnessing its raw power, propelling the searing shriek of a Japanese conceptual-artist-turned-siren.

While in London in 1966, Yoko recalled writing her first series of songs "before getting together with John." As she told author Paul Zollo, "the songs were in quite an interesting style, really. . . . It was mostly a capella, because I didn't have any musicians with me in London . . . a kind of mixture of Oriental rhythm and blues, I suppose."

The blues is an elastic art form that remains steadfastly true to itself no matter what changes or ornamentation people have tried imposing on it over the years. Although routinely dressed up with horns and string sections, the blues are often most powerful when played solo, on guitar, piano, or harmonica. Some of the greatest innovators of the music, like John Lee Hooker and Lightnin' Hopkins, boldly dispensed with its 12-to-the-bar structure and changed chords whenever they "felt like it." The blues are the perfect time-tested vehicle for conveying human emotions so deep at times that they have a way of overtaking the performer. In his early days, guitarist Buddy Guy's shows often ended when he broke down and left the stage in tears, unable to continue. This was also a staple of James Brown's act, when his emcee Danny Ray would drape a sparkling cape over the singer's trembling shoulders and lead him offstage in abject sorrow. And throughout his own career, Bob Dylan regularly bent the blues to his will, infusing the form with surrealist poetry, as in "Highway 61 Revisited" or the hilarious "Leopard Skin Pillbox Hat."

Clarifying the difference between creation and re-creation, the late blues scholar Albert Murray claimed that "re-creation was when Bessie Smith sang the blues.

She didn't actually *have* the blues at that moment she sang to her audience, but her performance was a 're-creation' of the feeling she'd had that first inspired the song." With Yoko, there was never any sense of re-creation or reenactment. What you heard and saw was completely improvised in that moment—wild and powerful with no filter. And John (along with a handful of their devoted fans) found it nothing short of exhilarating.

But the stunned and confused crowd of twenty-seven thousand attending the Toronto Rock 'n' Roll Revival offered little response beyond bewilderment in the wake of their performance. Between numbers, John leaned over and kissed Yoko, to reassure his wife, who smiled blissfully and began to sing, childlike at first before her voice turned into a ghostly bellow: "Jaaaaahhhhhhnnnnn . . . Jaaaaahhhhhhnnnnn . . . Let's hope for peace!"

Of Yoko's two mind-bending jams, "John, John (Let's Hope for Peace)" was the more radical and startling. Clapton aimed the pickups of his Les Paul toward his amplifier, manifesting waves of feedback in support of Yoko's haunted shrieks, while John stood by watching. Lovingly instigating the madness, Lennon occasionally hugged his wife, who punctuated the sizzling drone of the guitars with nerve-wracking yelps. After a few minutes, the musicians leaned their instruments against their amps and one by one abandoned the stage in a whirlwind of howling electricity.

"If it wasn't John, they would have thrown tomatoes," Klaus confided. Yet sharing a stage with Yoko had been an eye-opening experience for Voormann, who believed, "[it was] an amazing thing [what] she was doing—screaming. . . . You have to say one up for Yoko. [John] didn't give a shit what people said, [and] Yoko has a thick skin. There's not much you can do to throw her out of her balance."

"She was trying to transform herself into a rock star, but her singing was not going well," Dan Richter countered. "She had a way of wailing when she sang that belongs in a Japanese temple, not on a rock stage. The word *yowl* was used to describe it. John would not hear a word of criticism, but the more she sang, the more the people at Apple couldn't stand her. To them, she was not only an interloper but a terrible singer to boot."

In Clapton's estimation, the band's performance at the Toronto Rock 'n' Roll Revival was "nothing more than a glorified jam session." Yet he clearly enjoyed himself. "I could go on playing [old school rock 'n' roll like] 'Money' and 'Dizzy Miss Lizzy' for the rest of my life," Eric said enthusiastically. The set also included the premiere of Lennon's "Cold Turkey," a song he'd first offered to the Beatles but which Paul and George passed on, fearing its documentation of heroin withdrawal had crossed the line of good taste. Surprised by their response, Lennon allegedly countered that the song was not about kicking junk, but rather a case of salmonella he got after eating some bad turkey, a tale nearly as believable as "Lucy in the Sky with Diamonds" having nothing to do with LSD. But after playing the song in Toronto to a crowd who "dug it like mad," John was now anxious to get in the studio and record "Cold Turkey" with his new group, the Plastic Ono Band.

Thrilled with Yoko's performance, John described her portion of the show as "half rock, half madness." "It really freaked them out," he chortled. Yoko found performing live with Plastic Ono Band exhilarating as well: "In the beginning when I was sitting in the Beatles' sessions, I thought [their music] was so simplistic," she said, admitting to "a kind of classical-musician, avant-garde snobbery." "And then I suddenly thought, 'This is great!' I just woke up," Ono exclaimed. "There's an incredible energy [playing rock 'n' roll]. Like primitivism. It's a very healthy thing, and no wonder, it's like a heartbeat. It's almost like the other music [avant-garde] appealed to a head plane, like brain music, and then they forgot about the body."

Lennon, having played rock 'n' roll from the first moment he could get his hands on a guitar, came from the opposite direction: "On 'Twist and Shout,' I was letting go a bit," John told Jonathan Cott. He'd often felt the Beatles' vocal arrangements were too restraining for him as a singer. Always having to remain within the harmonic framework with Paul and George limited his emotional range and kept him from getting too far out. Now inspired by Yoko, who encouraged his nerve-wracked ululating on "Cold Turkey," John felt he was finally "beginning to let go again." But Lennon (who repeatedly claimed to hate the sound of his own voice) remained dissatisfied with his performance of the song. "It sounds like shit," he said, disappointed that he "hadn't really let go" and was "still sort of performing." But with the recording and release of *Plastic Ono Band*, John felt like he "finally broke through at last."

Despite an onslaught of nausea, John claimed to have "never felt so good in [his] life" following their short set. The Plastic Ono Band's electrifying performance at Varsity Stadium on that autumn night would give Lennon the extra boost of self-confidence he needed to inform Allen Klein he was through with the Beatles. While happy for John on a personal level, Klein, who had just beaten Capitol Records down to an unheard-of 25 percent royalty rate on retail sales, was determined to keep the lid on Lennon's shocking announcement for as long as possible.

One week later, on September 20, 1969, the Beatles convened for a business meeting at Apple's London offices. It wasn't long before the festering animosity within the band exploded. Ever the diplomat, Paul struggled to keep the mood light, when suddenly Lennon blurted out: "The group is over. I'm leaving. I started the band. I disbanded it. It's as simple as that."

Yoko later claimed she had no idea John was going to finally drop the bomb that had detonated within him long ago. While McCartney and Klein begged Lennon to maintain his silence for the time being, John claimed to have felt greatly relieved. Paul later likened Lennon's quitting the band to the moment when "he told Cynthia he was getting a divorce."

Momentarily bewildered, Yoko was suddenly confronted with the overwhelming prospect of not only being John's wife and muse but also his full-time artistic collaborator. "Those three guys were the ones [who had been] entertaining him for so long," she said. "Now I have to be the one to take the load."

Five days later, Plastic Ono Band (with Clapton on guitar, Voormann on bass, and Starr on drums) headed into EMI with John producing, singing, and playing guitar to record "Cold Turkey." Inspired by Yoko's feral vocals, John howled and growled on the song's coda, evoking the torture of kicking smack. Despite twenty-six takes, John remained unsatisfied and booked Trident Studios on September 28, only to return again two days later to EMI, where they finally nailed a take suitable for the single. The B-side, Yoko's "Don't Worry Kyoko (Mummy's Only Looking for a Hand in the Snow)" was, John believed, "one of the fuckin' best rock 'n' roll records ever made."

While various performances of the song have appeared over the years, the original version, titled "Mum's Only Looking for a Hand in the Snow" was first recorded on a portable cassette player as Yoko lay in bed recovering from her miscarriage at Queen Charlotte Hospital in October 1968. Later released on the 1997 CD reissue of *Wedding Album*, the homemade demo is considerably different from the more harrowing renditions that followed. The first version featured Yoko softly sighing "Kyoko . . . don't worry!" as John played a repetitive boogie riff on an acoustic guitar. By the time the piece was recorded as the B-side to "Cold Turkey" and cut again in yet another version for Yoko's 1971 album *Fly*, "Don't Worry Kyoko (Mummy's Only Looking for a Hand in the Snow)" had transformed into a staggering blitz of desperate yowls and howling feedback.

Ono's startling image of "a hand in the snow" originally appeared in her book *Grapefruit*. Written in the spring of 1964, "No. 3," the third section of "Three More Snow Pieces for Solo or Orchestra," instructed the reader to "Find a hand in the snow." Five years later, she employed the image again as a metaphor for the exasperating routine of trying to locate her daughter, Kyoko, who remained in her ex-husband Tony Cox's custody. Cox seemed to spend more time hopscotching the globe—from America to England to Denmark to Spain to the Virgin Islands—in the hopes of keeping their daughter away from Lennon and Ono than making art.

Reassuring someone not to worry is typically a calming act, usually accomplished by speaking in soft, soothing tones and perhaps accompanied by a gentle touch of the hand. But not in the case of "Don't Worry Kyoko," in which Yoko hysterically shrieks, "Don't worry! Don't worry!"

At Ono's first major recital at Carnegie Hall in 1961, she recalls trying to create a sound that caused tension to steadily mount within the audience, like "the sounds of fear and of darkness . . . [or] like a child's fear that someone is behind him." What Kyoko must have thought hearing her mother repeatedly scream her name in such a frantic, agitated state is anyone's guess.

* * *

In the meantime, the Beatles' slickest production to date, *Abbey Road*, was released on September 26, 1969. Little did their fans realize the band had fallen apart. A media circus continued to rage around John and Yoko from Amsterdam to Montreal at their Bed-Ins for Peace, while reporters took potshots at the "two gurus in drag." Dylan, the king of the finger-pointing song, remained surprisingly ambivalent when he commented on Lennon in *Rolling Stone*: "Well, everybody's doin' what they can do. . . . I don't mind what he does, really."

But when asked about John and Yoko's various "Life as Art" happenings and odd sonic explorations, George Harrison famously quipped, "I avant-garde a clue." According to Traffic's singer/guitarist Dave Mason, George likened Yoko's Svengali-like hold over John to "watching a Western movie [when] the love interest came in." By Harrison's estimation, Lennon/Ono were "out on a limb." Yoko, from his perspective, "was pushing him out of the band, inasmuch as she didn't want him hanging out with us."

There were plenty of reasons for George's mounting resentment toward John and Paul. He'd previously stormed out of the "Get Back" sessions, frustrated by McCartney's micromanaging his every guitar riff, along with John and Paul's refusal to record his new songs (many of which would appear on his forthcoming debut album *All Things Must Pass*). Lennon later confessed that their treatment of their junior partner had degenerated into "a festering wound." John acknowledged George had finally "realized who he is, and all the fucking shit we've done to him."

Despite his bandmates' abuse, Harrison seemed relieved, taking the Beatles' demise in stride. As he wrote in a diary entry dated 10 January 1969: "Got up went to Twickenham [Studios] . . . rehearsed until lunch time—left the Beatles—went home and in the evening did 'King of Fuh' [the controversial song by the eccentric New Jersey-based artist Brute Force, better known as Steve Friedlander to his mother] at Trident Studio—had chips later at Klaus and Christine's . . . went home."

"There was a point where enough was enough," Harrison reckoned. Perhaps George's friend and mentor Ravi Shankar, whom he respected above all others, understood him best when he said, "In spite of all the fame, all the hullabaloo . . . George had something we call in our language *tyagi*, which means the feeling of unattachment." Despite his tremendous notoriety and wealth, Harrison, for the most part, did his best to remain free of the entanglements of the material world. "It didn't seem to matter to him," Shankar pointed out, "Because he was searching for something much higher, much deeper."

Following their first LSD trip together, George and John would share a unique bond that allowed them to remain friends and continue working together despite the mounting differences and animosities within the band. On December 15, 1969, Harrison hesitantly took part in Lennon and Ono's Peace for Christmas benefit for UNICEF at London's Lyceum Theatre. The night's lineup featured an expanded seventeen-piece Plastic Ono Band that included Eric Clapton, Dave Mason, and Delaney and Bonnie Bramlett, whom George had recently joined on their Scandinavian tour. If that weren't enough, they were propelled by the frenetic pounding of the Who's lunatic drummer, Keith Moon.

When Delaney asked Lennon what key the first song was in, Harrison knowingly replied, "It doesn't matter." A moment later Yoko reaffirmed his flippant remark with a barrage of mind-bending vocals.

"It was beautiful . . . a fantastic scene," John said later. "The papers didn't think so. They thought it was a waste of talent." Lennon described the ninety-minute performance as "1984 music" that "simple-minded pop people" couldn't appreciate. Apparently half the audience, aggravated and bewildered, exited the theater before the performance was over.

Two tracks recorded that night were later released in 1972 on the band's double album *Some Time in New York City*. Side 3's live jam, credited to "John and Yoko/ Plastic Ono Band with a cast of 1000s," began with a nine-minute grinding version of John's "Cold Turkey," followed by yet another scorching version of "Don't Worry Kyoko."

Amid a gaggle of guitars tuning up, Yoko suddenly unleashed a haunted cry for her daughter Kyoko, a banshee's howl, echoing up from the deep, murky depths of an old, abandoned well. The band kicked off a hard-driving vamp reminiscent of Led Zeppelin's ballsy British blues-rock. Ono's voice was not merely irritating, it was merciless—a piercing sonic nightmare framed by four snarling guitars played by Lennon, Clapton, Harrison, and Mason, along with a punchy R&B horn section courtesy of Delaney and Bonnie's band. The piece eventually morphed into a hard-stomping temper tantrum with Yoko repeatedly screaming, "Ow! Ow! Ow!" like a screech owl being eviscerated, as the horns matched her every cry. The track demands great stamina (and/or a bizarre sense of humor) on the part of the listener to make it through. Yet there are many fascinating sonic flourishes to be found.

The sheer strength and audacity of Yoko's delivery is stunning. Punk rock has nothing on this stuff. Throughout this storm of sonic mayhem, Yoko continually screams, "Don't worry! Don't worry! Don't worry!" After the music ends, there is a moment of bewildered silence from the crowd before they reluctantly begin to clap, hoping perhaps to coax John back to the stage to sing a much-needed soul-soothing tune like "Across the Universe" or "Love."

Following the UNICEF benefit concert, Lennon/Ono returned to Canada again on December 16, 1969, to loan their celebrity clout to a three-day peace and music festival slated for July 3, 4, and 5 at Mosport Park, outside of Toronto. Although John boasted "to make it the biggest music festival in history" and claimed "everybody who's anybody" will perform, the event never materialized. After relaxing at "Rompin'" Ronnie Hawkins's farm for a few days, John and Yoko visited Ottawa, where they met for nearly an hour with Canada's Prime Minister Pierre Trudeau. Upon emerging from the PM's wood-paneled chamber, John told the press: "We spent about fifty minutes together, which was longer than he had spent with any head of state. If all politicians were like Mr. Trudeau there would be world peace."

What was discussed or accomplished was never quite clear. While loaning Lennon/Ono's peace campaign a bit of establishment cred, the meeting also helped further boost Trudeau's image among longhairs worldwide.

That night John and Yoko flew back to London for a quiet Christmas Eve together before dashing off once more to visit Kyoko in Denmark. The trip was memorable for several reasons. Marking the passing of the '60s dream, and symbolic of the changes they hoped the new decade would bring, John and Yoko surprisingly cut their hair. Once integral to their image, their locks, which had been artlessly lopped off, would soon be auctioned for charity. More importantly, the idea for John's next single "Instant Karma!" was inspired by a conversation between Tony Cox (Yoko's ex) and Cox's girlfriend, Melinda.

With "great hopes for the new year," John and Yoko proclaimed 1970 as "Year 1 AP (After Peace)." "The last decade was the end of the old machine crumbling to pieces," John said. "And we think we can get it together, with your help."

"Year 1" officially kicked off with the recording and release of "Instant Karma! (We All Shine On)." The experience, as John later explained, "was great, 'cause I wrote [the song] in the morning on the piano [and] I thought, 'Hell, let's do it,' and we booked the studio." Lennon then reserved Studio 2 at EMI and the session started that night at 7 p.m. on January 27, 1970.

According to George Harrison, "John phoned me up one morning . . . and said, 'I've written this tune and I'm going to record it tonight and have it pressed up and out tomorrow—that's the whole point, "Instant Karma," you know.' I was in [London] with Phil Spector and I said to Phil, 'Why don't you come to the session?' There were just four people: John played piano, I played acoustic guitar, there was Klaus Voormann on bass, and Alan White on drums. We recorded the song and brought it out that week, mixed instantly by Phil Spector."

Despite the Beatles' brief foray into psychedelia, Lennon was always first and foremost a rock-'n'-roller. "Phil came in," John recalled. "He said, 'How do you want it?' I said, 'You know, 1950 but now.' And he said, 'Right,' and *boom,* I did it in just about three goes. He played it back, and there it was. I said, 'A bit more bass, that's all.' And off we went. See, Phil doesn't fuss about with fuckin' stereo or all the bullshit. Just 'Did it sound alright? Let's have it.' It doesn't matter whether something's prominent or not prominent. If it sounds good to you as a layman or as a human, *take* it!"

The Beatles had loved and respected Spector's work for years. Phil, who had flown on the same plane with the Fab Four on their first visit to New York for their debut performance on *The Ed Sullivan Show* on February 9, 1964, famously said he believed that any plane carrying the Beatles wouldn't crash. The wildly eccentric producer was officially reintroduced to them years later by their brusque business manager, Allen Klein.

With a portfolio of songs integral to the history of pop music, Spector was immediately ushered in to clean up the unwieldly mess of the *Get Back* sessions (as the project was known before the album and the film were both finally released as *Let It Be*) and fashion them into a cohesive commodity for their fans, ever hungry for new Beatles product.

At the beginning of the *Get Back/Let It Be* sessions, Lennon admonished the Beatles' long-time producer George Martin, "I don't want any of your production shit. We want this to be an honest album. . . . I don't want any editing [or] overdubbing. We just record the song and that's it." But the Beatles had grossly underestimated the amount of rehearsal time it would take to get tight enough to cut an album's worth of new material in a single take. John would have to wait another year before achieving that sense of immediacy with *Plastic Ono Band*.

It's curious that the Beatles would hire the architect of the "wall of sound" to patch up their failed attempt at playing stripped-down live performances of their songs. The original idea behind "Get Back" had been for the Beatles to play once again as a cohesive unit, rather than John leading a backing band or Paul with a backing band or even worse, McCartney badgering George or Ringo to the point of making them walk out of the session and then playing their parts as well, which happened on more than a few occasions.

While he managed to get a good sound and stay out of the way of most of the material, Spector's treatment of McCartney's "The Long and Winding Road" didn't just cross the line of good taste, it obliterated it. The final mix sounded closer to a Liberace record than anything resembling the Beatles. One could almost envision Paul sitting at the piano in a lavender tux, illuminated by the warm glow of a candelabra, as the strings and choir of women's voices saturated his song with a layer of schmaltz as thick as any Phil had whipped up in his heyday. Spector's rococo rendition of Lennon's mercurial prayer "Across the Universe" would also run afoul, marring one of John's best later-day Beatle compositions nearly beyond repair. Eventually Spector would have his comeuppance for his excessive trespasses when the surviving Beatles released *Let It Be . . . Naked* on November 17, 2003.

While John and Yoko headed for Los Angeles in late April to continue their therapy sessions with Arthur Janov, Spector was hired to produce Harrison's long-awaited solo effort, *All Things Must Pass*. But as spontaneous and impatient as Lennon could be in the recording studio, George's slow, measured approach literally drove the high-strung, homesick producer to drink. Phil later confessed to journalist Robert Hilburn that he "started getting bored" with Harrison's tedious routine of overdubbing and second-guessing his performances. Klaus Voormann felt that Phil eventually became "obnoxious . . . [and was] fucking up the whole session," to the point where he wished the legendary producer would "please go home so we [could] get some work done."

Harrison's dry sense of humor and spiritual philosophy were particularly helpful when dealing with Phil. Believing the axiom that "we are all each other's gurus,"

George would claim that Phil Spector "had taught him the value of chanting Hare Krishna."

"You read these stories about Spector in the studio," session pianist Nicky Hopkins told author Dave Thompson. "And you think, 'Fuck, what a monster! I could never work with someone like that.'" But Hopkins's impression of Phil was decidedly different from the usual rumors floating about. While recording *Imagine* with John, Spector, from Nicky's perspective, was just "that little guy who sat in the corner chain-smoking. . . . He seemed okay."

John's Jukebox

While John acknowledged George's triumph with *All Things Must Pass* in *Rolling Stone*, Lennon was far from generous in his assessment of his former bandmate's new album when he remarked, "I wouldn't play that kind of music at home." John's back-handed compliment leads one to wonder just what "kind of music" he actually listened to at home.

In 1965 Lennon bought a British-made portable KB Discomatic jukebox that, as Jerry Leiber (of the great songwriting duo Leiber and Stoller) observed, looked "like a giant typewriter from 1943." John filled the big, clunky red-and-tan record player with forty of his favorite singles by his favorite soul and R&B singers, including Wilson Pickett, Smokey Robinson, Fontella Bass, and the Isley Brothers with their original "Twist and Shout" (which the Beatles covered and had enormous success with in 1963). There were 45s by Lennon's rock 'n' roll idols, Buddy Holly, Little Richard, and Chuck Berry, as well as more recent 1960s hits by Dylan, Donovan, the Lovin' Spoonful, and even Paul Revere and the Raiders.

In 2004 the British television series *The South Bank Show* presented an in-depth documentary titled *John Lennon's Jukebox* (soon followed by a thirty-nine-track companion disc of the same name), which delved into John's playlist with insightful interviews with Sting, Gary U.S. Bonds, and Steve Cropper and old voiceovers by Lennon, providing an invaluable music history lesson.

"I don't remember the chords or the lyrics or anything of the Beatles' songs," John explained. "I still go back to the stuff that the Beatles performed before they wrote." Whenever he'd pick up his guitar around the house, Lennon typically played "a bit of rock 'n' roll," forgetting about having "something deep to say," and sang "Be-Bop-a-Lula."

But John's passion for 1950s roots rock wasn't his sole inspiration for returning to the studio with Phil Spector in October 1973 to record an album of classics he simply titled *Rock 'n' Roll*. Lennon had been hit with a hefty lawsuit from the notoriously shady music publisher Morris Levy for having pilfered the opening line of Chuck Berry's "You Can't Catch Me" ("Here comes old flat-top, he comes groovin' up slowly") for the Beatles' "Come Together."

Sha-Na-Na's high-octane review of 1950s oldies at the Woodstock Festival in August 1969 had kicked open the door for a wave of nostalgic albums. This wave was spearheaded by Ringo's lushly produced *Sentimental Journey* in March 1970, which was followed by Laura Nyro's collaboration with Patti LaBelle on the gorgeous soul/doowop valentine *Gonna Take a Miracle* in 1971. Two years later, Harry Nilsson released an album of standards titled *A Little Touch of Schmilsson in the Night*, featuring sublime arrangements by Frank Sinatra's musical director, Gordon Jenkins. In June 1973, the Band's *Moondog Matinee* hit the street, giving fans a taste of the type of raucous, eclectic sets they once played while touring the Canadian hinterland as the Hawks.

While possessing one of the great voices in the history of rock 'n' roll, John's commitment to the material ultimately lacked the fire of his earlier performances, as heard on the Beatles' dramatic ballad "This Boy" or their smoldering cover of Roy Lee Johnson's "Mr. Moonlight," let alone the abandon of his feral vocal on Chuck Berry's "Rock 'n' Roll Music."

Ultimately the disappointment of Lennon's *Rock 'n' Roll* was its promise and failure to outshine all the other tribute albums of its day. The fault didn't lie with Lennon alone. Had John and Phil completed and released *Rock 'n' Roll* in 1973, it would have fit nicely into the trend of nostalgia happening at the time while still satisfying the nefarious Levy, who demanded Lennon record three of his tunes on his next album. But Spector suddenly, inexplicably, disappeared with the tapes, delaying the completion of the project until February 1975. At that point, *Rock 'n' Roll* (despite some great vocals by John) seemed like a half-hearted, uninspired effort by an over-the-hill '60s rock icon to remain in the game.

Fed up, Lennon then disappeared for the next five years to raise his "Beautiful Boy," Sean, and bake bread, before returning to the studio again in late summer of 1980 to record *Double Fantasy*.

While Lennon and Spector's collaborations on *Plastic Ono Band* and *Imagine* created a pair of great, enduring records, their relationship eventually went off the rails, thanks to unchecked artistic egos fueled by copious amounts of alcohol along with Phil's newly discovered passion for huffing amyl nitrate. Their third project together, Lennon/Ono's *Some Time New York City*, was a double album of agitprop anthems dedicated to radical activists John Sinclair and Angela Davis; the riots at New York state's maximum security prison, Attica State; along with the plight of the Irish and women's struggles for equal rights. Propelled by Manhattan's ragged street band Elephant's Memory, the much-reviled record limped to a disappointing No. 48 on the charts before nose-diving into oblivion. It seemed that John was more adept at writing autobiographical odes than ranting about the sins of Tricky Dicky and Rockefeller.

The sleeve notes to *Plastic Ono Band* listed Lennon, Ono, and Spector as coproducers—an odd combination of personality, style, and experience if ever there was one. The stripped-down album reflected the dark heart of Lennon's psyche more than the brand of pop that Spector was famous for.

Phil undoubtedly regretted putting his foot in his mouth a year earlier when he told Jann Wenner in a *Rolling Stone* interview that "Yoko may not be the greatest influence on [John]. I have a feeling that he's a far greater artist than she is." There was a double helping of crow waiting for Phil if he planned on producing Lennon's much-anticipated first solo album, as he would have to accept and work with Ono as his peer and coproducer, despite her inexperience in the studio.

Beyond Spector's erratic personality, Klaus Voormann found the producer "very quiet," "intelligent," and possessing "a great sense of humor." From Voormann's perspective, Phil was nothing short of "brilliant. . . . He didn't have to do his big sound. He could do something very fine, delicate, and sensitive, whatever was appropriate for the song and the moment."

"Spector was not of the staff producer ilk, that if it sounds fine, you leave it the fuck alone," Hal Willner stressed. "Some of the best productions I've ever done happened because I didn't do a damn thing! So few producers can do that. Or they can't do the psychological thing—to make the idea look like the artist came up with it. Maybe it was Stravinsky who said, 'If you're going to produce, you need the ear, you need to know the whole history of music in your head, and you have to be a child psychiatrist.'"

Spector had learned firsthand the inherent challenges in working with a "mom and pop band" after producing Ike and Tina Turner's brilliant/failed masterpiece "River Deep, Mountain High" in 1966. Yet Klaus found him surprisingly diplomatic, pointing out that whenever Yoko made a suggestion "that was completely wrong," Spector would "find a way to explain it to her or overlook it." Voormann believed Phil only cooperated with Yoko because he had to. Spector believed John was "like the brother I'd never had."

Shocked by Lennon/Ono's arrest at Ringo's apartment on October 18, 1968, Phil told *Rolling Stone*: "A multimillionaire in [John's] position just doesn't get caught in an English apartment house by the cops on a dope charge. I mean you have dogs, you have bodyguards, you got something to protect you. Lennon must really have been causing a disturbance or somebody must have been setting him up to get busted, cause it ain't no medal of honor. . . . Being busted for marijuana don't mean nothing . . . if anything, it just wasted his time. It may have even caused . . . miscarriages."

"There's nothing wrong with John Lennon doing whatever he wants to do," Spector told *Rolling Stone*. But he also wondered, "Just how bizarre he can get before he really blows it?"

Lennon's third single following the Beatles' breakup, "Instant Karma!" was probably Spector's greatest production since "River Deep, Mountain High" sent him into a deep depression. The recording was laid down in such haste that Klaus Voormann didn't even recall meeting the producer: "This guy came into the studio, and he had PS monogrammed on his shirt. It still didn't dawn on me. . . . . What followed just blew us away."

"It was not only the volume," Klaus recalled, "it sounded incredibly good. That was the moment when I knew it was Spector."

With a pair of acoustic pianos—one played by Lennon, along with George Harrison and drummer Alan White on the second—Voormann joined in, playing a third, electric piano, with Billy Preston on organ along with an ad-hoc crew of backup singers including Yoko and Allen Klein. Upon its British release just ten days later on February 6, 1970, Lennon remarked that he'd written the song "for breakfast, recorded it for lunch, and we're putting it out for dinner."

"Instant Karma!" would spend the next nine weeks on the charts, peaking at No. 5. The single's B-side, Yoko's hypnotic, gentle "Who Has Seen the Wind?" was produced by John. While the lyric evoked the imagery of Victorian-era poet Christina Rosetti (whose best work includes *Goblin Market and Other Poems* published in 1862 and 1882's *The Face of the Deep*), the harpsichord, the folksy recorder, and the charmingly amateurish/angelic vocal by Yoko are reminiscent of the Incredible String Band's ethereal singer Licorice McKechnie.

On February 11, 1970, John, Yoko, and the Plastic Ono Band performed "Instant Karma!" on the BBC's *Top of the Pops*. While Lennon sang live, the rest of the band mimed their parts. The always enigmatic Yoko appeared blindfolded, calmly knitting while sitting next to her husband, who hammered away at the piano. They both sported armbands reading "People for Peace."

"I met Phil quite a few times. And he was alright back then. Kind of a little bit of a weird character, but we got on with it," drummer Alan White recalled in a 2019 interview with *The Aquarian*. "Phil didn't come out of the control room very much [during the sessions for *All Things Must Pass*]. . . . George was kind of in control in the studio."

* * *

Engineer Richard Lush, who manned the boards for both *Plastic Ono Band* albums, considered the Starr/Voormann rhythm section "a great little unit," while Spector, he recalled, "was his inimitable self, pulling the strings, and Yoko was there nodding her head along too. There were some extremely funny moments and some good songs. It really was John speaking from the heart. He didn't want the huge Phil Spector 'wall of sound.' He wanted it to be pretty straightforward. We didn't end up doing hundreds and hundreds of takes, which is probably what would have happened if Spector had had his way!"

Like Lennon, Spector carried the scars of childhood trauma, having been abandoned by his parents. When Lennon howled "Father you left me, but I never left you," it addressed the deep bitterness within both men's hearts. John's dad abandoned the family when he was just nine; Phil's father committed suicide when Phil was the same age. Neither had known of the trauma the other had suffered.

While Yoko's lack of technical understanding challenged Phil, John's unconventional approach to recording tended to stretch everyone around him beyond their limits. After all, Lennon once famously instructed George Martin to make his music sound "orange." But from Lennon's perspective, their relationship was ultimately about what Spector could do for his music: "When I say to Phil, 'I want this,' he gets it for me!"

At the same time there was no love lost between Spector and Ono. While John's *Plastic Ono Band* was recorded over the period of a month, Yoko's album was cut in a single day, after the band had finished up recording Lennon's songs. Ono recalled how the engineers would immediately take a break, or "go to the bathroom." "[Phil] was the worst," she groused. "He would come back from the men's room and say, 'I just threw up,' to let me know how he felt."

Not only was Yoko insulted by Spector's callous remarks, she'd also been appalled by how cheap he was after he sent Lennon a bill charging them for "this crummy breakfast" he scrounged up after they spent a miserable night at his Alhambra home, sleeping on a "damp and musty" mattress.

Following John's murder, Yoko would hire Phil again to produce her new album, *Season of Glass*, "thinking it was a good idea to make the record really AM commercial so my message would get through." Although she respected Spector as a producer and considered him a friend, the odd pair soon parted ways once more after Phil cruelly remarked, "Don't worry, when we're finished with it, people will never recognize your voice."

"He meant well," Ono said . . .

4

THE ROMMEL OF THE COUCH

Whether he knew it or not, John Lennon had been a prime candidate for psycho-
therapy long before he discovered Dr. Arthur Janov's *The Primal Scream*. As Lennon
once observed, "If we cannot love ourselves, we cannot fully open to our ability to
love others or our potential to create."

Determined to heal himself and finally shed a traumatic past that continued to
loom over him despite his enormous success, John immediately agreed to work with
Janov, who claimed his unconventional methods were a cure-all for everything from
drug addiction to alcoholism, ulcers, and even homosexuality.

The initial inspiration for Dr. Janov's controversial primal scream therapy first
struck after one of his patients recalled a bizarre scene they'd recently witnessed during
an experimental theater performance. An actor, wearing nothing but diapers, curled
up in a fetal position and began to scream repeatedly for his mommy and daddy until
he began to wretch. Noticeably relieved after vomiting, the actor then wended his
way through the shocked and disgusted audience, sharing samples of his fresh puke,
distributed in sealed plastic bags, as if it were a sacrament or a souvenir.

Convinced that this gruesome ritual might be developed into a useful method
to help heal the deep wounds of early childhood trauma, Janov immediately began writing a book about a new cathartic process he coined *The Primal Scream:
Primal Therapy: The Cure for Neurosis*. Published by E. P. Dutton in 1970, an advance
copy was sent to John Lennon (as well as Peter Fonda) with the hopes of a celebrity
endorsement.

John Lennon's endless curiosity and impulsive nature often led him into strange,
uncharted territories. From his prolific use of LSD, to competing with his fellow
Beatles to see who could meditate the longest at the Maharishi's ashram, to his
and Yoko's brief dalliance with heroin, to their Bed-Ins for world peace, to their
fist-pumping revolutionary phase with Yippie Jerry Rubin, John's passion, no matter
how short-lived, was always total and complete until the next fad struck.

Suddenly fixated on Janov's ideas, Lennon would describe his primal therapy sessions as "the most important thing that happened [in his life] besides meeting Yoko

and being born." Interestingly, he didn't bother mentioning the Beatles or his former songwriting partner Paul McCartney, without whom he would never have become a world-famous musician.

In order to prepare themselves before the arrival of Janov and his wife/assistant Vivian, John and Yoko were sent a list of instructions demanding they abstain from all forms of stimuli—including drugs, cigarettes, television (which John watched habitually), and even the telephone. But the most difficult demand of all was the doctor's order to separate and take up residency in opposite sides of the mansion.

Upon his arrival at Tittenhurst, Janov discovered that John "was simply not functioning" and "needed help" immediately. Lennon agreed to submit to what was tantamount to a psychic bloodletting by "The Rommel of the Couch," as Albert Goldman, author of the poison biography *The Many Lives of John Lennon*, tagged Dr. Janov. Goldman's analysis of Lennon's "nervous breakdown," which he'd allegedly suffered following a year of hectic peace campaigns, exhibitions, and happenings—along with releasing three poorly received albums—sounded like amateur psychology run amok.

From all accounts John had reached a breaking point by February 1970 and sequestered himself inside his palatial estate until the first rays of daylight came in April in the form of Arthur Janov's new book *The Primal Scream*. Lennon recounted, it "came in the post and when I read it, I thought it was like Newton's apple. This must be it!"

"Being a Beatle nearly cost me my life, and certainly cost me a great deal of my health," Lennon wrote in the theater program for *The Ballad of John and Yoko*, a proposed Broadway show that never made it to opening night.

After scouring psychiatric textbooks, Goldman reckoned that Lennon's childhood traumas had caused his psyche to splinter into "subpersonalities." Goldman concluded that John's split with the Beatles was not merely a frustrated artist's need to express himself beyond the commercial limitations of a pop band he'd formed as a teenager, but rather evidence of a full-blown attempt at "psychic suicide." In a bit of catchy writing more akin to a Madison Avenue adman than a biographer, Goldman described Lennon as "a man with peace on his lips but war in his heart."

According to Arthur Janov, the primal scream originates from the "central and universal pains which reside in all neurotics." The controversial psychotherapist believed that our perpetual state of emotional unease is caused by "Primal Pains," triggered by "the original, early hurts upon which all later neurosis is built." "These pains," he explained, "exist in every neurotic each minute of his later life, irrespective of the form of his neurosis." Janov's radical method of healing his patients was initial-ly rigorous and even harmful. "I hurt people," he confessed. "The pain channels need to be opened. So, I dig in," he said in an interview with *Getty News*. Janov's intent was to force patients to relive their childhood traumas in hopes of finally freeing them from the lingering pain associated with disturbing events. While some reverted back to an infantile state, others claimed to have gone so far as to relive their birth. Janov's technique also involved punching pillows and other aggressive acts to help patients release years of pent-up frustration and anger. Although followed by a brief sense of relief, many believed this approach ultimately solved little and wound up generating negativity that came boomeranging back at them in unexpected ways.

After three weeks of private one-on-one sessions, Janov's patients were required to attend a series of three-hour group seminars, comprised of anywhere between twenty and fifty patients. Janov believed that meeting twice a week with fellow pa-tients would help patients release whatever deep-seated feelings remained within.

Janov soon determined that John and Yoko's daily routine at Tittenhurst was too distracting and implored them to continue the sessions in London if they were going to reap any benefit from the therapy.

While Lennon considered Janov's treatment "great," he added that he didn't "want to make it into a big Maharishi thing." "If people want to find out, they can find out. I have no idea about any other therapy. I don't think anything else would work on me so well," John explained. "I'm not through with it. It's a process that's going on. We primal almost daily." Lennon said he preferred not to delve any further into their personal experiences with Janov, as he found it "embarrassing."

"It is," Yoko concurred. "In a nutshell, primal therapy allowed us to feel feelings continuously, and those feelings usually make you cry."

Ironically, Dr. Janov was unable to scream himself, due to a throat condition that left his voice a mere whisper. In turn, Vivian Janov became the spokeswoman for her husband's radical healing method.

In response to those who wondered what became of them, John and Yoko re-leased a statement to the press on April Fool's Day, 1970, claiming they had both "entered a London clinic for a dual sex change operation" In reality, they were in the thick of therapy sessions with Janov.

On April 9, 1970, Paul McCartney phoned John to inform him of his plans to release his first solo album. "I'm doing what you and Yoko were doing last year," he explained.

"Good luck to yer," Lennon snapped. What McCartney failed to mention was his decision to publicly quit the band, which John and the rest of the world would discover the following morning on the front page of *The Daily Mirror*.

Barraged with questions from the press, Lennon maintained a cool façade, replying, "You can say he didn't quit. He was fired." However, CBS News in New York didn't take McCartney's announcement lightly. They considered the demise of the Fab Four "a landmark in the decline of the British Empire."

More turmoil ensued on April 18, when Dr. Janov suggested that, as part of his healing process, Lennon visit Cynthia and Julian to take responsibility for the failure of their relationship. Having become more conscious of the damage he suffered after his father left, John attempted to communicate with Julian. He also presented Cynthia a copy of *The Primal Scream*.

Emotionally distraught and fearing he might be tempted to return to his former life, Yoko resorted to drastic measures, calling John to demand he cut his visit short by threatening suicide if he didn't come home immediately.

On April 27, Lennon/Ono flew to Los Angeles and rented a house at 841 Nimes Road in Bel Air to continue their therapy sessions with Janov, who had to return to his patients and practice.

On its exterior, the Primal Institute was a nondescript, single-story stucco building in West Hollywood. Inside, however, the clinic's trendy décor resembled Youngblood Priest's Harlem pad in the 1972 Blaxploitation film *Superfly*, complete with, as *Rolling Stone* reporter Jerry Hopkins put it, "magenta wall-to-wall carpeting, indirect lighting, vermillion flock wallpaper, dark wood paneling, [and] padded black furniture." But Janov's unusual methods of "measuring brain waves" and observing patients in a dark, silent, barren "dungeon" for twenty minutes, where he hoped they'd drop all defenses and become more cooperative, sounds like a scene from a 1960s B-movie horror flick.

Prospective patients, Hopkins noted, were given "a complete physical, because Janov says a man with a weak heart literally won't live through what is in store for him." Beyond abstaining from all forms of stimuli (as John and Yoko were instructed), they were often requested to stay awake for twenty-four hours, "so that when [they report] the following day . . . [their] defenses will have been lowered by fatigue."

For Janov's patients, "this [was] a painful period," having to relive their past traumas. And then, as Hopkins observed, there were "the techniques employed by primal therapists in getting those experiences told; when Vivian or one of the long-haired,

Ivy League–suited young men on the staff punches the patient in the stomach to halt 'neurotic breathing' or brutally squeezes the muscles of the shoulders and neck to get the tension out." (Yes, people actually paid for this and believed it would help them.)

Beyond their one-on-one meetings (John with Janov and Yoko with Vivian), Lennon/Ono now attended group therapy sessions that met three times a week. Albert Goldman disparaged the scene as "a nursery . . . with oversize infants throwing tantrums." Images of *Marat/Sade* come to mind, with patients balled up in fetal positions, feebly sucking their thumbs while white-cloaked assistants brushed tears away from their cheeks as they relentlessly bawled in a cacophony of human misery.

"They are trying to open me up . . . reach deep, into my pain . . . the early pain and bring it out so I can get over it," Yoko explained. "It's always going to be there . . . and start to be like a cancer [and] destroy my body."

"Primal is just another mirror y'know," John explained. "You're so astounded about what you find out about yourself." While Yoko compared their experience with Janov to the Beatles' visiting the Maharishi's ashram, John, fishing for the right metaphor, compared their therapy sessions to "writers [who] take themselves to Singapore to get the atmosphere—in that way [*Plastic Ono Band*] is the first Primal album, like George's [*All Things Must Pass*] is the first Gita album."

Along with giving Charles McCarry, a reporter from *Esquire*, a copy of *The Primal Scream*, John described the punishing therapeutic process he endured: "You must go back through your emotions and feel . . . the mental pain that comes from childhood . . . actually feel it with your body."

According to McCarry, Yoko remained lonely and unhappy throughout her life until she met John, her "first friend." Foreshadowing Lennon/Ono's temporary split in 1973, John said, "We're both balmy people. [Without Janov's therapy] we would have blown up in a few years, we couldn't have kept up the pace we were going at." With her guard uncharacteristically down, most likely due to weeks in treatment, Yoko surprisingly described their relationship as "destructive." "We were in love desperately," she confessed. "Possessive and jealous and all that" (which helped shed some light on Lennon's remorseful songs like "Jealous Guy" and "Woman"). "We were really beginning to choke each other," John concurred, adding that their breakup, "would have suited everybody fine."

Despite everyone thinking he was crazy, Lennon sounded remarkably focused when recalling the intense workshops: "We'd go down to the session, have a good cry, and come back and swim in the pool," he explained. The therapy, usually followed by a dip in the cool blue, made him "feel like after acid, or a good joint . . . and every-thing was fine." But the sense of well-being soon vanished, he confessed, "and you'd go back for another fix." Or perhaps down to the local ice cream parlor, where John claimed to have systematically worked his way through all "twenty-eight different colors" to soothe his ragged vocal cords after hours of screaming away his pain. By the time he and Yoko returned to England at the end of September, John had gained nearly thirty pounds, thanks to a steady diet of sweet, creamy dessert.

* * *

A year after John and Yoko bought Tittenhurst Park, on May 22, 1969, workers dis-covered an unexploded bombshell in the basement of their Ascot estate. Thought to be a relic from World War II, this deadly weapon's unearthing undoubtedly triggered forgotten emotions in Yoko, whose mother fled Tokyo with her three children after finding a live explosive in their garden. The following day, a review in *New Musical Express* (*NME*) hammered yet another nail into the Beatles' coffin, calling their new album *Let It Be* "a cardboard tombstone."

On June 8, Janov instructed John and Yoko to see *Let It Be* while vacationing in San Francisco. Joined by *Rolling Stone*'s Jann Wenner, the three sat together, watching the depressing documentary in a sparsely attended matinee. While Janov thought the experience might help provide a sense of closure for his clients, the grim flashback on the big screen only left everyone depressed, with tears in their eyes.

Returning to LA, John began recording the first demos of the songs for *Plastic Ono Band*, laying down a rough version of "God" with an acoustic guitar on July 26 as he unburdened his soul singing, "I don't believe in Beatles."

Meanwhile, Yoko began having serious doubts about the effectiveness of Janov's therapy. She feared "The Hollywood Healer" (another of Goldman's pithy nicknames for Janov) was just another "daddy" in a long line of father figures that John constant-ly sought out.

"When I see something that is supposed to be so big and wonderful—a guru or a primal scream—I'm very cynical," she confessed. Ono suspected Janov was scheming to exploit her husband by videotaping his sessions with John. While Janov attributed Yoko's accusations to jealousy, Allen Klein claimed the real source of Ono's con-flict with their psychotherapist was due to his repeated attempts to try to convince Lennon to leave his wife. But a plausible and peaceful solution was suddenly reached after the United States Department of Immigration and Naturalization refused to extend their visas, allowing John and Yoko to gracefully bow out of the inevitable confrontation with Janov and return to England on September 24 after spending nearly five months in America.

John ultimately claimed Doctor Janov was no match for his wife, who, he believed, "watched everything he did" and "learned to do it better." But Janov harbored serious concerns that Lennon, who'd managed to get himself back on his feet after apparently suffering a devastating nervous breakdown, was now leaving before the therapy was complete. The doctor, it turned out, had good reason to fear for his most famous patient's future.

5

PLASTIC ONO BAND
(OR "JOHN'S SOUL")

Beatle John belongs to an era that is gone now.
But honest, ornery John Lennon belongs to the ages.

—Robert Palmer

John Lennon always preferred his rock 'n' roll raw, except for a brief excursion into the syrupy realms of psychedelia that began in 1966 with the mystical drone of "Tomorrow Never Knows" and peaked the following year with the surreal sound collage of "I Am the Walrus." After leaving the Beatles, John's music packed a surprisingly jagged edge, from the avant-garde musical explorations with Yoko to Plastic Ono Band's "Cold Turkey" and "Instant Karma!" Following months of therapy, John reserved a month of studio time at Abbey Road from late September to late October 1970 and got down to making his first "solo" album with old, trusted friends—bassist Klaus Voormann and Ringo on drums. Lennon "wanted, as quickly as possible, to get this feeling down before it changed," Voormann told *Rolling Stone*. Upon entering the studio, Klaus immediately noticed the ex-Beatle was "very much taken by that experience he went through."

"Plastic Ono Band was John and Ringo, half of the Beatles; and their old mate from Hamburg, Klaus Voormann," Peter Case pointed out. "Yoko replaced Paul as his partner-in-chief, and Phil Spector replaced George Martin. There was plenty of genius to go around."

Voormann considered *Plastic Ono Band* "extreme . . . because you just have John talking [about] the way he feels." In Japan the album was released as ジョンの魂 (*John no Tamashii*), which translates to *John's Soul*.

"He would always put it out there," despite whatever repercussions he was sure to face, Ringo concurred. As Arthur Janov surmised, John "was naked in front of his fame."

"The twin *Plastic Ono Band* records were released in the aftermath of the Beatles'
breakup and Altamont and so much falling ash in the waning hippie atmosphere,"
Nels Cline explained. "At first listen I was kind of baffled, verging on bummed out
because of what actually makes this record so timelessly great in retrospect. It is so
brutally naked and instrumentally stripped down. I wanted to hear 'production' or
something. And besides, there's all that screaming! But the power of *Plastic Ono
Band* was undeniable, like a bitter pill that needed swallowing, a harsh antidote to all
the illusory bullshit surrounding the Beatles, John and Yoko, and the dreams of the
counterculture."

"I missed the Beatles as a kid," said Sonic Youth drummer Steve Shelley. "I remember hearing 'Strawberry Fields [Forever]' and 'The Ballad of John and Yoko' on
the radio, because he said 'Christ,' and it was a very big deal at the time in Midland,
Michigan, where we used to buy our records at the grocery store down the street. You
never saw Plastic Ono Band records at *that* store!" Steve laughed. "I was only eight
years old in 1970, so I wasn't ready for 'God,' or 'Mother,' or any of that."

"*Plastic Ono Band* was a heart attack of an album . . . the antithesis to *Sgt.
Pepper*," proclaimed Marvin Etzioni, songwriter/producer and founding member of
Lone Justice. "The lyrics were direct, simple yet timelessly profound. The production
was something I had never heard before . . . the stark, minimalist sound . . . especially
with Phil Spector's name attached to it. Growing up, I gravitated toward George
Martin and Mickey Most's production. Phil Spector's wall of sound seemed distant.
It wasn't until I heard *Plastic Ono Band* that I went back to Spector's records and
realized his arrogant brilliance. He just turned off all the effects, and instead of a wall
of sound, John's *Plastic Ono Band* was just a wall, one that would stand through the
decades and never fall."

"It's crazy. In 1970 I was fourteen years old. I have a son that age now," Hal
Willner said, mystified by the passage of time. "I got both records on the same day,
the minute they came out. I brought John's album to school and played 'God' and
asked everybody what they thought. My friends knew about the record but didn't like
it. I still think John's *Plastic Ono Band* was one of the greatest albums ever made . . .
ever! The structure of the songs are drop-dead amazing. There's not one ounce of fat
on that record."

6

MOTHER

I didn't sit down to write about my mother.
They [the songs] just came out.

—John Lennon

Alf Lennon had it bad for Julia Stanley, the bubbly, beguiling usherette from the Trocadero. Not only did she have a vivacious smile and wicked sense of humor, but she loved to go ballroom dancing as well. Besides, they both possessed some modicum of musical talent. While Alf's imitation of Al Jolson impressed friends, particularly when he donned blackface and went down on one knee to bellow a rousing rendition of "Mammy," Julia sang and played the banjo, as well as accordion and ukulele.

Not surprisingly Julia's family disapproved of Alf, whom they considered no more than a lowlife. They doubted whether Lennon, employed as a ship's steward, could ever be a reliable husband, as he was often away at sea for long stretches of time. But despite their repeated warnings and protests, Julia impulsively married Alf in a private civil ceremony on December 3, 1938, after having taunted him to propose. Barely two years later, John Winston Lennon was born. By then the war was in full tilt, despite Hitler's flimsy promise of peace to Chamberlin. For two nights prior to October 9, 1940, Liverpool had been pummeled by the Luftwaffe's bombs. But on the night that John arrived, the city was strangely calm. Two nights later, the German bombers returned again.

With little hope of available employment in Liverpool, Alf's time away at sea steadily increased. He'd been gone for a six-month stretch, between September 1942 and February 1943, and then shipped out again the following July, this time for sixteen months. During this time he was arrested and jailed twice—once in Algeria—and then stranded in New York City before returning to Liverpool only to discover that Julia, who had no clue whether he was dead or alive, was pregnant with another man's child. To help curb the inevitable gossip and shame, the baby girl was immediately given up for adoption, renamed, and whisked off to be raised in Norway.

Throughout this period of domestic chaos, John was temporarily sent to live with Alf's brother, his Uncle Sydney, and his Aunt Madge until his wayward father, determined to repair his broken home, arrived to retrieve his young son. But in the interim Julia had taken up with yet another man with whom she would have two daughters. Although they were still legally married, she had no intention of ever returning to Alf.

Claiming he was just taking John out for a few hours to buy new clothes, Alf spirited his young son up north to the seaside resort town of Blackpool, where they stayed at the home of Alf's former crewmate for the next few weeks until Julia arrived unannounced after finally tracking them down. The confrontation that ensued would psychologically scar John for the rest of his life. Once again Alf begged Julia to come back to him and start over, but she would have none of it. To settle the issue, the child was commanded to make a choice between his mother and father. Having recently bonded with Alf, John initially picked his dad, until he saw his "mummy" getting ready to leave and ran to her in tears, desperately throwing his arms around her waist.

Although this family drama sheds a lot of light on John's overwhelming insecurity, we can't be certain the confrontation ever happened. While one biographer claims it as fact, others view it as an unconfirmable legend. Either way the story, which seems made for television, continues to be told and retold over the years and has become part of John's narrative.

While many of the Beatles' early songs were fabricated dramas reflecting the problems faced by young lovers, the lyrics to "Mother" sprang directly from Lennon's childhood experience, memories he'd struggled to repress and forget but was now determined to confront in hopes of finally freeing himself, once and for all, from the trauma that still lingered.

While musically simplistic, Lennon's latest batch of songs were unlike anything he'd ever written and recorded. Influenced by Bob Dylan, who'd bared his soul with bitter breakup songs like "Don't Think Twice It's Alright," and Roy Orbison, who fearlessly wore his emotions on his sleeve in tunes like "Crying," John first revealed his inner self in the "confessional" lyrics to "Help," which no one took seriously at first due to its catchy upbeat tempo. Besides, why would anyone think the leader of the world's most popular band could be "really down" and "so insecure?" Surely, it was just more role-playing, like so many of John's earlier songs. But with their following album, *Rubber Soul*, released in December 1965, it was clear the Beatles were beginning to grow up—fast! As Dylan keenly observed, the mop tops were "no longer cute anymore."

Rubber Soul featured Lennon's melancholy masterpiece "In My Life," taking us on a guided tour of his lost youth in Liverpool. Along with the surprisingly dark and tormented "Girl," John now wrote and sang songs that opened the book of his life for his fans to freely interpret. The lyrics to Lennon's "Nowhere Man" portrayed a self-absorbed layabout who couldn't care less that the world's passing him by. "Isn't he a bit like you and me?" John asked knowingly, while we wondered if he was talking about himself.

It had been barely two years since that fateful night when a joyous brand of new mayhem exploded across America (and the rest of the world) as the Beatles appeared on *The Ed Sullivan Show*. And now John Lennon was already taking joy in puncturing the myth that being a Beatle was as "fab" as we'd all imagined.

Having shed what he later ridiculed as the "gobbledygook" lyrics of earlier psychedelic masterpieces like "Lucy in the Sky with Diamonds" and "I Am the Walrus," John began writing with a bold, new emotional transparency, previously unheard in pop music. (It would take another five years and a jarring divorce before his artistic sparring partner, Bob Dylan, finally dropped his mask of surrealistic wordplay and revealed his most private emotions on his 1975 masterpiece *Blood on the Tracks*.) Lennon's introspection and honesty had reached an unprecedented peak with the elegiac portrait of his mother in the gently fingerpicked "Julia" on the *White Album*. With just an acoustic guitar and his lilting voice, John fearlessly laid his feelings bare for all the world to hear.

Plastic Ono Band's opening track, "Mother," was Lennon's ultimate attempt to free himself from the psychic umbilical cord that still bound him to the specter of his negligent mummy. The song began with four lumbering chimes of a church bell, which could be taken to symbolize the final laying to rest of the Beatles, with each toll representing a member of the group. Or perhaps John employed the doleful carillons to announce the death of the 1960s dream of peace and love, which he, the self-described "dream-weaver," once helped spearhead but now unceremoniously proclaimed "over" in the shocking lyrics to "God." As John told Jann Wenner in his famous 1970 *Rolling Stone* interview: "The dream's over, and I have personally got to get down to so-called reality."

No matter how one interprets them, the bells cast a gloomy, funereal atmosphere over the opening song and set the tone for the rest of *Plastic Ono Band*. John claimed the inspiration initially struck in Los Angeles, while he was watching an old horror film late one night on TV. Whether it was coincidence or something floating around in his subconsciousness (as John previously dismissed his pilfering of Chuck Berry's lyrics from "You Can't Catch Me" that he'd nicked for "Come Together"), *Black Sabbath* had also opened with the ominous tolling of bells. The eponymous debut by rock's (arguably) first heavy metal band was released on February 13, 1970, in the UK (and four months later in America, on June 1), well before Lennon recorded *Plastic Ono Band.*

Was John Lennon familiar with Black Sabbath? Their dark and gnarly debut had kicked and clawed its way up to No. 8 in England and subsequently No. 23 on the *Billboard* charts in America. And it was obvious where Ozzy Osbourne got his visual style from, aping John's *White Album*-era look by donning granny glasses and parting his shoulder-length hair down the middle. Either way, Lennon regularly kept an eye on the Top 40, as he revealed in the absurd/acerbic letter sent to Queen Elizabeth explaining the abrupt return of his MBE (the MBE, short for Member of the Most Excellent Order of the British Empire, is an award designating the third-highest ranking of the British Empire, most often given for great accomplishments in the arts, sciences, and charitable work). On November 25, 1969, Lennon wrote: "Your Majesty—I am returning this MBE in protest against Britain's involvement in the Nigeria-Biafra thing, against our support of America in Vietnam, and against 'Cold Turkey' slipping down the charts" (the song had pushed its way into the Top 20, peaking at a disappointing No. 14).

The next day Lennon held a press conference to read the letter, which claimed the Establishment had attempted to buy the Beatles with the honor. "Now I'm giving it back," John said. He then confessed, "I sold my soul when I received it. . . . But now [I] have helped redeem it in the cause of peace." Signing off to Her Majesty, Lennon reminded the Queen "to try and do everything with humor and keep smiling."

Aloof as they appeared at times, the Beatles did not exist in a total vacuum. Well aware of the music charts and current trends, they would lay claim to inventing heavy metal (a term originally credited to Beat novelist William S. Burroughs, from his 1962 novel *The Soft Machine*) with Paul's apocalyptic rocker "Helter Skelter" on the *White Album.*

Both "Mother" and "Black Sabbath" were slow, heavy, plodding dirges that exuded a dark, ominous atmosphere. While Yoko, nothing short of a force of nature in John's estimation, provided a whooshing "wind" (as she was credited in *Plastic Ono Band*'s liner notes), Sabbath employed the soundtrack of a full-blown thunderstorm on their song. Either way, the London-based Hammer Films, producer of fabulously tacky horror movies, was the probable source of the haunting bells for both artists.

But the reverberation of melancholy bells was just the beginning. From Al Jolson's black-faced tearjerker "Mammy" to the Rolling Stones' "Have You Seen Your Mother Baby, Standing in the Shadows" (which portrayed a struggling unwed mother confronted by the looming ghost of her own mother), songs about moms have usually spelled trouble. Nothing was more outrageous than the Doors' oedipal opus "The End," in which an unhinged Jim Morrison screamed, "Father, I want to kill you, Mother . . . I want to . . ." Hoping to dodge an inevitable storm of controversy, Elektra Records understandably substituted Jim's "fuck you" for an indecipherable feral groan that teemed with self-loathing. Lennon later confessed to having overwhelming oedipal desires towards Julia after he accidentally brushed his hand against his mother's breast as the two enjoyed an afternoon nap together.

Even naming one's band "The Mothers" was fraught with issues, as the mad maestro Frank Zappa discovered. Irked by the implications of the group's questionable moniker, Verve Records demanded the Mothers change their name, which led to Frank's playful bastardization of Plato's quote "Necessity is the mother of invention." Thus, any questionable notions their original name might have conjured were instantly quashed. After all, this was a gang of scraggly long-haired men who were dubbed "The Ugliest Band in Rock" and appeared in drag on the jacket of their third album, We're Only In It for the Money, a vicious/hilarious parody of the Beatles' Sgt. Pepper's Lonely Hearts Club Band that nearly cost Verve a lawsuit. Pressured by record company execs, the band eventually acquiesced and reversed the album's cover photo with the bright yellow gatefold image of Frank in a dress and pigtails, along with the rest of the Mothers of Invention looking like a motley crew of bearded spinster aunts.

It's interesting to note that after John and Yoko performed at the Fillmore East with Zappa and his crew on June 6, 1971, their impromptu jam would be credited to "The Plastic Ono Mothers" on side 4 of Lennon/Ono's Some Time in New York City.

Beyond the menacing presence of the four overdubbed bells, John's Plastic Ono Band was strictly a stripped-down affair, the antithesis of the over-the-top production that the album's producer, Phil Spector, was famous for. The record's credits left many wondering if the legendary music man had been John's "producer" in name only.

In fact, Lennon had bought a full-page ad that ran simultaneously in Billboard, Record World, and Cashbox on October 3, 1970, with the message: "PHIL! JOHN IS READY THIS WEEKEND!" printed in bold capital letters, in hopes the eccentric producer would see it and find his way to Abbey Road where John, Ringo, and Klaus had already begun recording without him. Starr apparently had "no real memory of

Phil producing" the sessions for Plastic Ono Band. As he recalled, "The engineer took down what we did, and John would mix it."

Spector had clearly left his mark on George Harrison's first solo outing, *All Things Must Pass*—released just a few weeks before *Plastic Ono Band* on November 27, 1970—nearly burying the wispy-voiced singer under his trademark "wall of sound" created by multitracked guitars, keyboards, horns, and drums.

In comparison, the making of *Plastic Ono Band* was more like a field recording than the typical multitracked, polished product of its day. Like an inspired jazz improvisor or bluesman brimming with emotion, Lennon wanted to get in the studio and lay the music down as quickly as possible before the feeling faded. Released shortly before Christmas, *Plastic Ono Band* seemed more like a portfolio of wounds and scars than John Lennon's first solo album. The bare-bones aesthetic of *Plastic Ono Band* was simply John's way of keeping the music fresh. With the recent release of "Cold Turkey" and "Instant Karma!" Lennon seemed more present in the studio than he had been in years. Many of the album's basic tracks were cut in a matter of two or three takes, captured at what the French photographer Henri Cartier-Bresson termed "the decisive moment."

"The album was recorded in an adrenaline rush, with little time expended on discussion or rehearsal," Klaus Voormann recalled. Lennon passed chord charts around with the song's lyrics "written bigger than normal," Klaus explained, prompting the musicians "to read the words and consider how their accompaniment might better fit the feeling that John was seeking."

"Klaus was 'the invisible bass player,'" says Bobby Whitlock. "You should *feel* the bass. It should just line up with the kick drum and not stand out. Klaus had a shining personality, so he never had to play flashy."

"Lennon must have wanted a friend in the studio to play bass after his squabbles with McCartney," said Violent Femmes bassist Brian Ritchie. "Voormann's bass playing is serviceable, minimal, and transparent. Just right for that material."

"The simplicity of what Klaus and I played . . . gave [John] a great opportunity to actually, for the first time, really use his voice and emotion. . . . There was no battle going on," Starr imparted in the *Classic Albums: John Lennon/Plastic Ono Band* documentary. "He would just sit there and sing them, and we would just sort of jam, and then we'd find out how they would sort of go and we did them. It was very loose actually, and being a trio also was a lot of fun."

While off in Spain filming the spaghetti western *Blindman* (in which Starr played a scruffy, sombrero-clad sidekick to Tony Anthony in the leading role of a blind gunslinger), Starr didn't bother trying to dispel the mounting rumors that Klaus Voormann had been tapped to replace McCartney. "I'll be in a group with John and George and Klaus and call it the Ladders, or whatever you want," he told *Melody Maker.* "But I don't think it would be called the Beatles."

"It was a good combo," Yoko said of the Plastic Ono Band. "When Ringo did this, I said, 'My god, he's really good.'"

"It's not easy to play that simple," D. J. Bonebrake, drummer with the legendary Los Angeles punk band X, explained. "On 'Mother,' Ringo put the kick on the 1 and 3 with the snare on the 2 and 4, with an added kick every couple of measures, on the 'and' of 4. His playing reminds me of Al Jackson Jr. [drummer with the funky Memphis instrumental band Booker T. and the MG's, whose nickname was 'The Human Timekeeper']."

"You can't get any better than that," he continued, "except maybe for Ringo. He's got perfect time and a perfect groove. At the end of the verses, he replaces one of the eighth notes with a sixteenth note. But on the third verse, the bass drum becomes more complicated. At the end of the song, his snare fills match John's vocals when he begins to scream, "Mama, don't go!" Suddenly he is playing in 7/8 time or 2/4 with a measure of 3/8 or 6/16. . . . Either way Ringo's fills always have a great shuffle feel to them."

Chosen as the album's single, "Mother" was issued by Apple Records on December 28, 1970. There was little doubt that many of John's derogatory remarks in the lengthy *Rolling Stone* interview that soon followed were inspired by the nagging fact that George Harrison's "My Sweet Lord" had spent the previous month atop the *Billboard* charts, while "Mother" peaked at a disappointing No. 43.

"I was a bit surprised by the reaction to 'Mother,'" Lennon complained to author Robert Hilburn. "Can't they see how nice it is?"

John's fans were unnerved not only by the song's stark lyrics but also by the series of feral screams and shrieks on its coda. Lennon's savage howls on "Mother" and "Well, Well, Well" were always recorded after the day's sessions, as they shredded his vocal cords. As engineer John Leckie told *Uncut* magazine in August 2010, "The screams were double-tracked [as] John didn't like the raw sound of his own voice. He always wanted lots of stuff on it." Leckie felt Phil Spector's greatest contribution to Lennon's *Plastic Ono Band* "was to be generous with reverb and echo."

Finding little support in Britain, the single version of the album's opening song was only released in America (there was no UK issue!) in a monoaural pressing and edited to down to 3:55 from its original length of 5:29. Gone were the ominous tolling bells, and the radio-friendly version of "Mother" quickly faded out after the last verse. The B-side, Yoko's explosive "Why," didn't do much to help John's anemic sales.

Nine years after the release of *Plastic Ono Band*, Roger Waters's "Mother" (from Pink Floyd's *The Wall*) addressed many of the same issues as Lennon's song by the same name, while taking an unflinching look at his life and delving into matters of morality, security, and trust.

As country singer Harlan Howard once famously said, a great song (no matter what style it is) only needs "three chords and the truth." Dynamics play an intrinsic role in both Lennon's and Waters's "Mother." While John punctuated his song's steady, hypnotic rhythm with primal screams of anguish, Pink Floyd relied on David Gilmour's soaring blues guitar riffs to up the emotional intensity of Waters's dark tale. The song's chorus resembles a modern version of a Grimm's fairy tale as its protagonist (whose father was killed during the war) earnestly searches for guidance while his mum assures him she will make his deepest fears "come true."

"John Lennon's a great example of someone who does it [draws from personal feelings and experiences to write songs] and Paul McCartney is a great example of somebody who doesn't," David Gilmour reckoned. "McCartney always seemed . . . frightened of exactly that, of letting anything of his true self out, which is a shame."

Recalling "a short moment in my life when I felt pretty desperate," Gilmour wrestled with whether to use personal pain as a source of inspiration, because, as he confessed, "it felt a little too close to me. . . . And that's a nervy thing to do." His bandmate Roger Waters apparently had nerves of steel when fearlessly mining his own life for the motivation to create *The Wall*.

"In the end, either you cheer people up with your songs or help them exorcise some problems they have," singer/songwriter Steve Earle pointed out. John Lennon apparently did more than his share of each.

Intrepid Interpretations: "Mother"

Covering Lennon's highly personal songs from *Plastic Ono Band* was a losing proposition for most artists. Delivering such powerful lyrics demanded that the artist enter a deeply emotional state to present John's hard truths with the same level of conviction with which he wrote them. These songs are in a world of their own when compared to the early pop confections Lennon and McCartney were famous for. Even John had difficulty sounding convincing when he performed the material live two years later, on August 30, 1972, at Madison Square Garden. "This song is another song from one of those albums I made since I left the Rolling Stones," Lennon quipped, attempting to lighten the mood for a moment before adding, "a lot of people thought ["Mother"] was just about my parents, but it was about 99 percent of the parents, alive or half dead."

In the year following *Plastic Ono Band*'s release, Barbra Streisand (of all people) recorded "Mother" (along with Lennon's gossamer-like "Love") on her album *Barbra Joan Streisand*. While the notion of Babs wailing Lennon's lament to his dead mother seemed nothing short of bizarre, the diva did a most admirable job with John's song. Kicking off with long, sustained, churchy organ chords, and supported by droning cellos, an unrestrained Streisand sang the wallpaper off the wall. Thankfully, she didn't try to outscream John on the song's coda. Instead Streisand's voice soared, sounding like she meant every word of this bitter farewell.

Maynard Ferguson gave Lennon's torturous dirge plenty of sizzling hot trumpet on the puzzling version of "Mother" from his 1972 album *M. F. Horn Two*. John would have had difficulty recognizing his own tune, as Ferguson's rococo arrangement packed none of the emotional power of the original song. "Mother" certainly seems like a peculiar choice to jazz up. Perhaps Ferguson chose it for its repetitive vamp (over which John screamed "Mother don't go!") as the foundation for Stan Robinson's burly tenor sax solo. But this and many jazz interpretations of Lennon and other Beatle songs in the past most likely spurred John to disparage jazz as "the worst kind of music . . . ever created or imagined."

Country rocker Shelby Lynne sang Lennon's heartbreaker as a cathartic way of dealing with the trauma suffered after her father shot her mother in an alcoholic haze, then killed himself when she was just a teenager. Bringing a bit of blue-eyed soul to the song while adding a few warmer chords to John's skeletal melody, Shelby's version morphed into a light grunge anthem. An echoey vocal mix adds a somewhat cerebral quality to the song. Perhaps the most effective aspect of her arrangement is the cliffhanging ending, which evokes the feeling that comes with being abandoned suddenly.

Years later in July 2011, Lou Reed performed a plodding, punishing rendition of "Mother" while on tour in the UK and Europe. It seems like an odd choice for

Reed, as the song's legato notes are clearly out of his vocal range. Instead he awkwardly recites the lyric, punctuated by occasional groans. As one YouTube detractor groused, Reed sounds "like he just got out of a mental institution." There's perhaps more truth to that quip than the commentator realized, as Reed had been subjected to electroshock treatment in his youth.

"Mother" spoke to Lou because, as he told author/journalist Bruce Pollock, it "had realism." Reed claimed when he first heard it, he didn't "even know it was him. I just said, 'Who the fuck is that? I don't believe that.' Because the lyrics to that are real. You see, he wasn't kidding around. He got right down to it, as down as you can get. I like that in a song."

From the opposite end of the spectrum came David Bowie's soulful rendition of "Mother," produced by Tony Visconti. Originally intended for a Lennon tribute album, Bowie's version was recorded in August 1988 in Nassau, with Visconti on bass and ace session drummer Andy Newmark. Remaining true to John's original, David's husky vocals bring an added theatricality to the song, taking it to new sonic heights with the help of guitarist Reeves Gabrels's slashing shards of sound. While the track remains unreleased and labelled "rare," it has received around five hundred thousand plays on YouTube.

Other covers of "Mother" include the Roots' powerful live performance in 2015 and Christina Aguilera, who sounds strangely enough as if she's covering . . . a Barbra Streisand song.

7

HOLD ON

By the time *Plastic Ono Band* was released on December 11, 1970, the counterculture dream was in shambles. While three days of peace, love, and music at the Woodstock Festival had offered a momentary tab of hope to the shaggy, mud-drenched masses, the remainder of 1969 grew darker by the minute. The Harvard-professor-turned-acid-guru Timothy Leary would escape from a California prison on September 12, while eight days later, the Doors' lead singer Jim Morrison was arraigned for "open profanity and indecent exposure" after having been arrested at a Miami concert, although no one in the crowd was sure whether they'd actually seen his offensive appendage. Two days after that, the Nixon administration ordered one thousand plainclothes FBI agents to infiltrate college campuses across the country to keep an eye on the mounting unrest among the students.

Then things turned seriously ugly on December 6, at the Rolling Stones' free-concert/free-for-all at Altamont Speedway. Mayhem ensued after the Hell's Angels, who were hired as security guards (on the recommendation of the Grateful Dead), ran amok. The beer-drenched, burly bikers first slugged Marty Balin, the Jefferson Airplane's singer, and then repeatedly beat members of the bewildered crowd with pool cues, ultimately killing the eighteen-year-old Meredith Hunter Jr., who was packing a loaded pistol with the intent to murder Mick Jagger.

While "The Woodstock Nation," as Abbie Hoffman had dubbed his fellow baby boomers, may have momentarily reclaimed "The Pepsi Generation" from Madison Avenue marketing execs, it was clear they had a long row to hoe if they were going to successfully usher in a new revolution on par with the country's forefathers.

The simple refrain of "Hold On John, John Hold On" seems like the perfect mantra that John might have chanted to himself while navigating the crazy time he and Yoko faced—from the bitter disintegration of the Beatles to the tsunami of criticism and hatred that rained down on them daily, from the controversy over their outrageous *Two Virgins* album to the drug bust led by the celebrity headhunter Sergeant Norman Pilcher.

Having previously arrested Keith Richards, Brian Jones, and Donovan, Sergeant Pilcher had had his sites on John and Yoko for some time before showing up outside Ringo's Montagu Square apartment around midnight on the night of October 18, 1968, with a crew of bobbies and dope-sniffing dogs. Relaxing in bed, Lennon/Ono refused to get up and answer the door, which later resulted in an obstruction of justice charge. After the police attempted climbing through the windows, Lennon finally acquiesced, opened the latch, and let them in.

Having been tipped off the bust was coming, John claimed to have previously disposed of any and all contraband before Sergeant Pilcher arrived. But it wasn't long before the dogs tracked down a small dope stash that Lennon swore had been planted on the premises by the crooked cop.

Pilcher's karma may not have been instant, but his comeuppance eventually did come. After retiring in Australia, "Semolina Pilchard," as Lennon immortalized him in "I Am the Walrus," was shipped back to England, where he was tried, found guilty for his corrupt practice of routinely planting dope on rock stars and alerting the press to their imminent arrest, and served four years in prison. But the problems that stemmed from possessing a small amount of hashish would later cause untold trouble for Lennon when attempting to emigrate to America. And it didn't help Yoko, who'd been trying to prove she was a suitable mother for her daughter, Kyoko. Add to that a car accident in Scotland, when John (whose dim eyesight didn't help his meager driving skills) lost control of their car, badly bruising all passengers within.

In response to his childhood traumas, John Lennon constantly searched for some sort of escape from life's harsh realities, a safe haven where he could hide, imagining a utopian world of his own design. "There's a place, where I can go . . ." he once sang in seamless harmony with his old pal, Paul McCartney.

In order to survive the world's slings and arrows, Lennon/Ono over time learned to dismiss the media's opinion of them. Once asked how she felt about the steady flow of vitriol toward her, Yoko slyly replied, "Roses need a lot of fertilizer."

Following the disappointing response to *Plastic Ono Band*, Lennon/Ono returned to the bucolic splendor of their seventy-two-acre Tittenhurst Park estate. With his home studio Ascot Sound Studios (which he affectionately dubbed ASS) finally complete, Lennon wasted no time getting back to work. Joined by Billy Preston on keyboards, the Stones' saxman Bobby Keys, and Voormann and White laying down the rhythm, John cut his hastily composed agitprop anthem "Power to the People" on February 15, 1971. With a nod to the Rolling Stones' "Street Fighting

Man," the song kicked off with "the sound of marching, charging feet," while buoyed by a chorus of voices (which featured Rosetta Hightower of the '60s girl group the Orlons) chanting Lennon's latest slogan. Released in the UK with Yoko's provocative B-side "Open Your Box," the American version was delayed for ten days due to Ono's lascivious lyrics. Reprinted with the "more suitable" "Touch Me" now on the flipside, John's revolutionary rocker finally hit the airwaves in the States, climbing to No. 6 in the UK charts while just falling short of *Billboard*'s Top 10.

Years later in his "unfinished" and somewhat fragmented memoir *Skywriting by Word of Mouth*, John confessed the tune was "rather embarrassing." Attempting to defend his obvious pandering to the left (after being pressured by Robin Blackburn and Tariq Ali of the radical magazine *Red Mole* to make a concise political statement following the confusion over "Revolution"), Lennon claimed the song had been "a quickie . . . something for the people to sing." Gonzo Journalist Dr. Hunter S. Thompson was considerably less charitable, slamming the single for coming out "ten years too late," which was, like much of Thompson's work, an exaggeration. The recent movement toward revolution actually began on January 11, 1968, in Split, Croatia (at that time part of the former Yugoslavia), when artists/activists Pave Dulčić and Tomo Ćaleta with a clutch of co-conspirators painted the peristyle (the town square) red. This defiant act—one part political protest, one part performance art—triggered a wave of dissent throughout Europe that helped ignite the Prague Spring and the Paris demonstrations of May 1968.

Next up on Lennon's hit parade of cause songs was "God Save Us" (backed with Lennon/Ono's groovy hokeypokey "Do the Oz"), a fundraiser for the Australian/British underground magazine *Oz*, which had been plagued with obscenity charges. The publication's desperate editors phoned John begging for help, but Lennon, who was on the verge of recording his next album, *Imagine*, balked at releasing what might be taken as another throwaway following "Power to the People." A compromise was quickly reached. Lennon/Ono would write the song, with a few lines tossed in by *Oz* editors. But as the original lyric, "God save *Oz* from it all," would mean little to Americans, they decided to go with "God Save Us." Anyone expecting a follow-up to *Plastic Ono Band*'s monumental "God" was sure to be disappointed. After recording the basic tracks at his Ascot studio on April 13, 1971, John, having played acoustic guitar and singing a guide vocal, turned the mike over to Bill Elliot, lead singer from the band Half-Breed, a Mal Evans discovery. Credited to the Electric Oz Band, the single was released in July backed with "Do the Oz." Despite Lennon's noble effort to

help the "Oz Three" (Richard Neville, Jim Anderson, and Felix Dennis), the journalists were found guilty, and the magazine soon folded. But perhaps worse was John's
comment that the song "really hurt my ears." Despite Lennon's disparaging remark,
Bill Elliot (whom John claimed sounded "like Paul") later reemerged as half of the
vocal duo Splinter, signed to George Harrison's Dark Horse label.

* * *

Determined to top his old bandmates' current releases, John rounded up an excep-
tional crew of musicians to fashion a more commercial/radio-friendly album. They
included LA session drummer Jim Keltner and Nicky Hopkins, whose keyboards
augmented records by legendary San Francisco bands Quicksilver Messenger Service
and Jefferson Airplane, and who had more recently become essential to the Rolling
Stones' mix.

Once again Klaus Voormann was on bass with George Harrison adding some of
the most sublime slide guitar playing of his career, while Phil Spector produced, this
time taking a more hands-on approach. Lacking the fire and gravitas of *Plastic Ono
Band*, Lennon's next offering had a broader sonic palate and appeal. "*Imagine*," John
quipped, was "just 'Mother' with chocolate coating."

"Those two records [Lennon/Ono's dual release of *Plastic Ono Band*] are such
genius," Peter Case exclaimed. "John's is the greatest record he ever made as a songwriter. *Imagine* is pale next to it. Though 'How Do You Sleep?' and 'I Don't Want
to Be a Soldier' are really strong, some of it is weak, like 'Crippled Inside.' . . . I'm
not sure what happened to him after that, I feel he really lost his way and never
recovered."

Following the dual release of their *Imagine/Fly* albums, Lennon/Ono would
leave the isolation of their English manor and dive headfirst into a tumultuous new
life in New York City. The "Two Virgins" returned to Yoko's old stomping ground to
kick up a creative tornado in the name of peace. They truly became "just a boy and a
little girl, trying to change the whole wide world" as John had sung.

Initially taking up residence at the St. Regis Hotel in Midtown Manhattan,
Lennon/Ono soon bought a small Greenwich Village two-room basement apartment
that previously belonged to Joe Butler, the drummer with the Lovin' Spoonful.

Holding court at their 105 Bank Street grotto (come on NYC, make it a landmark already!) John and Yoko took care of business with a passel of assistants and a
tangle of telephones from the comfort of their king-sized bed. What came next didn't
necessarily please Lennon's fans.

If you've been among those wondering what became of the Lewis Carroll-esque blubbering walrus of the Beatles' psychedelic phase, forget it ("I was the walrus, but now I'm John," Lennon revealed in "Isolation"). Lennon/Ono were no longer sending world leaders acorns wrapped with coy instructions to plant them in the name of peace. Nor were they content to lounge about in striped flannel pajamas in comfy hotel beds from Amsterdam to Montreal, playing host to throngs of journalists and friends, strumming guitar, flanked by hand-scribbled signs declaring "Bed Peace" and "Hair Peace."

Arriving in New York to promote their new albums, John (with Yoko offering occasional commentary) gave a marathon interview to *Rolling Stone* with the intent of driving a stake through the dying heart of the Beatles' legacy. "Lennon Remembers" filled two issues of the magazine with poison rants that John would later refer to as "Lennon Regrets."

Having been impressed with Jerry Rubin's anarchistic antics on *The David Frost Show* on November 7, 1970 (in which Rubin lit a joint on live TV and handed it to his flustered host, saying "It's an experience. . . . Try it!), Lennon/Ono began hanging out with the Yippie leader to map out the next American revolution. Just months before, John was in the thick of therapy, digging deep, mining the unbearable pain of his existence for what was the most stunning song cycle of his career. But the "Isolation" the couple experienced while living what appeared to be an idyllic life in England turned out a bit stifling and claustrophobic.

And now they were carefree, happily camping out in the bohemian West Village, walking arm in arm down city sidewalks and through shady parks, buying steaming hot dogs from street vendors (so much for the strict demands of a macrobiotic diet), and jamming with and producing the wild and woolly David Peel and his gaggle of Lower East Side street-rockers.

Like Woody Guthrie's homeless son, Peel (born David Michael Rosario to Puerto Rican immigrants and raised in the tenements of Brooklyn) regularly played for free in Greenwich Village's historic Washington Square Park. Instantly smitten upon hearing the ragged street singer crow his three-chord, radical, free-love/free-dope anthems like "Have a Marijuana" and "Up Against the Wall," John signed Peel to Apple Records and produced his third album, *The Pope Smokes Dope* in 1972. David's heavy "New Yawk" accent spoke directly to John's inner Scouse, helping to inspire (for better and worse) the grungy rock 'n' roll newsflash of *Some Time in New York City*. David even looked like Lennon, down to his dark, round granny sunglasses and long scraggly hair that he parted down the middle.

Despite the "Beatle burnings" in the wake of his "Bigger than Jesus" quip, John Lennon always claimed to love America, New York City in particular. "I should have been born in the Village," he told Jann Wenner. "That's where I belong."

With their combined vision for world peace and love of clever pranks, Lennon/ Ono now adopted the great unwashed with open arms. Their new proletariat attitude was reflected by their new fashion sense. Gone were the matching monochrome black-and-white suits (as Lennon sported on the covers of *Abbey Road* and *Hey Jude*), replaced by khaki army fatigues and combat helmets with raised fists, which suddenly became the new order of the day. With Lennon/Ono, the winds of change could suddenly shift at any time, with no warning. Very little missed their antennae. They sensed the zeitgeist and were quick to absorb and adopt any new concept that could be used to further their fervent world peace campaign.

John deeply understood the power of mantra—whether gleefully chanting "Hare Krishna" at the lotus feet of Srila Prabupad with George and a handful of saffron-robed devotees or reeling off a list of names of all the "beautiful people" who gathered around their Montreal hotel bed on the night of June 1, 1969, to record their proto-rap single "Give Peace a Chance."

"Hold On" seems to possess the power of a mantra as well. It's not hard to imagine John chanting the song's lyrics under his breath whenever stressful moments arose. With its lush chords and a melody that rolled and washed over you like waves, massaging the shoreline of your mind, "Hold On" picked up where *Abbey Road*'s "The Sun King" had left off. But the song's serene mood was abruptly disrupted after John suddenly blurted out, nearly belching the word, "Cookie!" in his best imitation of *Sesame Street*'s blue, gruff-voiced Cookie Monster.

Over the years, in dozens of interviews, Lennon openly confessed he was addicted to watching "the telly." And grumbling "Cookie" wasn't the first time Lennon referenced something as mundane as a TV show in his music. On *Sgt. Peppers'* rockin' "Good Morning, Good Morning," John sang, "It's time for tea and *Meet the Wife*," name-checking the popular British television series.

There were actually two versions of "Hold On." The original recording, released on the album, was a gentle, lilting ballad that John initially tracked as an instrumental, playing a tremolo-laden guitar with solid support by Klaus and Ringo. Needing to concentrate on his guitar performance, John laid down a guide-track vocal, singing gently only on the chorus. But as the tune ends, the band impulsively breaks into a loose, bluesy boogie. Lennon's lead guitar slips and slides, while Voormann walks a syncopated bass line over Ringo's bubbly shuffle. John, in one of recording session's more playful moments, calls out "Hold on John. . . . Hold on Yoko!"

All told, the original medley of the two-part "Hold On" clocked in at 5:01. While an interesting bit of studio spontaneity, this lost track reveals that the sessions for *Plastic Ono Band* had not been a solely angst-ridden affair. Beyond the double helping of pain and trauma John conjured up were many moments of levity. There was a rough sketch of a '50s-style ballad song with the trite title of "When a Boy Meets a Girl," which they kicked around for a minute and a half before Lennon apparently lost interest.

Although he claimed to no longer "believe in Elvis," John and the band, between takes, joyfully jammed on both "That's All Right Mama" and "Hound Dog," along with a foot-stomping cover of Carl Perkins's "Honey Don't." Phil Spector saturated his vocals in Sun Records-style reverb, and Klaus walked a punchy gangster bass line in the style of the great Chicago bluesman Willie Dixon.

Fumbling the guitar riff, John suddenly broke into a garbled version of "Don't Be Cruel," sounding like one part comedy and one part desecration. A steady rockin' version of "Matchbox" was propelled by Starr's thudding drums. The band came together nicely as John drilled a fuzzy lead guitar until suddenly losing interest or patience and dropping the jam in mid-flight, dismissing the old-school music with an indifferent "Okay. . . ." A loosey-goosey take of Perkins's "Glad All Over" (which the Beatles once covered back in 1963 at the Cavern Club, with George on vocals) seemed ironic in contrast to the severity of the rest of the album.

Years later, Yoko shed a ray of light on the inner workings of John's duality, or being of "two minds" as she described him in the introduction to a catalog for a retrospective exhibit of Lennon's art at the Kunsthalle in Bremen in 1995. "Once when John was in a dark mood, I looked over his shoulder and found him drawing a very funny picture. Another time, John was in a happy mood drawing a picture with black humor. Only John would do that."

With the next take, Ringo drove the song with a determined, heavier beat while Lennon's vocal turned to raspy sandpaper: "Hold on! Hold on darlin'," he shouted. But a moment later the track suddenly came crashing down. By take 24, "Hold On" took on a funkier feel, revealing the influence of Curtis Mayfield's breezy soul grooves, as John repeatedly begged an out-of-control world to come to its senses and "Hold On."

"It's pretty hard, ya see," Lennon groused after playing the song's lilting guitar figure repeatedly: "I'm gettin' [a] crimp!" But all the hard work eventually paid off once the band came together, evoking the gentle, floating feeling the Beatles once played on songs like "Don't Let Me Down" and "Sun King."

"You're gonna see the light" Lennon sang, just before stopping again. "I'm so sorry. I'm just crippled."

Intrepid Interpretations: "Hold On"

Released on September 23, 2008, the hip-hop duo Johnson and Jonson (comprised of "Blu," a.k.a. Johnson Barnes III, and Mainframe) sampled Lennon's intricate guitar figure and grooving rhythm as the framework for their freestyle rap number by the same name, in which Blu assures himself, "They say it's gonna be alright, but I'm just tryin' to make it through these hard days and dark nights. . . ."

8

I FOUND OUT

The sharp-talking King of the World was actually
a terrified guy who didn't know how to cry. Now I can cry.

—John Lennon

Years before Kurt Cobain's nihilistic anthems became the creed of another generation of malcontents, John Lennon's "I Found Out" created a new musical genre perhaps called "self-help grunge." Before the advent of Buddhism in America and the plethora of books, lectures, and workshops by popular "feel good" philosophers from Jack Kornfield to Pema Chödrön, Lennon had encouraged his fans not to run from their pain but to face it, embrace it, and stoically remain with it . . . until you begin to understand it and learn from it, no matter how scary and difficult the process.

John's vicious vocals and grungy guitar driving "I Found Out" were a harbinger of 1970s punk rock. Propelled by Ringo's thudding drums and Klaus's ballsy bass, the tune grooves along like "Batman" on three cylinders as Lennon lets loose with a flamethrower of blistering vitriol, rivaling any dis ever spit by Johnny Rotten, the Sex Pistols' gargoyle-esque front man.

Lennon growls like a crabby old man waving his cane, threatening the neighborhood to "stay away from my door." Suddenly, with no warning, John had turned his back on the very peace and love movement he'd helped create just three years earlier, on July 25, 1967, when the Beatles sat, singing and playing among bouquets of eye-bursting flowers and colorful balloons, delivering their celestial message of brotherhood with a global television broadcast of "All You Need Is Love."

Lennon's seething anger seemed even more shocking in contrast to the recent "War Is Over If You Want It" campaign, in which Lennon/Ono posted a series of giant billboards in twelve cities worldwide on December 15, 1969, begging everyone's personal involvement to help end the ongoing conflicts in Vietnam and Biafra.

The effervescent feeling of cosmic brotherhood percolating in the "We all shine on" chorus to "Instant Karma!" was unceremoniously flushed with one fell swoop.

And all those fledgling "superstars" would instantly be reduced to "fucking peasants" in John's "Working Class Hero." All talk of peace and love was suddenly vanquished. With the hard-rocking temper tantrum of "I Found Out," Lennon bitterly slammed the door in the face of his former bandmates, friends, and fans everywhere. But just a few months later, John would once more stretch out his hand, inviting the world to "join us" in "Imagine."

Sick and tired of the "freaks" who wondered where the yellow submarine went or were still waiting for the Magical Mystery Tour to come and take them away, John berated his old fans for infringing on his privacy. Then there was Michael X, who, along with a posse of self-appointed, self-important left-wing politicos, took John to task over which side he was on after the Beatles' "Revolution" (released in August 1968) seemed to straddle the fence with its vague lyrics, counting them both "in" and "out." Lennon/Ono apparently donated thousands of pounds to X's London commune, "Black House," along with, most notably, a bag of their shorn hair to be auctioned off at a benefit in February 1970.

Lennon/Ono then appeared on a TV talk show with Michael X (who had recently adopted the exotic moniker Abdul Malik). John claimed they planned to pose together with Malik for a poster proclaiming "Black and White Is Beautiful." (Yeah . . . but what about the Asian woman?) John also allegedly funded Malik to write his memoir, *A Black Experience*, which never saw the light of day.

A year later, escaping escalating problems in the UK, Malik returned to Trinidad, where he organized a new Black House commune. But the compound was soon engulfed in flames and its leader slapped with a murder charge after a pair of bodies was discovered buried near the smoldering ashes. Malik fled but was soon caught and convicted. Despite public and financial support from John and Yoko, along with his fellow activists Angela Davis and Dick Gregory, the high-profile lawyer William Kunstler, and blue-eyed soul singer Judy Collins, Malik was hanged on May 16, 1975.

* * *

Beyond John's unrestrained rage, there are moments of hope within "I Found Out"; as John admonished, "Don't take nobody's word what you can do." Like Dylan before him in "Subterranean Homesick Blues," John advised his fans, "Don't follow leaders." Whether hopeful or hateful, Lennon always encouraged his fans to think for themselves and create their own dream just as he had.

"When I was a kid, John Lennon was one of my biggest heroes," Peter Case said. "At sixteen years old, I read the *Rolling Stone* interview where he said something like 'I'm the kind of person, when I have a hero, if I find out they wear green socks I'll run out and buy green socks,' and I immediately started to wear green socks myself. I wore them for years. I know that's fucked up. But that's how I was about John Lennon."

Case wasn't alone—not in his newfound passion for green socks but in his belief that someone must have the answer to the world's endless problems, whether they be a songwriter, comedian, politician, or guru. Rather than praying for some supernatural intervention, be it Krishna or Jesus to come from the sky, John believed it was better to shoulder the responsibility for our own sorrow, disappointment, and anger.

Lennon urged us to "feel your own pain" and cry rather than numbing ourselves with alcohol and drugs. But the song's lyric comes off a bit preachy and hypocritical, considering Lennon/Ono's recent and much celebrated withdrawal from heroin.

Despite striving for inner peace, while conceiving of clever ways of helping the world come to its senses, John constantly struggled with the dark and light throughout his life (with and without Yoko). If he was, in fact, the genius he brazenly claimed to be in his *Rolling Stone* interview (and there remains plenty of brilliance to choose from over the years to prove the point), and if, as he insisted, "genius is pain," Lennon continued to wrestle with his emotions, which were sometimes easily triggered and not always well controlled.

Lennon's vast need for love and validation as a "genius" stretched beyond whatever affection or approval his troubled parents could provide to the world stage. In addressing Alf and Julia's shortcomings, John confronted an entire generation of mothers and father who lacked the warmth and understanding their children required by projecting unrealistic desires onto them rather than encouraging their own kids to follow their dreams. Feeling unloved and conflicted, both John and Yoko sought love beyond their own families from the world at large: "They didn't want me, so they made me a star!" Lennon howled, regurgitating years of anguish and guilt.

Surprisingly, John even berated masturbators in "I Found Out" as he growled the song's most shocking lyrics, directed at lonely pleasure seekers sitting "there with your cock in your hand." Not even Frank Zappa, ringmaster of the notoriously perverse Mothers of Invention, who once sang the lascivious "Catholic Girls" and "What's the Ugliest Part of your Body" ("your mind," of course!), had yet to push the boundaries of freedom of speech that far. But having exposed themselves on the cover of *Two*

Virgins, Lennon/Ono had already crossed into the land of "No Filter." Wanking off, Lennon reprimanded, "don't get you nowhere, don't make you a man." Outrageous as it was, John's attitude seemed macho and judgmental, like a school headmaster wielding a ruler to smack the "dirty" hands of his young fans for committing such abominable acts.

No one was beyond Lennon's reproach as he took aim at his former junior partner George Harrison and his "pie in the sky" quest for spiritual bliss, snarling, "Old Hare Krishna's got nothin' on you, just keep you crazy, with nothin' to do." In his ongoing quest for self-knowledge, John would passionately embrace numerous teachers and methods until he'd bitterly declare them fraudulent and then move on once more.

Disparaging the Hare Krishna movement was an obvious slap in George's face, a counterpunch to Harrison's earlier scathing remarks about Yoko. Lennon's insult was part of an ongoing squabble that had dragged on since they'd reportedly come to fisticuffs during the *Let It Be* sessions. A year later John would refuse to perform at George's gala *Benefit Concert for Bangladesh* on August 1, 1971, after Harrison stipulated that if Lennon were to appear, it would be only as a solo artist. Under no circumstances would he allow a caterwauling Yoko Ono to take Madison Square Garden's stage on his watch.

"If Yoko can't play, neither can I," John countered. When later asked why he didn't appear at the *Concert for Bangladesh*, Lennon glibly replied he "didn't feel like it." Between Harrison's haughty attitude toward Yoko, his nervousness over how his performance would measure up against an all-star cast, and the mounting fear of walking into a possible Beatle reunion, John opted to catch the first flight back to England, where Allen Klein maintained he had important business waiting. Lennon claimed his phobia over reuniting the band was inspired by a story Yoko once told him about a Japanese monk "who loved this fantastic golden temple so much that he didn't want to see it disintegrate. So, he burned it. That is what I did with the Beatles. I never wanted them to slide down, making comebacks."

Harrison's harsh feelings toward Yoko were no secret. According to Warner Bros. in-house producer Russ Titleman, George believed "the Beatles had ended the day Lennon brought Yoko into the studio."

"George just hated the idea of anybody hanging around the studio. He didn't even like George Martin to be there," Tony Bramwell (Harrison's boyhood friend and Beatles former tour manager) claimed. "George could not stand to be in the same room with [Yoko]. She was interfering with everything."

Catholic by birth, Harrison was the most spiritual member of the Beatles. As his sister Louise once explained, their father Harold had been "a bus driver in Liverpool who'd always been kind and patient with his passengers, as he believed each one of them was a small part of God." George would later discover this compassionate approach was a precedent of the Hare Krishna philosophy. Having read and been entranced by Yogananda's memoir, *Autobiography of a Yogi*, as well as delving into the practice of transcendental meditation with the Maharishi Mahesh Yogi, Harrison was eager to receive Krishna's message "from inner space," as he later sang in his 2002 song "Rising Sun."

While on his initial visit to India, George claimed to have crossed paths with a mysterious stranger who sensed the young rock star's inner restlessness. The spiritual master recognized that while Harrison already possessed "youth, fame, fortune, [and] health," all of those blessings were still not enough for him. "You want to know about something else," the guru surmised, sensing George's deep spiritual hunger. Harrison claimed the auspicious meeting was "like a door opening," which helped him understand that he was "fortunate enough . . . to realize there's something else to life" beyond the desire for sensual pleasure and material possessions.

Soon after, Harrison met a Hare Krishna devotee named Shyamsundar at Apple Records, who had come in hopes of persuading the label to release a recording of kirtans (call-and-response devotional songs) that he'd made. By happenstance (or more specifically, as George liked to say, "By Krishna's arrangement") Harrison entered the office to discover the shaven-headed, saffron-robed devotee patiently waiting. "Where have you been?" George exclaimed. "I've been trying to meet the Hare Krishna people for the last couple of years."

George invited Shyamsundar, a former Fulbright scholar and professional skier, to his home in Esher the following Sunday for lunch. Harrison explained, much to the disciple's delight, that he already owned a copy of Swami Prabhupada's album of sacred mantras, and that he and John once strummed ukuleles as they joyfully chanted "Hare Krishna" together for hours on end while sailing around the Greek islands on vacation. George immediately invited a gang of saffron-robed devotees down to Trident Studios to record a demo of their ecstatic singing, drumming, and chiming finger cymbals. Delighted by their transcendental sound, Harrison booked a date at Abbey Road studios in July 1969. Transforming the old recording studio into a temple, lighting incense, and applying tilaks to every willing forehead, the devotees cheerfully served prasadam (fresh, organic food first offered to Lord Krishna before it is eaten) to everyone present. Joining the devotees, George contributed supporting guitar and bass parts to the tracks.

John and Yoko's flirtation with Krishna consciousness was typically intense and brief. In search of new living quarters, Lennon (who'd previously been joined by a handful of devotees from the Radha Krishna temple when recording "Give Peace a Chance") offered fifteen devotees and their itinerant guru Srila A. C. Bahktivendanta (a.k.a. Prabhupada, the spiritual leader of the International Society of Krishna Consciousness [ISKCON]) temporary lodging in the old servants' quarters of his Tittenhurst estate in return for some renovation work.

Meanwhile, on August 22, 1969, Apple Records released the single of the "Hare Krishna Mantra," which quickly sold seventy thousand copies. A few weeks later, a bunch of blissed-out devotees appeared on the popular TV show *Top of the Pops*, glee-fully chanting the Maha Mantra. Impressed with their nimble carpentry skills after they'd efficiently installed a new marble floor in his mansion, Lennon queried Srila Prabhupada what his secret was for inspiring such powerful devotion and enthusiasm in his followers.

Although intrigued by the swami and his orange army, John remained skeptical. "There ain't no guru who can see through your eyes," Lennon cried in "I Found Out." After branding the Maharishi Mahesh Yogi with the cruel nickname of "Sexy Sadie" for his alleged sexual indiscretion among his female disciples, Lennon decided to become his own guru, appearing on the album cover of *Abbey Road* dressed in white from head to toe, aloof, with a flowing beard that rivaled the facial hair of any Hindu holy man.

Not only did John disparage Harrison's spiritual beliefs, he criticized his musi-cianship as well. When Jann Wenner asked John how he rated his own guitar playing against that of his bandmate's, he dryly replied, "I prefer myself. I have to be hon-est. . . . George produced some beautiful guitar playing, but I think he's too hung up to really let go."

According to Lennon, it took his vindictive valentine to Paul, "How Do You Sleep?" to really inspire Harrison to cut loose and "do the best [guitar playing] he's ever fucking played in his life. He'd never get that feeling again!" John declared.

A methodical player who worked out tightly arranged, memorable leads that could be hummed almost as easily as the song's melody, Harrison carefully shaped each phrase he played while never wasting a note. But his slow, studious approach had a way of consuming costly studio time while driving both the perpetually impatient Lennon and the technically proficient McCartney to the brink of madness.

"Lennon's guitar playing was a big influence on me, the one-note solos on 'Yer Blues' and the punching, screaming, almost vocal-like solos on 'I Found Out,'" said Peter Case. "On *Abbey Road*, during the guitar trade-offs, his playing is so basic, visceral, and rocking. He projects a powerful emotional hit that the other Beatles' solos don't have."

"John was always the wildest guitarist in the Beatles as both an avant-gardist and as a bluesman," Gary Lucas concurred. "Paul and George may have outplayed him technically on the *Abbey Road* medley, but his guitar is so feral and guttural."

The rough demos of "I Found Out" that Lennon recorded in California during the summer of 1970 are nothing short of a revelation. John relentlessly pounds a bluesy A7 chord on a tremolo-soaked National steel guitar, as he repeatedly accents his coarse voice with a series of slashing slide riffs. The swampy groove is straight from the Bayou, reminiscent of "Green River" by Creedence Clearwater Revival, one of the few bands Lennon publicly praised at the time for their gritty, no-frills roots rock. John's voice sounds positively tortured, more akin to the feral howl of the street-singing holy blues man Blind Willie Johnson than the sweet, melodious vocals heard on the Beatles' records. While the rawness of "Cold Turkey" both surprised and alienated some fans, this was John Lennon sounding thoroughly possessed, with the same "hellhound on his trail" that once stalked Mississippi blues man Robert Johnson.

There are a few instances in which the lyric on the demo of "I Found Out" varies from the final version of the song. Perhaps fearing the repercussions certain to follow from singing the word *cock*, Lennon initially sang, "Some of you sit there, your *axe* in your hand, won't get you nothin', won't make you a man." And the lyric "now that I found out about dope and cocaine, don't even want to see Mary Jane" quickly morphed into "Don't let them fool you with dope and cocaine, no one can harm you, feel your own pain," a vast improvement over the original and one of the most important messages John could offer his fans through his personal experience.

The home demo of "I Found Out" also allows John's fans a deeper understanding of his writing process, which became clearer with each lyrical revision. Such is the case when John initially sang "I've seen 'neurosis' from Jesus to Paul," which became clearer after changing the word to *religion*.

Working swiftly in the studio, John retained a natural, spontaneous approach while recording *Plastic Ono Band*. "Just play it how you feel it," he advised Klaus and Ringo before kicking off the song. The unvarnished honesty with which Lennon expressed himself on the *White Album* on tunes like "Yer Blues" and "I'm So Tired" was delivered here in a raw, stayed-up-all-night-until-dawn voice, while his guitar sounds as if it was strung with barbed wire. Klaus, as always, stuck to simple bass patterns, while Ringo repeatedly kicked the bass drum hard and floppy.

"My view of the Ringo/John engine was that their right hands were identically in sync, rhythmically," explains Michael Blair (percussionist with Tom Waits, Lou Reed, and Elvis Costello). "The iconic, open swish-swish sound that Ringo made on his hi-hats and ride cymbals locked in perfectly with John's right-hand guitar-strumming groove. It was absolutely spot-on in every song they recorded. Not tight or stiff, but in fucking sync. It was there from the beginning," Blair emphasized. "Go back and watch *The Ed Sullivan Show* videos sometime and focus on their right hands. It's really wonderful."

"It's hard to describe how beautiful this beat sounds," D. J. Bonebrake concurred. "The first verse of the song begins in half time with Ringo opening the hi-hat on the 2 and 4, just enough to accentuate the backbeat. He also accents the *ands* on the hi-hat as well. Then he comes in with that great double-time feel on the chorus. After that, Ringo plays the verses in double time too. The balance between the various drums are so important!"

"I Found Out" ends with John shouting "Ow!" like a coyote with its foot caught in a steel trap. As the song fades out Lennon mutters another of his classic non sequiturs: "It must be yours 'cause mine don't look like that!"

Intrepid Interpretations: "I Found Out"

While lacking John's inherent rawness, the Red Hot Chili Peppers' version of "I Found Out" was recorded with a big stadium rock beat and gobs of reverb on Anthony Kiedis's lead vocals. Kiedis does an admirable job of covering the song. Menacing and full of swagger, lead guitarist Dave Navarro's solo is the sonic equivalent of spitting out his gum in English class. A moment later the song comes crashing down unexpectedly, adding to the grim atmosphere of it all.

On September 16, 2013, Elvis Costello, backed by the Roots, delivered a menacing version of "I Found Out" live at New York's Brooklyn Bowl. With a straw porkpie hat pushed down over his eyes and his trademark tortoiseshell Buddy Holly glasses, Costello ground out the rhythm on his trusty Fender Jazzmaster. Elvis and the Roots would also perform a thundering encore of "I Found Out" at the Capitol Theatre in Port Chester, New York, on March 12, 2014.

9

WORKING CLASS HERO

If you get any more serious than Lennon at his most serious,
you throw yourself under a train.

—Roger Waters

John Lennon loved Bob Dylan. As he confessed in 1965, the Beatles had gone absolutely "potty" over the rough-hewn bard from Hibbing, Minnesota. The influence that "The Voice of His Generation" exerted over the Fab Four was clear with one listening to John's melancholy waltz "You've Got to Hide Your Love Away" (allegedly inspired by the love troubles faced by their closeted gay manager Brian Epstein). And while Bob never said much about the Beatles' songs, harmonies, or hair, he was wowed by their guitar chords. Beyond their mutual musical respect, Dylan and the Beatles inspired each other in a variety of ways, including fashion. On the cover of his 1963 eponymously named debut album, a pudgy, somewhat skeptical-looking Bob Dylan appeared with his collar up, clasping his guitar neck, wearing a peaked "Dutch boy" cap similar to that donned by his hero, the rambling Oklahoma troubadour Woody Guthrie. The look was quickly adopted by John Lennon, who struck a familiar pose for the cover of his 1964 book of absurdist poems, stories, and doodles, *In His Own Write*. Noticing the striking resemblance, Ralph J. Gleason (pundit of the hip and original editor of *Rolling Stone*) wrote a hilarious letter to the editor of the folk magazine *Sing Out!* in March 1965, begging their readers to "Look at the picture of Lennon on the cover of his book . . . and look at the picture of Dylan on his first Columbia LP and draw your own conclusions. And even more significant! *Has anyone ever seen them together?* I intend to investigate further and ask Joan Baez, who is the only person I know who knows both."

Although conspiracy theories about the Kennedy assassination ran rampant at the time, such wild rumors as "Dylan is a quadriplegic" (following his 1966 motorcycle accident) and the raging gossip "Paul is dead" had yet to begin circulating within the rock world.

Following his 1964 British tour, Bob triumphantly returned to America no longer appearing like a disheveled farmhand but instead looking slick in a black turtleneck and a pair of sleek Beatle boots. It wouldn't be long before he strapped on
a Fender Stratocaster and shocked the crowd at the Newport Folk Festival when he
"went electric" on July 25, 1965, with the help of the greatest guitarslinger of the day,
Mike Bloomfield of the Paul Butterfield Blues Band. Defiant in a black leather "sell-
out jacket" (as the New York Times described it), Dylan howled "Maggie's Farm,"
drawing a bold line in the sand and alienating older folk fans, while Bloomfield
punctuated his every lyric with a series of scorching riffs. But Bob's "outrageous"
performance shouldn't have surprised anyone who'd been paying attention, as his
monumental hymn to uncertainty, "Like a Rolling Stone" (released just five days
earlier on July 20), had been pouring out of every radio from New York to California.
At the same time as Dylan was topping the charts with his disaffected electric anthem, the Beatles began strumming acoustic guitars and expressing themselves with
sophisticated sentiments that stretched beyond the simple joys of adolescent hand
holding. Overnight the Fabs began crafting lyrics that revealed a surprising hipness,
while pulling the plug on their early perky-boy-band routine.

Although startling, George Harrison's bitter put-down "Think for Yourself," in
which he scolds some ditzy bird with an "opaque" mind to "try thinking more if
just for your own sake," it could hardly rival Dylan's "Positively 4th Street," which
portrayed the cold-hearted betrayal by a former "friend." But there was little doubt
who inspired the "Quiet Beatle" to speak his mind in such an overtly blunt fashion.

While Dylan inspired the Beatles, he was not above taking pot shots at Lennon
and McCartney's songwriting. Although he refuted it in the press, Bob's surreal waltz
"Fourth Time Around," which appeared a year later on his 1966 masterpiece *Blonde
on Blonde*, was a blatant parody of Lennon's obtusely poetic "Norwegian Wood." As
cultural rivals, John and Bob had something of a tense relationship, as depicted in
a dreary scene from D. A. Pennebaker's film *Eat the Document*. Lennon would later
admit that Bob's intimidating imitation had made him "very paranoid."

"Lennon never recovered from his Dylan envy that followed after he heard
Freewheeling," Peter Case pointed out. "He began feeling like a fraud, imitating
Dylan's hat and singing 'I'm a Loser' with its harmonica and lyrics about being a
'clown,' which was a big Dylan word at the time. Then there was 'You've Got to Hide
Your Love Away,' which was just 'The Times They Are a-Changin' but with flutes
instead of a Dylanesque harmonica, and again he used the image of a 'clown.'"

"'Working Class Hero' was the first song I learned on guitar," recalled Marvin Etzioni. "With just a couple of chords, it said it all. I grew up in a working-class family. My dad was a carpenter, and my mom worked for the state in an office. 'As soon as you're born, they make you feel small . . .' I immediately connected. I was writing songs in junior high school and had high ambitions, without lessons or encouragement. I believed in the power of song. It's what got me through school, and still gets me through life to this day."

There is a humorous old adage in folk music that claims someone dies whenever a minor chord is played. With "Working Class Hero," a two-chord minor-key ballad, John suddenly trod into the same bleak territory as Dylan's harrowing "Ballad of Hollis Brown," which recounted the shocking tale of a starving farmer whose growing desperation drives him to murder his own family.

The inspiration for "Working Class Hero" had been lingering in the depths of Lennon's consciousness for years. Irish folk music has long been part of Liverpool's cultural landscape, and the name *Lennon* has Irish origins, most likely derived from O'Lanian or O'Leannain. While John's mum, Julia, played banjo and sang, his grandfather John (a.k.a. Jack), for whom he was named, was a traveling songster born in Dublin in 1855. Pressured to become a priest, Jack Lennon migrated to New York in the late 1880s and quickly found work in the minstrel shows, touring the country, donning blackface to perform bawdy "coon songs" (as they were known at the time) with Andrew Robertson's Colored Operatic Kentucky Minstrels. But Jack would eventually hang up the grease paint and return across the Atlantic once more to settle in Liverpool, where he married and raised a second family and found employment as a clerk while performing occasionally in local pubs for the rest of his days.

Although John Lennon openly disparaged folk music, the Quarrymen were primarily a skiffle band, whose repertoire featured a chugging cover of Lead Belly's "Rock Island Line." (And as George Harrison once said of "The King of the 12-String Guitar," "No Lead Belly—No Beatles!")

Peter Case, whose own work has alternated between intimate acoustic ballads and raging rockers, found "Working Class Hero" "strong, but John didn't really have the background, the roots, that would have fed that direction. Dylan had spent years learning folk songs and ballads, Woody's tunes, poetry, country music, and blues, all of which have a richer vein lyrically than most of the Motown, Brill Building, and Sun Records stuff that John understood."

Lennon found out just how difficult recording a simple folk tune, although only two chords, could be. According to engineer Andy Stephens, John spent days and "an endless number of takes . . . well over one hundred" cutting "Working Class Hero." In the August 2010 issue of *Uncut* magazine, Stephens recalled how Lennon became more frustrated with each failed attempt until his temper finally boiled over: "If the mix in his headphones wasn't exactly what he wanted, he would take them off and slam them into the wall . . . then walk out of the studio."

"Working Class Hero" was eventually spliced together from two separate performances that had been recorded at two different studios. With careful listening the edit can be detected by a slight shift in the tonality of both Lennon's voice and his acoustic guitar.

With "Working Class Hero," John revisited the abuse he'd suffered for being different from his classmates, groaning: "They hate you if you're clever and they despise a fool." It's no surprise to learn that Lennon was a misfit in the Liverpool educational system. John had already figured out the game by the time he was five years old, when he claimed, "My mother always told me that happiness was the key to life. When I went to school, they asked me what I wanted to be when I grew up. I wrote down 'happy.' They told me I didn't understand the assignment, and I told them they didn't understand life."

In recent years, records of John Lennon's detentions while attending Liverpool's Quarry Bank School between 1955 and 1956 were discovered and put up for auction, bringing a hefty price tag of nearly $4,000. John had been made to stay after school on a regular basis for a range of incorrigible acts from "shoving" and "fighting in class" to "talking," "shouting," and "silliness." And then there was the crime of having "just no interest whatsoever." But most interesting of all was the mysterious and inexplicable charge of "sabotage." These written accounts of Lennon's numerous detentions were slated to be burned back in the 1970s, but when the teacher appointed the task spotted John's name on them, he wisely put them aside for safekeeping.

Like millions of baby boomers, Lennon also felt alienated by the overwhelming demands of church, school, and society, as he wearily sang in a hoarse whisper of a voice: "Till you're so fucking crazy, you can't follow their rules." With one line, Lennon managed to sum up the inarticulate restlessness of 1950s cinematic rebels James Dean and Marlon Brando, who'd become idols to an entire generation of postwar teens, who, as the Welsh bard Dylan Thomas once wrote, refused to "go gentle into that good night."

In 1998 Yoko told *Uncut* magazine that John explained his cursing in the song was "part of being working class. It won't be working class if what you say is all very clean and very proper."

In what sounded like a terse note from the headmaster's office, an EMI spokesman addressed Lennon's flagrant use of profanity by alerting the press that "This matter is under discussion with the Beatles' management. . . . There will be a definitive statement next week and some action may be taken." To which an Apple Records representative (most likely Tony Bramwell or Derek Taylor) knowingly replied, "We don't think it will affect sales."

While John's "foul" language prevented "Working Class Hero" from receiving commercial airplay, it had the opposite effect to EMI's concerns. In fact, the ex-Beatle's shocking vulgarity helped spike the album's sales. Although John once again stunned many of his old fans by slinging around the F-word, not once but twice in the same song, what was even more disturbing was that he'd flatly dismissed them all as "peasants."

In the popular 1960s antiwar anthem "Where Have All the Flowers Gone," Pete Seeger begged, "When will *they* ever learn," as if the world's multitude of problems were the fault of someone other than ourselves. The song exemplified a pervasive attitude at the time that portrayed the well-meaning (younger) "us," who routinely felt wronged by the short-sighted and greedy (elder) "them." But the truth remains to this day that "we"—the human race—have yet to learn. Perhaps the answer to Seeger's nagging question was best summed up by the cartoonist Walt Kelly in his classic comic strip *Pogo* (syndicated from 1949 to 1975), when the hero, a sensible possum named Pogo from the backwater of Okefenokee Swamp, drolly pointed out, "We have met the enemy and he is us!"

In singing "*you're* still fucking peasants," Lennon revealed an elitist attitude that only helped further isolate Yoko and him from his fans, like the very "folks on the hill" that he clearly detested. As a millionaire rock star, John triggered a storm of criticism for such hypocritical attitudes. Had he chosen instead to sing "*we're* all fucking peasants as far as I can see" (as Marianne Faithfull would in her 1979 cover of the song), he might have taken some responsibility in the social dilemma that continues to this day: the denigration of the poor while the rich continue to get richer.

In the Beatles' early days, Brian Epstein continually struggled to steer the Fabs clear of whatever controversy he felt might damage their cute and cuddly image. But Epstein soon realized that controlling John Lennon's impulsive outbursts was a fool's errand. Other than George Harrison's scathing "Taxman" (for which John contributed a handful of lines), in which the guitarist bitterly complained about the severity of the tax bracket that came with his newly acquired wealth, the Beatles remained strangely silent on divisive issues of the day, from the Vietnam war to mass starvation in Biafra, until Epstein's sudden death in 1967. John tended to respond to political events emotionally, with a naïve knee-jerk reaction rather than taking time to assess the situation and make a well-researched, cool-headed reply.

And while the Beatles' 1968 hit single "Revolution" smoldered with grungy fuzz tone, it immediately brought the band another firestorm of controversy. The Beatles recorded both a hard-rocking and a slow, easy-grooving version of John's first protest song, both of which triggered a harsh round of criticism from left-wing politicos, who'd been waiting for the leader of the world's most famous band to finally make a political statement. When it came to the issue of "destruction," Lennon remained ambiguous, weighing both sides of the issue. Recording two versions of "Revolution," Lennon was unable to decide whether he was "in" with militants or "out" with pacifists.

Either way, he couldn't win. It turned out everything was not going to be "alright," as he repeatedly chanted on the song's coda. While his first stab as a protest singer was deemed "sloppy and irrelevant" by John Hoyland in the Keele University student paper, years later, in a 1974 *Melody Maker* interview, Todd Rundgren got nastier, claiming, "John Lennon ain't no revolutionary. He's a fucking idiot, man. Shouting about revolution and acting like an ass. . . . All he really wants to do is get attention for himself. . . . He's an important figure, sure. But so was Richard Nixon. Nixon was just like another generation's John Lennon. Someone who represented all sorts of ideals but was out for himself underneath it all."

Witty and sardonic as ever, John Lennon shot back a quick reply at "Sodd Runtlestuntle," replying in an open letter on September 30, 1974: "I have never claimed to be a revolutionary. But I am allowed to sing about anything I want! Right? . . . It sounds like I represented something to you, or you wouldn't be so violent towards me. The one thing those Beatles did was to affect *peoples' minds*. Maybe you need another fix?" Then Lennon signed off with a humorous twist: "However much you hurt me darling, I'll always love you, J. L."

Much to his credit, when it came to finger-pointing songs, Lennon was never above criticizing himself. When he sang, "Keep you doped with religion, sex, and TV," in "Working Class Hero," he could have easily been berating himself, the former "Nowhere Man," who once floundered in his comfortably numb mock-Tudor mansion in the London suburbs.

For someone with such an acute intellectual capacity and strong antiestablishment streak, Lennon's love affair with television always seemed surprisingly bourgeois. Perhaps it was endemic to his generation, who'd been enthralled by the novelty of the new medium as children. But being a songwriter and visual artist, John was a dedicated observer, and TV provided constant inspiration for him. So did newspaper headlines, as in the case of the death of his friend Tara Browne (heir to the Guinness fortune), which triggered Lennon's opus "A Day in the Life."

"Working Class Hero" is arguably *Plastic Ono Band's* most powerful song, if not the album's most famous. Lennon delivers the solemn lyrics not in an anxiety-fueled scream but in a defeated whisper, which clobbers listeners as if they'd been suddenly struck over the head in a knock-down at the local whisky bar.

Resigned to the fate that came with his enormous fame, Lennon, nearly paralyzed by the lingering misery that tainted his youth, barely muttered, "If you wanna be a hero, then just follow me."

Just days before his death in 1980, John told *Rolling Stone* "what nobody ever got right [about 'Working Class Hero'] was that it was supposed to be sardonic—it had nothing to do with socialism, it had to do with 'If you want to go through that trip, you'll get up to where I am, and this is what you'll be.'"

In truth, John was the least working-class member of the Beatles. Raised by his Aunt Mimi at Mendips, Lennon's upbringing was overtly middle class when compared to that of George Harrison, whose father barely supported his wife and four children on a bus driver's paycheck. For much of his childhood, George's family home at 12 Arnold Grove had no proper bathroom, just an outhouse. As for Paul, he and his brother, Mike, were raised by a single father following their mother's death from breast cancer, while Ringo's childhood was one of illness and poverty. But as John knew, there was nothing romantic about being middle class.

While inventing themselves as footloose troubadours, everyone from Pete Seeger to Bob Dylan to Bruce Springsteen eschewed their middle-class roots, wagering that whatever tales of personal hardship they'd endured (or invented) might add allure to their image.

"We were the first working-class singers who stayed working-class . . . didn't try to change our accents that in England were looked down upon . . . probably still are," John told Tom Snyder of the *Today Show* in 1975.

With the twin release of *Plastic Ono Band*, John and Yoko's wardrobe would change too. Gone were their matching all-black or all-white outfits that helped link them with the avant-garde. They now posed for photographer Annie Liebovitz for their two-part *Rolling Stone* interview clad in denim overalls (the all-purpose uniform of American working-class mechanics, plumbers, and carpenters). Lennon/Ono also chopped off their hair and donated the precious clippings to Michael X, who auctioned their shorn locks off for charity. John had also cropped his flowing *Abbey Road* beard and now stared intensely into Leibovitz's lens through his wire-rimmed glasses with the air of a Marxist professor.

"Somewhere along the line, John became a politically minded person, which he definitely was not in Hamburg," recalled singer Tony Sheridan, who once hired the Beatles as his backup band in the early '60s. "I don't know where all that came from." Lennon's old friend believed John always felt he had to be "something beyond a rock 'n' roll musician," if he was going to "impress the whole world."

Lennon himself had been born into a world of conflict when he came screaming into this life on October 9, 1940, in the dreary port of Liverpool. "We were Hicksville," Lennon told Jann Wenner. For the most part, people from Liverpool were considered no more than "animals" by Londoners. While Paul, George, and Ringo had all been raised working class, it was John, brought up by his Aunt Mimi in her prim and proper Mendips home, who enjoyed the perks of a suburban upbringing.

Lennon's political spark continued to spread with his 1971 single "Power to the People," along with *Imagine*'s scorching "Just Gimme Some Truth," in which he attacked "Tricky Dicky" (then-President Richard Nixon) and addressed the ongoing quagmire in Vietnam with the ghostly "I Don't Wanna Be a Soldier."

Intrepid Interpretations: "Working Class Hero"

With her sensual sandpaper voice, Marianne Faithfull's unique interpretation of "Working Class Hero" is built off a driving blues rhythm propelling her jaded delivery, as she spits out the words "but *we're all* fucking peasants as far as I can see." According to Marianne's long-time guitarist/collaborator Barry Reynolds, the song's startling arrangement began with Mark Miller Mundy, producer of Marianne's 1979 new-wave opus *Broken English*, "who wanted more electronic sound in the mix. Steve Winwood came up with the [keyboard] vamp and from there it just developed organically."

Then there was the Brooklyn-born soul/folk singer (and surprise star of Woodstock) Richie Havens, who recorded highly personal versions of Beatles' songs throughout his career, interpreting "Eleanor Rigby," "Strawberry Fields Forever," and most successfully "Here Comes the Sun" (which climbed the charts to No. 16 in 1971), delivered John's "Working Class Hero" in his distinct, deeply resonant voice on his 1987 album *Sings the Beatles and Dylan*.

Havens gravitated to Greenwich Village in 1959, drawn by its bohemian atmosphere, and soon began singing politically charged, socially conscious songs like "Tear Down the Walls" by the legendary Fred Neil (author of Harry Nilsson's hit "Everybody's Talkin'") and "A Hard Rain's Gonna Fall" by a young Bob Dylan. With his intricate strumming patterns inspired by the Indian raga (Richie, like many '60s guitarists, also played the sitar for a brief time), Havens employs open chords that ring over a 6/8 Afro-Cuban groove as he delivers John's weary message in a husky/honey voice.

Green Day's cover of "Working Class Hero" (2007) kicks off with a gingerly strummed acoustic guitar, as Billie Joe Armstrong's nasal delivery sticks closely to Lennon's original phrasing and emphasizes the inherent Irish quality of the ballad. The drums come in with a crisp, hard punch, as the guitar and bass grinds and snarls. It can be found on YouTube with over nine million views.

While "Working Class Hero" has been covered by everyone from Cyndi Lauper to Marilyn Manson and Ozzy Osbourne, an instrumental version of the song by guitarist Bill Frisell may be the most unique interpretation of all. "I don't know if I'd even be playing the guitar if it hadn't been for the Beatles . . . and John Lennon," Bill explained. "This music is such an important part of my life. It's in my blood." While most of Frisell's Lennon-tribute album *All We Are Saying* featured a full band, his bare-bones take of "Working Class Hero" (which appeared as a bonus track on the 2011 release) highlighted Bill's delicate solo acoustic guitar work. "I didn't try to change anything . . . reharmonize anything . . . or jazz this up," he pointed out. Interpreting such an "intense and personal" song as "Working Class Hero" without John's startling lyrics seems like an impossible task until you hear Frisell's gentle, moody meditation.

10

ISOLATION

It's always lonely where I am.

—Bob Dylan

For all their bold concepts and outlandish avant-garde antics, John and Yoko appeared rather delicate at times. "We're afraid of everyone, afraid of the sun," John confessed in the lyrics to "Isolation." Different as they were, both Lennon and Ono had reasons for their moments of overwhelming shyness. The daughter of a wealthy banker, Yoko, along with her siblings and mother Isoko, was forced to flee Tokyo during World War II. Thrust from a world of privilege, she attended school and played with poor farm children. Feeling alienated in her strange, new circumstances, she became an object of ridicule. The poems, songs, and art that Yoko Ono created were not just the work of a highly imaginative child finding a way to cope with uncertainty, but they helped create a barrier, a self-made cocoon where she could escape and find safety from a troubled world.

As Ono once told journalist Jonathan Cott, she was incapable of explaining "to people how shy [she] was." Yoko confessed that whenever her family had visitors, she "wanted to be in a big sort of box with little holes," which would allow her to peer out while preventing anyone else from seeing in. This eventually manifested as her "Bag Piece."

When John sang of "eating chocolate cake in a bag" in the "Ballad of John and Yoko," it was not about enjoying rich deserts on the run but rather referred to one of Yoko's bags, which they would occasionally occupy like a suit of armor when fielding questions from the press.

Yoko's ritual of taking refuge in a bag eventually made its way to the stage during Plastic Ono Band's first concert at the Toronto Rock 'n' Roll Revival. This deliberate shielding of one's personality can be traced to a tradition in Japan during the Edo period of 1600–1868 among the Zen Buddhist Komusō monks. They donned woven wicker baskets over their heads as masks, known as *tengui,* from which they would peer out at the world between cracks of woven straw. Some claim that *tengui* were also worn by shakuhachi flute players to help quell the musician's ego and keep the audience focused on the music rather than on the personality of the performer.

Lennon/Ono eventually created Bag Productions as the umbrella for their joint ventures. "Bag," as in hippie slang "what's your bag?" was a metaphor for one's "thing" or niche. Most folks first got hip to the term from Fred Neil, who sang the groovy blues number "That's the Bag I'm In," while Richie Havens titled his classic 1966 album *Mixed Bag*, referring to the diversity of musical styles found on the record.

"They didn't know what to call me. My music has always been a mixed bag, and it's still a mixed bag today," Havens said in 2008.

* * *

Through the constant media blitz of television, radio, movies, their own Saturday morning cartoon show, and every form of marketing from tin lunchboxes to ny-lon stockings to tons of newspaper and magazine features, the Beatles' adoring fans (whom Lennon mercilessly berated within the verses of "Isolation" for having un-wittingly "caused so much pain") came to believe they actually "knew" John, Paul, George, and Ringo.

"As powerful as 'I Want to Hold your Hand' was in 1964, *Plastic Ono Band*, which was only six years later, was light years away from the innocence of hand holding," Peter Case explained.

> Lennon was looking for God, love, and wanted mommy and daddy to come home. No matter who you are, one yearns. Not everyone has the gift of expression like Lennon. No one had lyrics so impactful, singing, "Some of you sit there with your cock in your hand, don't get you nowhere, don't make you a man." How did he know?
>
> If one judges an album just on the merits of commercial success, then this album may not meet your standards. It had no hit singles, but it was an album that defined "heavy," as in real. It's a lot easier to listen to any Beatles album, where you can feel the comradery of a band. But with John's *Plastic Ono Band*, you feel the desperation of an artist in "Isolation."

Little could fans comprehend the isolation and lack of freedom that huge stars like Elvis, the Beatles, and Michael Jackson experienced, constantly locked away in hotel rooms, unable to freely walk the streets, just go to the movies, or get a bite to eat without being recognized and possibly mobbed. While Richard Lester's *A Hard Day's Night* portrays hordes of kids gleefully chasing the Beatles down cobblestone streets, D. A. Pennebaker's documentary *Don't Look Back*, about Bob Dylan's triumphant 1964 British tour, reveals the brilliant but brutal folk singer learning to cope with his new life in the eye of fame's hurricane.

Surrounded by a throng of adoring fans and singer-songwriter wannabes, Bob plays cruel mind games on everyone assembled, arbitrating who's cool and what's not as his kowtowing clique nervously hangs on his every whim. And if he happened to shred somebody with an acerbic barb, well, it just came with the territory. They were only collateral damage. Someone was bound to get hurt. As he sang in "Sooner or Later, One of Us Must Know," "You just happened to be there, that's all."

It seemed the greater influence the Beatles had, the smaller their world became. But after retreating from the world's madness, John Lennon, within the confines of his sprawling Tittenhurst Park estate, would soon confront his own psychosis.

Recorded at Abbey Road on October 6, 1970, "Isolation" begins with John singing gently over his pulsing piano as Voormann and Starr lay a simple, soulful foundation.

"The piano does it all for you. Your mind can do the rest. [You] don't need anything else," Lennon said, explaining his simple, pristine keyboard work. The song's stripped-down production is given an extra shine with an uncredited organ part in the bridge, whether played by John, Billy Preston, or even Mal Evans, who once added a bit of Hammond to the Beatles' *Rubber Soul*. John's voice is doubled as he delivers the song's soaring punchline: "You're not to blame, you're just a human, a victim of the 'insayane'. . ."

"Ringo's drum pattern," X's drummer, D. J. Bonebrake, explained, "defines the song poetically, as he plays quarter notes on the kick and snare. Even the drum fills are all quarter notes, until before the bridge where he adds a twenty-sixth note—an eighth dotted note with a sixteenth."

"Sorry! I don't mean to sound like a technical manual," D. J. joked. "On the bridge he plays quarter notes on the bass drum alone! It's so effective. Coming out of the bridge is so good. There's a triplet build-up that segues back into double time. The transition was so perfect, timewise. I wonder if they used a click track or if they edited or cut the tape? That's why people give Ringo a hard time. Could he really be that good, or was he enhanced by technology or ghost drummers?"

Intrepid Interpretations: "Isolation"

Although a deeply personal song, "Isolation" has been recorded by a long list of singers, most notably by Ann Wilson of Heart, who shreds "Isolation" with her raspy, raw delivery over pulsing keys as the drummer's fills tumble, shifting gears from funky to raucous.

With its expansive emotional range, from navel-gazing to accusation, "Isolation" was a favorite of singers from Harry Nilsson, with his lithe delivery; to Joe Cocker, who gives it a rockin' Ray Charles/gospel feel; to Marianne Faithfull, whose reading appeared on *A Perfect Stranger: The Island Anthology* in 1998. While Matthew Sweet's acoustic rendition (an outtake from his 1991 classic album *Girlfriend*) floats on a bed of reverberating guitars, the most original interpretation of "Isolation" was concocted by the Scottish band Snow Patrol for the 2007 benefit compilation album *Instant Karma: The Amnesty International Campaign to Save Darfur*.

While John refrained from adding any extra production or "sweetening" on *Plastic Ono Band*, Lennon (who remained insecure about his voice throughout his career) double-tracked his vocals in the song's middle section. There was also a thin icing of organ audible on the song's final verses. An outtake of "Isolation" was later included in the John Lennon *Anthology*.

11

REMEMBER

Friday October 9, 1970, John Lennon's thirtieth birthday, had been a memorable day for many reasons. Through his recent primal therapy sessions with Dr. Arthur Janov, John had confronted and struggled to overcome all lingering feelings of abandonment by his parents. But Janov would voice concern over Lennon, who left California in haste before completing the demanding program. Sounding like a passage from Mary Shelley's *Frankenstein*, the curly-haired pop psychologist worried that he had taken John apart but didn't have enough time to properly finish putting him back together.

Despite the terrible memories and deep-seated contempt John had harbored for his father, Alf, who later became known as Freddie, it appeared their relationship, for the time being, was on the upswing. Now fifty-eight, Freddie, with his twenty-year-old girlfriend, Pauline Jones (who'd recently suffered a miscarriage), had just returned from Scotland, where they'd secretly eloped, much to Pauline's mother's consternation. John had not only been rooting for the mismatched pair but even helped foot the cost of their trip, along with buying them a new home in Brighton.

Freddie had hoped the release of Hunter Davies's much-anticipated new biography, *The Beatles* (published in August 1968), would irrevocably set the record straight. Davies had interviewed Freddie, who finally was allowed to tell his side of the story: how his philandering wife, Julia, had been dating a handful of men while he was away at sea and had become pregnant and then refused his plea to reunite with her hapless husband. But the ever-controlling Aunt Mimi would have none of it and demanded Freddie's testimony be stricken from the record. Upon its publication, John would immediately dismiss the Davies book as "a whitewash," claiming the author had "copped out" in omitting the darker details of his childhood. Having finally heard his father's side of the story for himself, John at last seemed to understand Freddie's dilemma and the difficult decisions he'd had no choice but to make.

Although John invited Freddie and Pauline to lunch in good faith, it didn't take long before he exploded with an onslaught of vitriol that shook Freddie to his core.

John chided his father about how as a young boy he spent "day after day screaming for my daddy, sobbing for you to come home. What did you care, away at sea all those years?" John shouted, determined to have it out with his no-account father at last.

Janov had hoped Lennon might finally come to a point of resolution with the help of his therapy, but once again John bolted (as he'd previously done in Rishikesh) and failed to reap the full benefits by completing the entire program. When John laid eyes on Freddie again, he suddenly snapped and flew into a rage, throwing his father and his young wife out of his house, while making what Freddie nervously told a solicitor were violent threats against his life. John's father recalled how John had lost his temper, repeatedly pounding the table with his fist as his "voice rose to a scream" while admitting he was "bloody mad, insane."

"He had gone to America at great expense to have some kind of treatment through drugs," said Freddie, to return and relive his early childhood traumas, which the elder Lennon believed "he should have been happier to forget." Freddie was convinced that "the evil intensity" of this confrontation was "the result of this treatment." He was shocked how John "reviled his dead mother in unspeakable terms." No one except Yoko was exempt from John's tantrum, in which he took shots at everyone—even his devoted Aunt Mimi, close friends, and bandmates. "I sat through it all, completely stunned, hardly believing that this was the kind, considerate 'Beatle' John Lennon." Judging from the naivety of that statement, John's own father, who in truth barely knew his son, like the rest of the world, had bought into Brian Epstein's well-crafted image of Beatle jocularity.

Freddie was convinced that John "meant every word he spoke. His countenance was frightful to behold, as he explained in detail how I would be carried out to sea and dumped 'twenty, fifty, or [as John threatened] perhaps you would prefer a hundred fathoms deep?'" Struck by how his son took pleasure at the notion of doing him in, Freddie claimed his outrageous threat had been "uttered with malignant glee, as though he were actually participating in the terrible deed."

Following their explosive confrontation earlier that morning at Tittenhurst Park (the last time John would ever see his father), Lennon sought the familiar shelter of Abbey Road Studios, where he spent the rest of the day and well into the early hours of the following morning recording "Remember."

While trying to free himself from frustration and rage at nearly everyone in his life, John's muse was never sharper. The recent experience of taking such a savage journey within would inspire Lennon's greatest solo album—a rollercoaster ride of emotion that rose and fell sharply, alternating between peaks of love and valleys of fear and despair. Lennon addressed the pain inflicted on a generation of kids by parents "just wishing for movie stardom" rather than having realistic expectations of their children. John also took aim at the black-and-white simplicity of good guys and bad guys as portrayed in old Westerns when he begged, "Do you remember when you were young, how the hero was never hung?"

Two years later the Kinks' Ray Davies would cover similar territory when he wished his "life was a Hollywood movie show" in his melancholic "Celluloid Heroes." Davies ultimately preferred to live in a fantasy world rather than reality, as he wistfully sang, "Celluloid heroes never feel any pain, 'cause celluloid heroes never really die . . ."

An earlier version of "Remember" stretched over nine minutes long. As John hammered a staccato piano vamp, he instructed his rhythm section to "Get ready!" Voormann's loping bass helped propel the song while Ringo's snare snapped, keeping Lennon's occasionally straying rhythm on a tight leash. John's vocals revealed a sharper, more biting edge, as he growled, "Don't be sorry about what you've done," deeply understanding the power of those words.

His piano playing reveals a gospel feel. On the first verse, Lennon quotes Sam Cooke's 1965 hit "Bring It on Home to Me" (which John later recorded for his tribute album, *Rock 'n' Roll*), singing, "If you ever change your mind about leaving it all [rather than "leaving me"] behind." As the tune ends, Lennon quotes the old poem *Remember, Remember, the Fifth of November,* followed by a startling explosion that shredded your speakers. John was referring to England's great antihero Guy Fawkes.

As the song's final verse ends, John cracks up laughing while continuing to improvise until the tune eventually stops, clocking in at around eight minutes. For the album, Lennon made an abrupt edit, like that used on "I Want You (She's So Heavy)" from *Abbey Road*, substituting a surprise ending of an explosion that never happened. Lennon's fictional blowing up of the House of Parliament was a "poignant" way of punctuating the end of the song. "It was a good joke," he explained. From Sam Cooke to Guy Fawkes in a single leap, no one could second-guess what direction John Lennon's muse would take.

On yet another early take of "Remember," John hammered a minor-chord introduction on the piano, transforming the song into a lurching, Kurt Weill–style cabaret number as he ad-libbed, "This here's a story of me and you, and you and me." "Welllll . . . remember," he jokes, suddenly shifting gears and singing in his best rockabilly imitation of Elvis.

John's voice grows grittier as he growls the words "always got away" and "always let you down," emphasizing the disillusionment of becoming an adult. "Hold the rhythm! Get on! Don't lag behind. . . . Remember!" John instructs Ringo and Klaus with a maniacal laugh. A moment later the song falls apart.

A rehearsal take of "Remember," lasting barely three minutes, revealed a fluctuating tempo as the song was still being worked out. This version later appeared on the 1998 *John Lennon Anthology* box set. Other early takes of the song included an organ overdub (whether played by John or Billy Preston, whose gospel piano illuminates "God," is unclear). As usual Lennon double-tracked his vocals, and most surprisingly (and perhaps a first in Beatles-related musical history), a thrumming Jew's harp played by John added a funky percussive rattle to the mix but, in the end, failed to make the final cut.

"As a drummer, my take is that John was just throwing Ringo those songs," Steve Shelley said. "It was all pretty immediate, whether soft or loud, whether 'Hold On' or 'Remember,' which had a pretty punky beat."

The song's groove is reminiscent of Doug Clifford's drumming on Creedence Clearwater Revival's ominous "Bad Moon Rising," while the bridge offers one of the few moments of vocal harmony to be found on *Plastic Ono Band*.

"'Remember' is a beautiful, rocking song," Peter Case concurred. "He's really reaching out to his audience in a way he'd rarely do again. John usually pointed a finger [in both his songs and interviews], and that hasn't aged well. Maybe he was singing to himself, [but] his empathy on 'Remember' is moving. The piano with all its overtones and swinging riff, over Ringo's groove, makes it one of his best."

"I always love the way that songwriters play piano, whether it was John or Paul, George or Tom [Petty], or Bob [Dylan], who is a really cool piano player," said Benmont Tench, keyboardist with Tom Petty and the Heartbreakers. "If you have any facility and understanding at all of how to present a song, it doesn't matter if you're John Lennon, who could play a little piano, or Paul McCartney, who could really play. . . . When you play and sing a song that you wrote on piano, that's the way it should be played.

"'Remember' is really moving," Tench remarked. "When it finally reaches the chorus [which is also referred to as the bridge, due to the song's odd format] and goes into a straight backbeat from the double time . . . that's gorgeous. Was John's playing primitive or simple? That's the question . . . John could write! And he had rhythm like crazy. But Lennon was not this primitive, unsophisticated musician. Listen to the changes he wrote on 'Strawberry Fields [Forever]' and 'I Am The Walrus.' He wrote 'Remember' on piano and played the notes that went under the melody he sang. It sounds primitive because it's rock 'n' roll. But those songs work best with those chord voicings. If you use big chords under songs like 'Remember' or 'Mother,' you'll lose the directness John had."

The "Remember" sessions revealed Lennon's wide spectrum of moods at the time. In one outtake of the song John could be heard gleefully singing "Happy Birthday . . . to me!" as Ringo and Klaus provided some playful instrumental backup to his self-celebratory ditty.

A moment later Lennon can be heard chortling "Geohaorge!" at the sight of his former bandmate, who strolled through the door of Studio Three and presented him with a plastic flower and a brotherly hug. Harrison also gave John a fresh-cut acetate recorded earlier that August at the Saville Row studio. The track, "It's Johnny's Birthday," a twisted rendition of Cliff Richard's "Congratulations," soon appeared on the "Apple Jam" bonus disc included with Harrison's three-album set *All Things Must Pass*.

According to recording engineer Andy Stephens, Lennon's little birthday celebration continued with Yoko presenting John with "a sensory box," which he described as "about twice the size of a shoebox, with lots of holes . . . to put your finger in. One hole would be warm and mushy [while] one would be wet. One would have a pin in it. John had such a ball with it."

* * *

Lennon/Ono's "Remember Love" reveals a remarkable tenderness that shed an empathetic light on the "Dragon Lady" accused of domineering John's life. Recorded on their first night together at John's home studio in Weybridge, the song's Zen-like lyrics are buoyed by a simple, repetitive, soul-soothing melody that gently assures the listener that everything is alright, at least for as long the song lasts.

A hypnotic lullaby that remained unreleased until 1997, when it was finally included as a bonus track on the CD version of *Two Virgins*, "Remember Love" was gently fingerpicked on an acoustic guitar by Lennon (who later recycled the song's lilting feel for *Abbey Road's* "Sun King") while Yoko's cooing delivery is nearly as shocking as the album's controversial cover. It's unfortunate that Ono's more intimate vocals have been all but ignored, whether due to an overwhelming disdain for her abrasive scream or her enigmatic personality.

While Yoko's "Remember Love" is a gentle reminder of how to cultivate love, John's "Remember" triggers the pain and disillusionment we all carry from childhood while reminding us to take joy in puncturing the obsolete myths we've been taught.

Guy Fawkes

On a mission to restore Catholic Sovereignty to Great Britain, Guido "Guy" Fawkes (April 13, 1570–January 31, 1606) hatched a scheme that famously became known as "The Gunpowder Plot." As a young man, Fawkes joined the Spanish forces as a mercenary to fight the Protestant Dutch in the Eighty Years' War in the Netherlands, Belgium, and Luxembourg. But as Spain began to lose control of the lowlands, Fawkes headed for Madrid to seek support to instigate a Catholic uprising in his English homeland; he would return disgruntled and empty-handed. Along with Thomas Wintour and Robert Catesby, Fawkes plotted the assassination of King James I (who later claimed to admire his would-be killer's stout "Roman resolution"). Securing a cellar beneath the House of Lords, Fawkes and his ad-hoc rebel crew managed to smuggle in thirty-six barrels of gunpowder, which were discovered on the morning of November 5th, 1605, after Lord Mounteagle had been alerted to the devious plot. Imprisoned and tortured, Guy Fawkes quickly confessed. But in the end he managed to have the last laugh, when on January 31, 1606, as he ascended the scaffold where he was to be hung and then drawn and quartered, Fawkes lost his footing. He fell from the platform and broke his own neck, thus denying his executioners the satisfaction of their grim trade.

Critic/author Johnny Rogan interpreted Lennon's use of a loud, sudden explosion to end "Remember" as a romanticized recasting of history, as if the failed Gunpowder Plot had actually succeeded and Fawkes was, in turn, to be celebrated for blowing those "Scotch beggars back to [their] native mountains."

Written circa 1870, the poem commemorating Guy Fawkes's epic failure that every English schoolboy once was expected to memorize begins:

> Remember, remember the Fifth of November
> Gunpowder, treason and plot
> I know of no reason

why gunpowder treason

should ever be forgot

Guy Fawkes, Guy Fawkes

'twas his intent to blow up

the King and the Parliament

Three score barrels of powder below

Poor old England to overthrow

To this day the Fifth of November remains a holiday in England, cele-brating the assassin's failed attempt with dazzling fireworks and the figure of Fawkes being burned in effigy. The legend of Guy Fawkes has only continued to grow over the centuries. In September 2011, Fawkes would become the poster boy for a two-month-long protest known as Occupy Wall Street at Zuccotti Park in New York's financial district, when hoards of the disgruntled 99 percent took a stand against the American ruling class to demand wealth redistribution and equality. With demonstrators braving the autumn elements, camped out in sleeping bags, in tents, and under tarps, the park was eventu-ally deemed unsanitary. On November 15, the NYPD forced everybody to va-cate the premises or face arrest. The smirking, mustachioed mask donned by thousands of protesters was said to be none other than Guy Fawkes. Keeping up with the times, Fawkes even has his own Facebook page. In a post from April 2013, "Fawkes," who was then 443 years old, thanked his 30,000 fans for their continued support and for emulating his trademark "mustache and tall hat."

Intrepid Interpretations: Remember

While most Lennon fans were initially shocked by the raw emotional quality of his first solo record, Manel Guerrero of Barcelona became so thoroughly obsessed with it that he recorded a tribute in 2013 titled *Plastic Ono Man*, covering all ten songs, as well as creating a website on which he wrote copious notes for each song. Recorded, mixed, and mastered at his home studio, Guerrero does justice to some of Lennon's most difficult material. His mission was not to simply duplicate Lennon's most highly personal songs but also to honor "one of the most important rock records ever to be created."

12

LOVE

While Phil Spector's gossamer-like piano leads the song in, Lennon whispers and sighs its deceptively simple lyric. Like love itself, John's lilting song is a mirror, as each line reflects the words that begin the phrase "Love is real—real is love." The song is as perfectly balanced as a Zen rock garden. There isn't an unnecessary syllable or breath. Every note and word is essential. The melody gently pulls you along, leading to each new phrase. While seeking inner peace, John Lennon wrestled with various inner demons throughout his life. But beyond all the drugs and self-help methods he dabbled in—from pot to acid to meditation and Primal Scream therapy—John ultimately believed in the power of love. His razor-sharp wit, whether hilarious or cruel, never brought him much satisfaction; the only way to tame his wild mind was to "sing my heart," as he whispered in the tender lyrics to "Julia."

"To work on this relationship with Yoko is very hard," Lennon once explained. "We've got the gift of love, but love is like a precious plant. You can't accept it and leave it in the cupboard. . . . You've got to water it . . . and be careful of it and keep the flies off it."

While the tune "Love" exudes a fragile beauty, the atmosphere in the recording studio was decidedly different. Spector would later confess that his piano track on "Love" "took twenty takes" and was filled with "a million mistakes." As John and Yoko sat watching behind the recording console, the cocky producer fumbled over his part repeatedly while Lennon took pleasure in taunting him: "You don't like being on the other side of the goddamn fuckin' glass, do ya?"

***

Rubber Soul was an album for lovers. It was virtually a user's guide on the subject. Nearly every stage of love, every phase of relationships, was addressed within its lyrics—from infatuation to lust, jealousy, rejection, and loss, as well as another brand of love the Beatles had yet to address beyond their girl/boy musical dramas: the notion of universal love as portrayed in "The Word."

Recorded in 1965, "The Word," as Barry Miles pointed out, was "one of the first hippie anthems." Over their funkiest beat yet, the Beatles' music delivered a prevailing message: Love has the power to save humanity. Many of the Beatles' later songs like "Within You and Without You" and "All You Need is Love" would continue this theme.

Intrepid Interpretations: Love

Recorded for *Make Some Noise: The Amnesty International Campaign To Save Darfur*, the Cure's cover of "Love" was beyond odd, bordering on psychotic, as the rhythm surged like a panicky heartbeat pounding in Robert Smith's chest, while his echo-laden vocal swirled through the chambers of a fearful mind. Smith repeated the lyric "We can be" on the song's coda as if suddenly realizing that beyond all dread and doubt, he and his lover might make it somehow.

13

WELL, WELL, WELL

Driven by John's grungy guitar, "Well, Well, Well," is a great example of Lennon's dedication to raw-edged rock 'n' roll. "The playing itself, to him, was not that important. It was more important to capture the feeling. We did one or two takes. There's a lot of mistakes in there," Klaus Voormann confessed. "But [my bass playing] was just like a pulse. [It was] exactly what John wanted. He loved it."

"He did not want to make a production with lots of instruments and great arrangements," Klaus explained to Anthony Curtis in *Rolling Stone*. "The main thing was that he wanted to do something fresh and direct as possible . . . [in] a real close, intimate atmosphere. He just played the song and Ringo and I played the simple way we both enjoy playing . . . and it seemed to be exactly what he was looking for."

"Voormann is just perfect on *Plastic Ono Band*," said Dave Dreiwitz, bassist with Ween. "He has a fantastic sound and hits all the right notes. Sometimes he gets really gangsta, like on 'I Found Out.' But he also plays some nice Motown/James Jamerson kind of runs too. His sound is so heavy, and he grooves so well to compliment the music. He locks in with Ringo so nicely, but Klaus is not afraid of getting heavy in a Black Sabbath kind of way."

"Taking stock of John's guitar work around this time, I find his playing to be supremely direct and emotional, economical, contributing to the tracks in crucial ways," Nels Cline observed. "On 'Well, Well, Well' and 'I Found Out,' one gets the distinct impression that the guitar and voice were tracked at the same time and that they are inextricably linked. There is no layering, no sweetening. The guitar on both these tracks adds serious drive to these songs and gets me thinking about Bo Diddley, about Muddy Waters . . . about what a brutally direct guitar can do for a song."

"John's guitar playing was not about gymnastics. . . . Imagine trying to get Clapton to play like that?" Hal Willner mused.

Like the best rock 'n' roll, "Well, Well, Well" is raw and loose, careening along until nearly falling apart after the chorus. Klaus picks up the pieces, leading John and Ringo back into the groove again as the bass drum kicks a menacing heartbeat while John howls, flailing away at his guitar until both he and the tune are spent.

"Ringo was a lyric drummer," Marvin Etzioni pointed out. "As a singer himself, he played after the lyric. John sings, 'Well, well, well . . .' followed by a crash on an open hi-hat. You can sing his drum parts. I don't know a drummer who thinks that way!"

"For John, the song was the essence. Add to that the best White rhythm-and-blues drummer—Ringo Starr! Holy moly!" said Benmont Tench, who's performed live and recorded with Ringo on a handful of albums. "I was playing with Ringo and just stopped and turned around and said, 'You really are the greatest drummer in the world!' It just came out of me without meaning to. . . . But he swings like crazy and he's listening to the song."

"I never heard Yoko's *Plastic Ono Band* album at the time it was released," D. J. Bonebrake confessed. "When I listened to 'Why' recently on YouTube, I thought it was a modern-rock-based commercial preceding the track. That might seem like a put-down, but it demonstrates how modern it still sounds! The tape starts in the middle of the groove! I really love the intertwining of John's guitar and Yoko's vocal. They're in the same range, weaving around each other. The drums are driving and intense, with Ringo playing constant eighth notes against Klaus Voormann's melodic bass line in 4/4, with random measures of 2/4 thrown in. This would have been a good record to play at parties to verify my freak membership."

"She looked so beautiful I could eat her," Lennon sang in "Well, Well, Well," a line one might expect from Mick Jagger, whose sultry "Let It Bleed" invited his lover to "come all over me."

Ono not only revolutionized John's mind, she also helped unleash Lennon's sexuality. Lennon, who once had been so nervous he could barely speak when meeting his teenage dream, Bridget Bardot, was now doodling pornographic depictions of going down on his wife for the world to see.

Intrepid Interpretations: Well, Well, Well

Backed by Elephant's Memory, Lennon/Ono played their last concert together at Madison Square Garden on August 30, 1972. Billed as *One to One*, the show also included Stevie Wonder and Roberta Flack to benefit the Willowbrook State School for Retarded Children. An album of Lennon's set, including "Well, Well, Well," was posthumously released in 1986 as *Live in New York City*. Chewing gum as he sang, John delivered the song's suggestive lyric: "She looked so beautiful I could eat her," adding, "I did!" as his wife, dressed all in white with wraparound shades and playing an inaudible keyboard, smiled knowingly. The song ended with "Winston O'Boogie" (as he dubbed himself) shredding his vocal chords over a surging beat.

"I produced a reggae version of "Well, Well, Well" by [Ghanaian singer/songwriter] Rocky Daruni for *Instant Karma—The Amnesty International Campaign To Save Darfur*," Marvin Etzioni recalled. "It featured [Carlton] Santa Davis on drums, who played with both Marley and Tosh. The Lennon version of the song has one of my favorite guitar tones ever recorded. I made sure we cut the vocal live along with the band, as if it was an original reggae song. We didn't listen to Lennon's version."

Daruni's version of "Well, Well, Well" works nicely as a bouncy groover, with Etzioni's lead wah-guitar "singing" riff evoking Sly Stone's "talkbox" on "Don't Call Me Nigger, Whitey." The song fades out with Rocky and crew repeatedly chanting "Well, well, well," transforming it from Lennon's primal shriek into a calming mantra reminiscent of the chorus "Every little thing is gonna be alright" from Bob Marley's "Three Little Birds."

Long Beach, California, indie rockers Cold War Kids gave "Well, Well, Well" a swift kick for the Lollapalooza crowd in 2015, staying true to its blues/metal guitar grind and thudding beat, while an off-kilter descending keyboard riff brought a moment of originality to the mix.

Mama don't go! John Lennon (age 8) with his mother, Julia, in Liverpool, UK, 1948.
(ARCHIVIO GBB/Alamy Stock Photo)

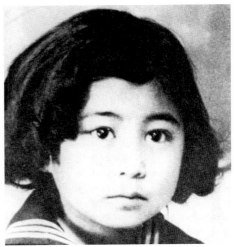

Yoko Ono circa 1940.
(Photofest)

John Lennon with Yoko Ono at *You Are Here* art exhibition, July 1968.
(Trinity Mirror/Mirrorpix/Alamy Stock Photo)

John and Yoko attend the opening night of the Old Vic Theatre adaptation of *In His Own Write*, London, June, 1968. This was the first public appearance of John and Yoko together.
(Trinity Mirror/Mirrorpix/Alamy Stock Photo)

John and Yoko busted for cannabis at Ringo's London apartment, October 18, 1968.
(Trinity Mirror/Mirrorpix/Alamy Stock Photo)

On the set of the 1968 Rolling Stones *Rock and Roll Circus* concert show; *l to r:* John Entwistle, Keith Moon, and Pete Townsend of the Who; John Lennon; Yoko Ono; and the Rolling Stones.
(Pictorial Press Ltd/Alamy Stock Photo)

John and Yoko live at
Cambridge University,
March 2, 1969.
(Tracksimages.com/
Alamy Stock Photo)

John and Yoko back in
Paris after their wedding,
March 21, 1969. John's
coat was made of human
hair and purchased for
1,000 British Pounds.
(PictureLux/The Hollywood
Archive/Alamy Stock Photo)

John and Yoko on the first
day of their Amsterdam
Bed-In, March 25, 1969.
(BNA Photographic/
Alamy Stock Photo)

John and Yoko appeared twice on *The Dick Cavett Show* (ABC) to premier "Imagine" on September 11th, 1971, and returned again on May 11, 1972; *l-r:* John Lennon, Yoko Ono, and Dick Cavett.
(ABC/Photofest)

Above: John and Yoko join NYC street rockers David Peel & the Lower East Side. *l-r:* David Peel, Yoko Ono, Yippie founder Jerry Rubin (on percussion), and John Lennon.
(20th Century-Fox/Photofest)

Left: John and Yoko declare "War Is Over! If You Want It" on the steps of the Apple building, Savile Row, London, December 15, 1969
(© KEYSTONE Pictures USA)

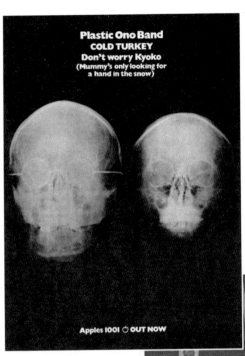

Left: 1969 British advertisement for the single "Cold Turkey" by the Plastic Ono Band on the Apple label.
(Neil Baylis/Alamy Stock Photo)

Below: John Lennon and Yoko Ono at the Lyceum Ballroom in London, December 16, 1969.
(PictureLux/The Hollywood Archive/
Alamy Stock Photo)

After their haircuts, January, 1970.
(Penny Tweedie/
Alamy Stock Photo)

John Lennon, Yoko
Ono and her 5 year-
old daughter, Kyoko
Cox, at Apple Records'
Headquarters, May 1969.
(PictureLux/© JRC The
Hollywood Archive/
Alamy Stock Photo)

John Lennon/Plastic Ono Band
released by Apple Records in
December, 1970 (cover photo by
Dan Richter).
(sjvinyl/Alamy Stock Photo)

Spontaneous surrealist radio
at its best! John and Yoko
visit New York's WPLJ's DJ
Alex Bennet (AKA "The
Youth Guru") twice in the
summer of 1971. Yoko sings in
Japanese, cries, screeches, and
asks questions like "What did
you do for the world today?"
as John mumbles nonsense
answers, laughs and coughs.
(Pictorial Press Ltd/
Alamy Stock Photo)

John Lennon and Yoko Ono at a *Grapefruit* book signing in Selfridges, London, July 15, 1971.
(Tracksimages.com/ Alamy Stock Photo)

John Lennon's *Imagine*, released by Apple Records in September, 1971, co-produced with Yoko Ono and Phil Spector.
(Moviestore Collection Ltd/ Alamy Stock Photo)

Some Time in New York City, released by Apple Records in June, 1972, by John Lennon and Yoko Ono, with Elephant's Memory and Invisible Strings.
(Directphoto Collection/ Alamy Stock Photo)

Reproduction of John Lennon and Yoko Ono's *War Is Over* billboard, Greenwich Village, New York City, 2006. (From *U.S. vs. John Lennon* (2006), written and produced by David Leaf and John Scheinfeld

(Photofest)

From *The U.S. vs. John Lennon* (2006) documentary film, written and produced by David Leaf and John Scheinfeld.

(Lions Gate Films/Photofest)

14

LOOK AT ME

Following the sweltering groove of "Well, Well, Well," Lennon's gently fingerpicked "Look at Me," with its cooing chorus, comes as a temporary dose of sweet relief. John wrote "Look at Me" in Rishikesh while practicing Transcendental Meditation with the Maharishi Mahesh Yogi in August 1967; he would learn the finer points of fingerpicking an acoustic guitar from the Scottish psychedelic folk singer Donovan, who was part of the elite entourage assembled at the giggling guru's feet (along with actress Mia Farrow, her sister Prudence, and Beach Boys singer Mike Love). Employing the delicate syncopated rhythm, Lennon immediately wrote both "Julia" and "Dear Prudence."

A navel gazer of the first order, the song begins with a bit of gibberish, reminiscent of the drowsy babble on the end of "I'm So Tired." "Okay?" Lennon asks himself. "Yes, thank you!" he replies. "Look at Me" bears the mindset of someone who has experienced the ego-quelling effects of LSD. While providing colorful, swirling visions that stretch day-to-day realities beyond the limits of our imaginations and create a sense of interconnectedness between all people and living entities, acid (particularly when ingested regularly in large amounts) has a way of making our lives' ambitions and problems seem rather inconsequential when compared to the profound experience of glimpsing eternity.

With its light, ethereal feel, "Look at Me" initially seems like a toss-off, coming between a pair of "heavy" numbers like "Well, Well, Well" and "God." But Lennon's song gently questions the very foundation of his soul, as he begs "Look at me, who am I s'posed to be?" Unshackling his psychic armor with the vulnerable lyrics of his 1967 masterpiece "Strawberry Fields Forever," John Lennon now revealed a deeper level of openness for the world to analyze. Whenever Paul McCartney found himself in the midst of conflict with John, he recalled his partner dropping all defenses and glancing at him over the rims of his glasses to say: "It's just me." Making such unpretentiously naked music was ultimately a much bolder act than posing nude for the camera with his Japanese earth mother.

"'Look at me, who am I supposed to be?' This was John addressing the end of the Beatles and telling everybody to 'Stop it!' It's over now. . . . Enough!" Hal Willner said. "Who the fuck knows what it was like being them?"

"Julia"

To better understand *Plastic Ono Band's* two most tender offerings, one must listen again to "Julia" from the *White Album,* where John, hoping to diffuse the ticking time bomb of his mother's memory, wrote and sang one of the most nakedly honest and poetic songs of his career. Composed during the summer of 1968 while on retreat at the Maharishi Mahesh Yogi's ashram in Rishikesh, India, the haunting melody was built on a gentle fingerpicking pattern John had recently learned from the "master of mellow," Donovan, while sitting "in the shade of a jacaranda tree." Donovan claimed he first picked up the technique from a folk musician named "Dirty Phil"; Lennon's sharp intellect and guitar skills apparently allowed him to absorb the style in half the time it took the Scottish psychedelic folk-rocker to learn it. Donovan, who'd previously thrown a few lines McCartney's way in "Yellow Submarine," also claimed to have helped John write the lyrics to "Julia." Fingerpicking an acoustic guitar opened a new world of possibilities to Lennon, who quickly composed "Julia" and "Dear Prudence," along with the sweet and soothing "Love" (which would eventually surface on *Plastic Ono Band*).

The daily ritual of transcendental meditation inspired Lennon to compose "songs that came from his deeper self," Donovan claimed. "He was feeling for his lost mother in a most loving way when he wrote 'Julia.'"

Donovan's rosy memories of India didn't completely match with those of Lennon, who, despite the laid-back atmosphere of Maharishi's meditation camp, claimed: "I wrote six hundred songs about how I feel," filled with thoughts of "dying, crying, and committing suicide. But I felt creative." At the same time Lennon felt nostalgic for his doomed mother, he wrote the startling "Yer Blues," uninhibitedly howling, "Yes, I'm lonely, wanna die!" paving the way for the raw personal songs to come on *Plastic Ono Band*.

Intrepid Interpretations: Look at Me

Joseph Arthur recorded a lilting "Look at Me" for the *Lennon Covered #2* CD issued by *Q* magazine in 2005. With lightly fingerpicked guitar and multitracked, reverb-drenched vocals, the tune floats downstream on rumbling soft-mallet tom-toms, taking on a lazy, psychedelic feel.

Canadian punk rockers Sum 41 released a song called "Look at Me" on their 2007 album *Underclass Hero*, whose opening verse begins with the lines "Look at me, who am I supposed to be?" The album's title song, a high-gear teen freedom anthem, also references Lennon's "Working Class Hero."

15

GOD

You're born in pain . . . and pain is what we're in most of the time.
I think the bigger the pain, the more gods we need.

—John Lennon

With his quick wit and sharp tongue, John Lennon was, not surprisingly, a discipline problem back in his school days. Although a voracious reader, John performed poorly in his academic studies, particularly in science and religion, which held little or no interest for him. In fact, God, as Lennon later admitted, rarely entered his consciousness until he first heard Elvis Presley sing "Heartbreak Hotel."

While fond of composing whimsical poetry, drawing humorous doodles, and listening to *The Goon Show*, Lennon became thoroughly obsessed with Elvis, falling in love with his reverb-drenched hiccupping voice, cool clothes, and slicked-back hair. But it was the sound and shape of his guitar that drove John to humble himself and beg the Lord's divine assistance in helping him get his hands on one. Although Aunt Mimi did everything within her power to save John from the social repercussions of dressing like a Teddy Boy (she drew the line at skintight drainpipe pants), it was his banjo-playing mother Julia who fueled John's love of music by buying him his first guitar through a mail-order catalogue.

God in one form or another was apparently alive and well in John Lennon as he flew home on April 12, 1968, after spending nearly two months at the Maharishi's ashram in Rishikesh, India. Whether inspired by too much sun or blinded by his own inner light, Lennon evidently experienced some sort of an epiphany. "I'm Jesus Christ; I'm back again," he informed his childhood pal Pete Shotton. Eager to reveal his identity to his fellow bandmates and the crew at Apple Records, John called an impromptu meeting on May 18. Well acquainted with the delusionary effects of LSD, the Beatles' press secretary Derek Taylor took the incident in stride, chalking John's outrageous proclamation up to a moment of temporary "insanity or eccentricity." Whether due to the overwhelming effects of drugs or fame, John determinedly gathered everyone around to announce (to their general amusement) that he was, in fact, the reincarnation of the Son of God. Without further word, the meeting was adjourned, and everyone rushed off to lunch.

Hoping to catch the public's eye while expanding their consciousness, Lennon/ Ono kicked off their "War Is Over If You Want It" campaign on December 15, 1969, by posting large, bold-typefaced antiwar billboards in twelve cities worldwide. While John was fielding questions from the press in Toronto, a journalist asked him about his faith in God.

"Yes, I believe that God is like a powerhouse, like where you keep electricity, like a power station," Lennon replied. "He's a supreme power, and he's neither good nor bad, left, right, Black, or White. He just is. And we tap that source of power and make of it what we will."

The opening line to Lennon's monumental song, "God is a concept by which we measure our pain," was at once startling and revelatory. The phrase suddenly popped into his head while in the thick of therapy with Dr. Arthur Janov. "Like a lot of the words, they just came out of me mouth," John later told *Rolling Stone*. "I had the idea 'God is the concept by which we measure our pain.' So, when you have a [phrase] like that, you just sit down and sing the first tune that comes into your head."

The tune, as the original demo tape of Lennon singing "God" solo reveals, was nothing special musically speaking, just typical 1950s standard chord changes (G–E-minor–C–D) steadily strummed on an acoustic guitar, reminiscent of old, emotion-ally charged Beatle ballads like "This Boy" or "Yes It Is."

"John always hated his voice," Barry Reynolds said. "That's why he usually dou-ble-tracked it. The *Plastic Ono Band* album was so immediate and raw, but his sing-ing on the last verse of 'God' is just sublime."

While critic/author Greil Marcus shared Reynolds's observation, he took it one step further, claiming John's vocal on "God" was "the finest in all of rock."

"'God' was definitely the end of something . . . the Beatles!" Hal Willner ex-claimed. "And the beginning of something else. Not long after that . . . two, maybe two and a half years later, punk rock started. Rock music, with bands like the Eagles, had gone stale, and everything was suddenly about sparseness, like we'd heard on the *Plastic Ono Band* albums."

"I don't know if Lennon and Spector were aware of it, but in a lot of ways, *Plastic Ono Band* was exactly the same template as Dylan's *John Wesley Harding*," Benmont Tench pointed out. Released three years earlier in 1967 at the height of psychedelia,

John Wesley Harding was a stripped-down affair, with Dylan delivering his apocalyptic sermons plain and simple, without any icing from Al Kooper's organ or Robbie Robertson's snarling guitar leads.

"It was just Bob with a really good rhythm section," Tench continued, "Charlie McCoy [on bass] and [drummer] Kenny Buttery. And it's one of Bob's best records. The songs are killer, and the fact that it's so empty . . . there's nothing on it that doesn't need to be there. The Beatles records were generally not cluttered until you get to their ornate, baroque period. But *Plastic Ono Band* cut everything down to the core. The only way to have outdone that would have been to record it with John on just one instrument, which he did on 'Working Class Hero.'"

As Lennon had once told Tony King (Klaus Voormann's friend who worked for Apple): "The instrument you compose a song on determines the tone of the song. A number originally written on the piano sounds totally different to one worked out on the guitar." This clearly was the case with the early demos for *Plastic Ono Band*. Whether playing guitar or piano, Lennon defined his songs with simple, solid rhythm patterns over which he phrased his vocals. On the studio recording of "God," John moved to keyboards in lieu of the original six-string sound, creating a more dramatic call and response between his voice and the piano. He was joined by Billy Preston playing a second piano, giving the tune a distinct gospel feel along with Klaus's minimal bass part and Ringo's drums.

"The very first Lennon solo album was very interesting," engineer Richard Lush recalled in an interview with the Australian online music magazine *Happy*. "I'd already worked with Phil Spector on George Harrison's *All Things Must Pass*. We had some fabulous sessions; I mean Billy Preston came in to play the piano on '*God*.' We had both John and Billy playing piano!"

John first met Preston in Hamburg in 1962. Billy was the real deal. Having played with Little Richard, Sam Cooke, and Ray Charles, he brought the spirit with him everywhere he went. Hoping to rescue the sour mood of the *Get Back/Let It Be* sessions, George brought Billy in to play electric piano on a few tracks.

"Billy Preston was an absolute wonder . . . a miracle," Benmont Tench marveled. "He was one of the best we ever, ever had. He was just in his own field. Think about his electric piano on 'Don't Let Me Down,' or his solo on 'Get Back!' He's so crazily good! The Beatles never credited anybody on a single except Billy! He was a gospel player and could shine more joy into a room than anybody. And to have him play on 'God' made a whole lotta sense."

Although Preston's keyboards were integral to the Beatles' sound on *Let It Be*, he was featured just briefly in cameo shots throughout the film of their final rooftop concert on January 30, 1969. Lennon allegedly had wanted to make Preston a full-time fifth Beatle, while McCartney demurred, claiming "It's bad enough with four."

According to Ono, Phil Spector "knew how to accommodate John's wishes. He just walked in when we were doing 'God' [which had yet to jell]. Spector listened for a moment and, following his sharp instinct, suggested Billy Preston come in and lay down an overdub over John's rudimentary gospel keyboard work.

"And Billy did such a brilliant, brilliant piano," Yoko said. "You can never think of 'God' without Billy's piano playing. . . . That was Phil's idea . . . that's how he just made that track shine."

* * *

While Ringo's drums once propelled Lennon's acid-fueled visions of "Tomorrow Never Knows," with "God," he laid down a rock-of-ages solid foundation for John's gospel-tinged testimony. Starr always claimed he never played a fill the same way twice, and "God" offers a veritable sampling of Ringo's unique expertise of the sticks, from basic timekeeping skills to a heavy, pounding fist as John rebuked Hitler.

"Magic, the I Ching, and the Bible" were "the first three or four [ideas that] just came out," John said, explaining his writing process to Jann Wenner. "I was putting down all these things I didn't believe in. I could have gone on . . . it was like a Christmas card list . . . where do I end? Churchill? And who have I missed out?"

Lennon speculated over whether he should've left "a gap," to encourage fans "to fill in [their] own, for whoever [they] don't believe in. It just got out of hand," he confessed. "But Beatles was the final thing because it's like I no longer believe in myth, and Beatles is another myth. I don't believe in it. The dream's over. I'm not just talking about the Beatles is over, I'm talking about the generation thing. The dream's over, and I have personally got to get down to so-called reality."

For George Harrison, the dream had unequivocally ended as well. Upon first glance, his debut album, *All Things Must Pass*, seemed like a dismal affair. The three-record box set sat on your lap, heavy as a tombstone, with Harrison's name and the album title etched in granite-like letters into the gray English sky above him. Balanced on a chair in his gardening clothes, George posed for Barry Feinstein's camera on his sprawling estate's lawn, surrounded by four grotesque gnomes that seem to symbolize himself and his former bandmates. The Beatles were history, and this was George's droll way of making the point, telling his fans to get over it and move on with their lives, rather than screaming their lungs out like his old friend or shamelessly airing their dirty laundry to the world's most popular music magazine.

McCartney publicly dealt with his "times of trouble" in his own way, gently evoking his deceased mother Mary, who returned to her son in a vision, advising him the best thing he could do was to "Let It Be." But Lennon was never one to hold back and spelled it out, loud and bluntly. "The dream is over," he sang, over a simple, repetitive, gospel-infused piano vamp. His voice, a raw scab, chanted a refrain of ideas and people he'd renounced, from magic to "Zimmerman" (Bob Dylan) to God and the Beatles.

It seemed like Lennon's litany of denouncements was his way of settling scores with old friends and disposing of philosophies he'd suddenly forsaken after his defenses had been stripped bare during primal scream therapy sessions.

1. Magic

First on John's list of abandoned heroes and discarded practices was magic. Those nostalgic for the '60s often claim it was a "magical" time. While the decade began innocently enough, with the effervescent type of enchantment found in a "young girl's heart" (as the Lovin' Spoonful sang in "Do You Believe in Magic?"), it was soon replaced by the black variety—a murky pool of inspiration that fueled the dark side of British bands from the Rolling Stones to Led Zeppelin and Black Sabbath. If the Beatles had ever dabbled in anything remotely resembling black magic, it was, at best, a momentary fascination. Lennon, who took pleasure in pushing people's buttons, had knowingly included the nefarious occultist Alistair Crowley in the rows of famous faces that adorned the cover to *Sgt. Pepper's Lonely Hearts Club Band*. EMI, the Beatles' British record label, immediately nixed two of John's other choices—Hitler and Gandhi—finding them too provocative. Crowley, the self-proclaimed prophet of Thelema, a home-brewed religion based on the spiritual practices of ancient Egypt, remained on the album's jacket, thanks in part, to his relative obscurity.

By the end of 1967, the Beatles would appear as four magicians in a scene from their charmingly aimless home movie, *Magical Mystery Tour*. At the same time, Mick Jagger donned a black cape and peaked magician's cap on the cover of the Stones' 1967 disasterpiece, *Their Satanic Majesties Request*. No one took Mick's posturing as the rock 'n' roll Mephistopheles too seriously, although Jagger's occult dabbling ultimately led to the Stones' brilliant "Sympathy for the Devil" and later "Dancing with Mr. D" (that's right boys and girls, "the Devil!") on 1973's disappointing *Goats Head Soup*. But like everything else with the Stones, from the blues, to fashion, to sex and drugs, it was Brian Jones who was always on the cutting edge. While most people attributed Brian's tragic death at age twenty-six to his voracious appetite for all things wicked, some believed Jones died shortly after witnessing the ritual sacrifice of a goat in Morocco. The band's blonde dandy was said to have allegedly gasped, "That's me!" just moments before the poor animal with the flaxen fringe hanging over its eyes had its throat slit.

With his new-found fame and wealth, Jimmy Page purchased Alistair Crowley's mansion in Loch Ness, Scotland, where rumors flourished of shrieking phantoms and skulls rolling down the stairs in the dead of night. Legends aside, the Who's guitarist/songwriter, Pete Townshend, took great pleasure in demystifying Led Zeppelin's image in his 2012 memoir, *Who I Am*, referring to them as "a couple of Ernies from the Highlands."

But Lennon's affront on "magic" might well have been triggered by Yannis Alexis Mardas, the Greek "electronic wizard" whom John generously dubbed "Magic Alex" after attending an exhibit of his kinetic light sculptures at the Indica Gallery. With a surplus of intriguing concepts, from paint with invisible properties to building the world's first 72-track recording console, the stoned and very gullible Beatles impulsively appointed Mardas to spearhead the electronics division of their new multimedia company, Apple Corps, offering him a substantial stipend and free reign to develop any idea that popped into his head.

It wasn't long before something began to smell foul. An inexplicable fire in Mardas's studio damaged or destroyed many of his creations beyond repair, but no one seemed too concerned. Lennon was happy, as long as he could stay stoned and keep peering into Magic Alex's "Nothing Box," a small, handheld plastic cube that enhanced his acid trips with bright, flashing lights.

According to John Dunbar (who curated the Indica Gallery with Barry Miles), Mardas was "quite cunning" and knew "how to wind people up." Sizing him up as a charlatan, Dunbar wasn't buying any of that "'Magic Alex shit." "He was a fucking TV repairman!" John Dunbar exclaimed. Meanwhile, the custom studio he was supposedly building in the basement of Apple headquarters on Savile Road remained a total shamble. Not only did the fanciful visions of this silver-tongued flimflam man turn out to have no basis in reality, they cost the Beatles over five million pounds.

In truth, Mardas had no formal training in any of the electronic media he claimed to have mastered. After bilking the Beatles, he used his "magic" powers to shake down various monarchs of the Mideast, including the Sultan of Oman and King Hussein of Jordan, whose royal limos somehow failed to withstand repeated rounds of live ammunition despite Mardas's special method of bulletproofing.

* * *

Years later, on May 27, 1979, a full-page advertisement (allegedly costing $18,240) entitled "A Love Letter from John and Yoko to People Who Ask Us What, When and Why" appeared in the *New York Times*. The expensive missive was designed, in its coy way, to fill the public in on their lives behind the walls of Manhattan's ominous Dakota apartment building. It had been three years since Lennon/Ono had made any form of public statement. Painting a portrait of domestic bliss, they assured us that all was well: "The plants are growing. The cats are purring," and "Magic is logical."

2. I Ching

Next on John's scornful list was one of the world's most renowned books—the *I Ching*, also known as *The Book of Changes*. This ancient divination manual has endured for centuries, having been employed as an interactive oracle with which the reader, whether by tossing three coins or a clutch of yarrow stalks, can question and receive inscrutable wisdom from its mysterious source, often referred to as "The Sage." The results are often uncanny and brimming with moral judgment.

Read and venerated around the world, the *I Ching* was originally developed in ancient China during the first half of the Western Zhou period, between 1000 and 750 BC. Its "Great Commentary" has been sought for everything from battlefield strategies to love troubles.

It was no surprise to discover that Bob Dylan was enthusiastic about "a book called the *I Ching*," an essential accoutrement of counterculture truth seekers. "I'm not trying to push it," Bob said in a 1965 interview. "But it's the only thing that is amazingly true, not just for me. . . . You don't have to believe in anything to read it. [But] besides being a great book to believe in, it's also very fantastic poetry."

Syd Barrett, the original founder/singer/guitarist of Pink Floyd, was also a great believer in the *I Ching*, consulting its ancient pages for inspiration when writing his 1967 song "Chapter 24," which is built of direct quotes from Fû (复), the hexagram symbolizing the concept of "Return."

"All movement is accomplished in six stages, and the seventh brings return," Barrett sang straight from the text in his lilting, loopy voice.

The following spring (1968), George Harrison, disheartened by the acrimonious atmosphere tainting the *White Album* sessions, consulted the oracle by randomly opening the mystical book and reading its pages. Seeking divine inspiration, he discovered the phrase "gently weeps," which triggered his greatest composition to date, "While My Guitar Gently Weeps."

3. The Bible

While Lennon found little inspiration in the Bible, Bob Dylan's 1968 comeback album, *John Wesley Harding*, teemed with apocalyptic visions equal to those of the holy book's final chapter, the Revelation of Saint John. Beyond the ominous lyrics to "All Along the Watchtower," there were poetic descriptions of the fifth-century Algerian bishop Saint Augustine wandering alone "in the utmost misery" while nature seemed to hasten an impending Armageddon, as leaves tumbled to the ground and "the seas began to part" in "The Wicked Messenger."

Throughout his career, the Bible was standard equipment in Dylan's lyrical toolkit. In his imagist rocker "Changing of the Guard," which opens his 1978 album *Street Legal*, Bob warned mankind that if we refuse to change our evil ways, we must all prepare to "face elimination." A year later, the mercurial bard shocked the world again after releasing the gospel-tinged *Slow Train Coming*, which brimmed with Christian imagery, while admonishing everyone from ambassadors to rock 'n' roll addicts and state troopers that the time had come that they "Gotta Serve Somebody."

A growing number of '60s musicians, from George Harrison to Cat Stevens and Van Morrison, would eventually turn their backs on rock 'n' roll's hedonistic lifestyle and transform into spiritual seekers of various beliefs and degrees.

In the early '70s, the world was first introduced to the funky, infectious groove of reggae. But few outside of Jamaica took the Wailers' Rastafarian creed seriously. Most folks enjoyed its lively rhythm and the effects of strong dope, which was considered an essential part of the laid-back Caribbean lifestyle.

"We know when we understand, mighty God is a living man," Peter Tosh sang in the Wailers' righteously indignant "Get Up, Stand Up." Although Haile Selassie heroically braved his country's invasion by Mussolini's troops, the Ethiopian emperor was still considered mortal by the rest of the world. But in the hearts and minds of the rapidly growing Rasta cult, Selassie would soon attain divine status, which he asserted was his due through his alleged lineage to King Solomon (the reason Rastafarians often wear "Solomon's Seal," better known as the Star of David). The Wailers' charismatic front man, Bob Marley, would also soon transform into a messiah-like figure, preaching peace and equal rights before tragically dying of cancer at the untimely age of thirty-six.

In 1976 Cat Stevens had a near-death experience in which he nearly drowned while swimming in Malibu. After desperately crying for God's help, he found himself immediately washed upon the shore. Following this life-changing event, Stevens began to search in earnest for answers in everything from "Buddhism, Zen, the *I Ching*, numerology, tarot cards, and astrology" until his brother David presented him with a copy of the Qur'an, which spoke directly to his soul. Changing his name to Yusuf Islam in 1978, Cat Stevens walked off the stage in search of the truth, turning his back on a tremendously successful career to become a devout Muslim. Claiming he'd finally "found the spiritual home I'd been seeking most of my life," Stevens auctioned off his guitars for charity and never looked back . . . for twenty-five years, until 2003 when he re-recorded "Peace Train" and began performing again.

In 1980 Van Morrison sang the joys of having become a "Common One," wandering the bucolic English countryside with just his "red robe dangling," free from the greed and madness of the dog-eat-dog world. Throughout the decade, Morrison sought the holy ("Veedon") fleece and evoked Blakean visions over simple chord changes that gently rose and fell, as on 1986's *No Guru, No Method, No Teacher*.

On the coda to the original demo for "God," Lennon jokingly testified, "Hallelujah! Eureka, brother! I got the news. It came to me in the night!" in imitation of shyster television evangelists. The second take of the demo reveals a more complete list of John's bitter denouncements, which also included Buddha, Kennedy, and Dylan, whose name he would later change back to "Zimmerman." "Dylan is bullshit," Lennon told Jann Wenner in *Rolling Stone*. "Zimmerman is his name."

In 1980 Lennon and Dylan's ongoing tiff was alive and more twisted than ever when John recorded "Serve Yourself," his sardonic reply to Bob's judgmental "Gotta Serve Somebody" (from his shocking 1979 born-again album *Slow Train Coming*). Mashing up Woody Guthrie with the Ramones, John pounded out a relentless punk rhythm on his acoustic guitar, unleashing a flood of sarcasm and vitriol in his best Liverpool Scouse (reminiscent of "Polythene Pam") that was so thoroughly absurd, it bordered on parody. "You say, you found Jesus Christ, he's the only one . . ." John snarled. "You got to serve yourself," he admonished Bob. "Ain't nobody gonna do it for you."

Along the way he also took pot shots at George Harrison for his devotion to Krishna, as well as Cat Stevens for his recent conversion to Islam. But it's important to note that the song ended with a winded laugh from Lennon after he violently shredded the tune's last chord on his guitar.

Re-recording the song with a clunky Fats Domino–style rocking piano that August, Lennon toned down the rougher edges of his punk attitude (only slightly) and edited out some of the tune's more rambling lyrics. Six months later John was murdered, and we can only speculate whether he would've included this vicious/hysterical farce of Dylan's funky fundamentalist warning on his follow-up album to *Double Fantasy.*

4. Tarot

Along with bashing magic, Lennon also disparaged the practice of reading Tarot as a means of divining the future. A deck of cards, divided into four suits of aces, kings, queens, and jacks, the Tarot was originally found in Italy, France, and Austria in the fifteenth century. The striking images and symbolism of Tarot enjoyed a great resurgence with the '60s counterculture, along with such pseudosciences as astrology and numerology.

Despite John's disapproving view of the occult, his own wife (who'd been called a witch for years) regularly employed various archaic mystical practices, from consulting the *I Ching* to basing important business decisions on the position of the stars. While in the thick of the Beatles' breakup, Yoko claimed the best defense against the constant barrage of lawyers and accountants was to employ the supernatural for guidance. As she told *Rolling Stone* in 1981, "The only power I had was to manage to move the date of the meeting. . . . If you have a meeting when the moon is void, everything you decide will later be annulled."

Years later, Yoko would transform into a formidable businesswoman, overseeing the couple's reported $150 million empire and investing in beachfront real estate and bucolic farmland where they raised herds of prized Holsteins (one of which allegedly sold for $265,000 at the New York State Fair). Like Nancy Reagan, Yoko would also rely on various occult practices to guide her.

In 2007 Ono finally confessed to the world's mounting suspicions that she was indeed a sorceress by titling her new album of remixes (which featured a slew of younger artists from Antony, DJ Spooky, and Cat Power to the Flaming Lips) *Yes, I'm a Witch.* While a joke, this admission only brought Yoko more scorn from those who questioned why, with all of her occult powers, didn't she sense that her husband was in mortal danger?

5. Hitler

It might seem like an arbitrary leap from Tarot to der Führer, but the madman who'd stolen Charlie Chaplin's mustache had also been an ardent fan of the occult, appropriating India's sacred swastika and reversing its direction as the symbol for the Nazi party.

Whether hoping to push people's buttons or for reasons known only to himself, John tried but failed to include images of Jesus, Hitler, and Gandhi among the cast of characters appearing on the cover of *Sgt. Pepper's*. A cutout of Gandhi had originally stood stage left, between the figures of Lewis Carroll and the platinum-blonde British bombshell Diana Dors, but the Mahatma was soon removed out of fear of insulting millions of Hindus.

Outtakes from Michael Cooper's famous photo session reveal a cutout of Hitler originally standing in the front row beside the famed vaudeville songster Izzy Bonn, whose waving hand above McCartney's head was interpreted by obsessive Beatlemaniacs worldwide as one of the many signs that Paul was dead. Set designer Sir Peter Blake later addressed the potential controversy: "After what John said about Jesus, we decided not to go ahead with him, but we did make up the image of Hitler. If you look at photographs of the outtakes, you can see the Hitler image in the studio. With the crowd behind [the Beatles] there was an element of chance about who you can and cannot see, and we weren't quite sure who would be covered in the final shot. Hitler was in fact covered up behind the band."

It seems the dichotomy between Hitler and Christ was never far from John's mind. As Lennon said in the ongoing series of interviews that he gave with Yoko during the Montreal Bed-In in May 1969: "Everybody's an artist. Everybody's a poet. . . . Who told you you weren't? Because some square-head said it when you were eleven and now you can't draw. . . . You are infinite. You have all the possibilities of being Hitler or Christ, whichever way you want to go."

6. Jesus

Although he claimed to the BBC that he was "one of Christ's biggest fans," Lennon would continue to court controversy when he recorded "The Ballad of John and Yoko" in April 1969. While the music (cut in a flash of inspiration by John and Paul one afternoon while George and Ringo were out of town) evoked the Beatles' sound circa 1965, the startling lyrics "Christ, you know it ain't easy, you know how hard it can be, the way things are going, they're gonna crucify me," managed to still shake up both fans and detractors alike.

Anticipating another backlash for his latest transgression, John sent Tony Bramwell a memo: "No pre-publicity on 'The Ballad of John & Yoko,' especially the Christ bit. So, don't play it 'round too much or you'll frighten people. Get it pressed first." John was well aware that his "blasphemous" exclamation of "Christ!" might cause the song to be banned from the radio altogether or at the very least bleeped!

But the repercussions from Lennon's outrageous antics would one day catch up with him in ways no one could imagine. While not initially stated as a motive for slaying John Lennon, his assassin (who shall remain nameless in these pages to deny him any more of the attention he so desperately craved), who self-identified as a born-again Christian, claimed to have been deeply offended by John's sacrilegious statements and verse.

7. Kennedy

The Beatles' meteoric rise to fame in America directly followed the collapse of Kennedy's idealized White House, affectionately nicknamed "Camelot." In some ways the Fab Four's enormous success was abetted by it. Originally scheduled to appear on the *Ed Sullivan Show* at the end of November 1963, Brian Epstein wisely postponed the band's debut until February 9, 1964, in hopes that the American public would be ready for the Beatles' unbridled enthusiasm. In the wake of JFK's shocking assassination on November 22, 1963, a fog of pain, confusion, and disillusionment hung over the country.

8. Buddha, 9. Mantra, 10. Gita, and 11. Yoga

The next four balloons that John unceremoniously popped were the foundations of Eastern mysticism: Buddha, Mantra, Gita, and Yoga, which all began to blossom in the West during the mid-'60s, thanks in part to the Beatles' fascination with Indian culture and spirituality. Only four years earlier, John had fashioned passages from *The Tibetan Book of the Dead* along with bits of LSD guru Timothy Leary's cosmic spiel into the lyrics of the hypnotic "Tomorrow Never Knows," the final track of the Beatles' 1966 masterpiece *Revolver*. Inspired by Leary's slogan "Turn on, tune in, and drop out," John coaxed millions of fans to "surrender to the void" and seek the perfect Buddha nature within themselves. "Turn off your mind," he commanded with his vocal drenched in reverb, resembling the disembodied voice of the Dalai Lama beckoning from distant snowcapped Himalayan peaks.

Both George Harrison and Lennon appreciated the power of mantra, having chanted the Hare Krishna Maha Mantra together, while John dispelled anxiety and fear by singing in Sanskrit: "Jai Guru Deva om . . . [in praise of Maharishi's spiritual teacher Guru Dev] Nothing's gonna change my world" in his gorgeously ethereal song "Across the Universe." John's use of mantra would eventually morph into popular slogans, which he and Yoko repeatedly chanted in "Give Peace a Chance" and "Power to the People," in hopes of getting their political message across. As John explained, "Power to the People" [was] "something loud and clear to break through all the unfeeling and repression that had been coming down on [the] kids."

Following the Beatles' breakup, both Lennon and Harrison employed vocal techniques outside the norms of pop singing, while quite different in their method and outcome, to induce new levels of consciousness. While George's chanting "Hare Krishna" evoked a feeling of bliss and unity with God within the spiritual novice, John's employment of Janov's primal scream technique would help free him from the lingering bondage of his traumatic past.

At the same time, Lennon mocked whatever new spiritual trend was in vogue, taking aim at people who (like himself) were anxious to expand their consciousness. The old paradigm of going to church, eating meat and potatoes, drinking a pint down at the local pub, and watching "the telly" started to give way to alternative diets, along with seeking inner peace through meditation.

In repudiating the Hindu holy book—the Bhagavad Gita—John was clearly taking a swipe at George Harrison. Yoga was next on the list. Lennon confessed to journalist Maureen Cleave that he had a strong aversion to any form of exercise, beyond whatever physical benefits might be gleaned from having sex. Yoga demands discipline, and John, a notorious layabout, couldn't be bothered twisting himself into a human pretzel, despite whatever physical or spiritual benefits he might derive from doing a "downward dog."

12. Kings

Abandoned by Freddie at a young age, Lennon constantly sought new father figures throughout his life. He temporarily found them in a series of older and what he expected to be wiser men—from Brian Epstein, to the Maharishi Mahesh Yogi, to Allen

Klein (who was more of a protector or hired bully) and finally Dr. Arthur Janov. But John inevitably found them all flawed and disappointing.

Having renounced any belief in Jesus, "the King of Kings," Lennon then condemned the monarchy. Whether his negation of "kings" referred to the myth of King Arthur and his Royal Court or Shakespeare's tragic *King Lear*, Richard the Lion-Hearted, or any variety of Henrys, it was most likely the response of a young man raised under the looming specter of England's crown, whether in history or literature, which persistently hung over his "working class" head.

In contrast to McCartney's affable praising of "Her Majesty" as a "pretty nice girl," John's swipe at "kings" may have stretched beyond British royalty to include the Kings of Rock 'n' Roll, who first led Lennon down the primrose path to fame and fortune. John would not merely join them at the royal table but would ultimately dethrone many of them as well.

While Lennon initially found Bill Haley (more a plaid-jacketed, spit-curled duke than a king) disappointing in *Rock Around the Clock*, the impact of Elvis and the deviant crew that followed, particularly Chuck Berry and Little Richard, not only thrilled John but also gave vision and purpose to a deeply troubled teenager's life.

Fronting the newly formed Plastic Ono Band, John would top the bill at the Toronto Rock 'n' Roll Revival, where, donning a white suit (whether inspired by Hank Williams, Elvis Presley, or Dylan's recent return to performing at the Isle of Wight), he shared the stage with a veritable who's who of rock 'n' roll "kings," including Jerry Lee Lewis, Bo Diddley, Gene Vincent, and Little Richard.

13. Elvis

At 11 p.m. on the night of August 17, 1965, the Beatles' limo pulled into the driveway of Elvis Presley's Bel Air, California, home, to find "The King" lounging in his plush living room, bathing in the glow of a large color TV screen. Their managers, Colonel Tom Parker and Brian Epstein, found a quiet corner to talk business while the Fab Four sat on a sofa, stupefied, gawking at their hero in awed silence, until an aggravated Presley finally stood up and announced he was going to bed. But rather than abandon his guests, Elvis graciously remedied the awkward situation by passing guitars around to John and George, while Paul sat down at the piano. Elvis plunked an electric bass while Ringo found something to pound on. No one dared take the lead, so they opted to play along to some old rock 'n' roll records for a while, until Lennon, always quick to blurt out whatever came to his mind, began pressing Elvis over why he abandoned rock 'n' roll. When Presley complained that his acting career ate up all his time, John wisely dropped the subject rather than criticize the batch of shabby films the King had starred in. The Beatles hung around for a few more hours until finally bidding their stoned and lonely idol goodnight. Upon saying farewell, Elvis gave the boys some souvenirs on their way out, including hand-tooled leather pistol holsters, while half-heartedly inviting them to come visit him at Graceland the next time they were in Memphis (although everyone knew he was only being polite). As they piled into the limo to head back to their hotel, John quipped, "Where's Elvis?"

Although Presley harbored deep resentment and jealousy of those long-haired louts who came across the sea and dethroned him, he would take Lennon's nagging question to heart, squeezing into a snug black leather suit just long enough to play his legendary comeback special on December 3, 1968.

Just over two years later, shortly before Christmas, 1970, Elvis suddenly arrived unannounced at the White House, hoping to receive an official badge from the Bureau of Narcotics and Dangerous Drugs. As "a concerned citizen," he tried to convince Richard Nixon that the nation's drug problems and the blight of ill-mannered, draft-dodging hippies was, in fact, due to the evil influence that the Beatles exerted· over American youth.

The irony of Presley—who would soon become a mumbling, stumbling pharmaceutical Frankenstein—planting the seed in the foul swamp of Nixon's paranoid mind about the benefits of deporting John Lennon is both profoundly hilarious and pathetic.

14. Zimmerman

Following Elvis, John disavowed Dylan, tagging him "Zimmerman," as it was "his real name," he told *Rolling Stone*.

"It's not what Dylan sings," John once said, "it's the way he sings it." The omnipresent '60s journalist/scenester Al Aronowitz had been dying to introduce the two songwriter/cultural heroes, but an anxious Lennon continually delayed the meeting, claiming he wanted to wait until he wrote something that would level the playing field and make him Bob's "ego equal."

Aronowitz, who finally made the much-anticipated introductions at New York's Delmonico Hotel in August 1964, described the awkward atmosphere as "Billy the Kid and the Jesse James gang acting like little girls." When the Fab Four offered Bob a glass of scotch and a handful of pep pills, Dylan demurred and responded by rolling a couple of "jazz cigarettes," turning "the James Gang" onto the pleasures of pot for the first time. In return, Dylan's ragamuffin troubadour image got a serious make-over. (According to Al Kooper, George Harrison had told Bob "when the Beatles first arrived in America, it wasn't just about the music, it was to show you guys you didn't have to dress like that anymore.") Overnight Bob began sporting Beatle boots and trendy Carnaby Street togs, before plugging in a Fender Stratocaster and turning the atrophying folk world upside down at the 1965 Newport Folk Festival.

The following spring, they met again in London at the Mayfair Hotel following Dylan's concert at Royal Albert Hall. Marianne Faithfull described everyone as "fan-tastically nervous," claiming the Beatles sat on the edge of their chairs, rapt, "waiting for the oracle to speak," while Dylan treated them "like strangers at a railway station." When Lennon complimented Bob's performance, Dylan carped about the squareness of the crowd who "didn't dig [his new song] 'That's Alright Ma.'" John assured the great bard it was because he was "ahead of [his] time." Dylan scoffed, already wary of the fleeting nature of fame: "I'm only about twenty minutes, as it is."

Trading barbs and caustic one-liners was modus operandi for this mismatched pair of insecure superstars who had more in common than either realized. Both Lennon and Dylan managed to create some of the most original music of their decade, despite the numbing conformity of their respective Northern industrial hometowns. Documentary filmmaker D. A. Pennebaker unflinchingly captured the strained dy-namic between the pair in a scene from his 1972 film *Eat the Document*, as Lennon and Dylan were chauffeured through the streets of London on a May afternoon in the back seat of Mick Jagger's borrowed Rolls Royce. Stoned and chain-smoking, they babbled on and on, attempting to spontaneously compose a witty script for the camera.

Whether drunk or drugged, a forlorn Dylan wound up clasping his miserable head in his hands, apparently nauseous, on the verge of vomiting as John continued to nonsensically jabber on: "Do you suffer from sore eyes, groovy forehead, or curly hair? Take Zimdawn!" Bob groaned as John chortled, "Come, come, boy, it's only a film. Pull yourself together."

Lennon later admitted to *Rolling Stone* that he'd been "nervous as shit" and that they both had been on "fucking junk," with "all these freaks around us." Despite whatever mixed feelings John harbored about Bob, a cutout of Dylan (circa *Highway 61 Revisited*) was included in the cover photograph of *Sgt. Pepper*'s graduating class of 1967.

Although most likely a coincidence, Yoko Ono's 1969 slow-motion, forty-two-minute film of Lennon's erection, titled *Self Portrait*, was followed a year later by Dylan's disastrous double album also entitled *Self Portrait*. While Ono quipped that "the critics wouldn't touch" her tribute to John's manhood, Greil Marcus was so incensed by Dylan's careless collection of country covers, live tapes, and various throwaways that he began his odious review in *Rolling Stone* by begging "What is this shit?"

By the end of the '60s, both Dylan and Lennon/Ono had reached such an extreme point of fame and self-absorption that their unchecked egos convinced them they could do and get away with anything. But both *Self Portraits* would represent the nadir of their collective careers.

In 2012 Bob Dylan released his 35th studio album, *The Tempest*, which featured "Roll on, John," an epic eight-verse ballad that juggled enigmatic imagery with various details of Lennon's life and fragments of Beatles lyrics and William Blake's poetry (with Bob singing lines from "A Day in the Life" and "The Tyger") to create a beautiful portrait of his fallen friend.

15. Beatles

Last on Lennon's list, not surprisingly, was the lingering specter of his old band. As John had told his mates, he wanted "a divorce." "I no longer believe in myth," Lennon explained. "And Beatles is another myth. . . . We were four guys. . . . I met Paul, said, 'Do ya wanna join me band?' And then George joined. And then Ringo joined. We were just a band that made it very, very big, that's all."

"I don't believe in Beatles," John cried, nearly regurgitating the words as he pounded the piano, slamming shut a chapter of his life. Interestingly, Lennon failed to mention the woman he loved and himself as a couple on the song's earlier takes, when he sang "I just believe in me" rather than "Yoko and me, and that's reality."

"You know the Beatles are something else quite apart from me," George would explain in gentler terms. "I'm not really 'Beatle George,' I'm sorry to disappoint you, but that is just a little part that got played through in this life. . . . There is much more to me than 'Beatle George.'"

Author Bruce Spizer pointed out that while John's "God" "declared 'the dream is over,' with 'Imagine' it was reborn." The *Imagine* album cover photograph portrayed Lennon once more as "the dream weaver," with his head literally in the clouds.

"Lennon created the monster and then destroyed it on his first album," Marvin Etzioni said. "'I don't believe in Beatles,'" he sang, while the rest of the world still did. No other artist has ever turned their back and attempted to cut the cord of success in such a brutal fashion. By the time *Imagine* came along, it was time to prop up the Beatle record-making machine again and add strings and bring in George Harrison to round things out. It was another spectacular solo effort, but what happened on *Plastic Ono Band*—the self-realization and starkness—never happened again for Lennon.

Intrepid Interpretations: "God"

Brian May's live performance of "God" manages to never mention god. Dropping the stunning opening line on which Lennon built the song—"God is a concept by which we measure our pain" —May begins instead with "The dream is over, what can I say," referring to the demise of his legendary band, Queen. Shaping the song to make it fit his personal history, Brian sings: "We were the fab ones, but now it is gone. I was the gentle one, but now I must be strong."

Lennon had claimed he originally conceived of leaving the song "unfinished" so everyone could add their own list of personal denials, which is exactly what Brian did. May simplified Lennon's concept. Rather than tagging Elvis or Kennedy, he simply sang, "I don't believe in heroes. I don't believe in fame. I don't believe the newsprint . . ." And then he goes on to include "history" and "race" until, like Lennon before him, he arrives at disavowing his own past, claiming he no longer believes "in being in Queen anymore. I just believe in me. . . . Just you guys and me, and that's reality." Where John's song ends, as his voice gently trails off, May finishes his tribute to Lennon by encouraging the cheering crowd to "Dream on!"

Recorded live at the Trans Club in Szczecin on April 21, 1996, the Polish prog-rock group Collage offered an elaborate version of "God," featuring a David Gilmour/Pink Floyd/*Wish You Were Here*-era scorching guitar solo over pounding war-horse drums and the haunted whoosh of a goth-style synthesizer. Guitarist Mirosław Gil employed a Coke can as a slide on the song's coda, shredding up a sonic tornado, as lead singer Robert Amirian added "Krishna" to the long list of Lennon's denouncements.

On December 8, 2010, in Charlottesville, Virginia, Jeff Tweedy performed "God" live at a concert commemorating the thirtieth anniversary of John's passing. Backed by members of his band Wilco and the Autumn Defense, Tweedy's version brings a lovely, weeping pedal steel to the mix.

The Brief and Incomplete History of God in Popular Song

Beyond Irving Berlin's patriotic World War I anthem "God Bless America" (written in 1918 and popularized by the microphone-melting voice of Kate Smith), "God" was generally considered a taboo topic in popular music.

Offended by the lofty attitudes of Berlin's song, Woody Guthrie responded by writing "This Land is Your Land." As Joe Klein, Woody's biographer, wrote: "'God Bless America' . . . told people not to worry, that God was in the driver's seat. Some sort of response obviously was called for."

Originally recorded in 1944, Guthrie's signature tune wasn't released until twelve years later in 1956, following the Senate's censure of Joe McCarthy's anti-Communist campaign. Woody rightfully feared retribution for singing his working-class anthems, knowing he would be publicly branded as a Communist, along with hundreds of writers, musicians, actors, and artists, for questioning the fairness of wealth distribution in America's democracy.

Frank Loesser's jingoistic World War II anthem "Praise the Lord and Pass the Ammunition" was said to have been inspired by the words uttered by a heroic chaplain named Howell Forgy, who'd been aboard the USS New Orleans on the morning of December 7, 1941. While in the midst of praying, the holy man allegedly put his Bible down and manned a gun turret, firing back at the incoming bombers attacking Pearl Harbor, as he shouted the famous words to what became the chorus of Loesser's gung-ho hit.

The true story eventually came out that Forgy had been making the rounds of the men fighting the Japanese and patting them on the back while repeating the clever phrase "Praise the Lord and pass the ammunition" to help boost the troop's morale. Years later, the next generation of Vietnam war protestors regarded such xenophobic sentiments as demeaning, portraying the Japanese (who were now our friends) as godless and barbaric.

Then in 1964 came Bob Dylan, crowing "With God on Our Side," challenging everyone (particularly the older generation) who came within earshot of his raspy voice and penetrating harmonica to take a good look at their beliefs and the lives they led.

While Dylan claimed sole authorship of his controversial ballad, the melody to "With God on Our Side" was boldly borrowed from "The Patriot Game" by singer/songwriter/novelist/playwright Dominic Behan, who based his song on an old traditional Irish folk tune called "The Merry Month of May." The practice of grabbing a good melody and making it one's own with a new set of lyrics was known as "the folk process," a common habit among folk singers up through the early '60s, when a sudden emphasis on originality became a major selling point for record companies. Behan didn't take Dylan's plagiarism lightly and publicly brandished the young upstart as a thief. Bob ignored Behan's accusation, explaining he'd previously heard the tune by way of a Scottish folksinger named Nigel Denver, and its lilting melody "must have somewhere stayed in the back of my mind."

While most people have little interest in the origin of the music they listen to, listeners were immediately struck by the power of Bob's stark history lesson of devastation that war has wrought throughout the centuries. If ever there was a song powerful enough to end war, "With God on Our Side" remains a likely candidate.

Even the nonoffensive, fun-loving Beach Boys managed to cause some controversy in 1965 when Brian Wilson broached the unthinkable by addressing the almighty with the lilting "God Only Knows." But after Wilson humbly explained that their gorgeously orchestrated opus *Pet Sounds* (on which the song appeared) had been conceived as "a teenage symphony to God," most, if not all, accusations of blasphemy were immediately dismissed. All dissent apparently melted away once the offended got an earful of the Beach Boys sublimely singing like a clutch of choir boys. While Brian Wilson's fans wrote off his eccentric behavior as that of "a crazy genius," whatever trouble John Lennon managed to stir up never slid easily off his back. Instead, it clung to him like hot glue. Regardless of Brian Epstein's constant efforts to polish off John's many jagged edges, Lennon habitually opened his mouth to spontaneously spout his most unabashed ideas. In 1966 he'd inadvertently whipped up a tempest after predicting Christianity's imminent demise to reporter Maureen Cleave. John's irrefutable proof was his own band's enormous popularity, which he pointed out was currently beyond that of the Son of God's. "Christianity will go," Lennon declared. "It will vanish and shrink. I needn't argue about that; I'm right and I'll be proved right. We're more popular than Jesus now. I don't know which will go first—rock 'n' roll or Christianity. Jesus was all right, but his disciples were thick and ordinary. It's them twisting it that ruins it for me."

While causing minor controversy in England, in America it unleashed an ugly backlash after his comment appeared on the cover of the teen magazine *Datebook*, thanks to journalist/A&R director (and no fan of the Beatles) Danny Fields.

Overnight, "Beatle burnings" spread across the South, instigated by a pair of infuriated DJs named Tommy Charles and Doug Layton from WAQY in Birmingham, Alabama, who incited their listeners to rid themselves of their "Beatle trash" by joining their fellow insulted Christians down at their local church parking lot and incinerating whatever tainted souvenirs they'd collected. While John Lennon had a great gift for bringing people together, on this occasion (August 14, 1966), he'd inadvertently united an angry, riotous mob. Radio stations across the South and Midwest, as well as in Spain and South Africa, immediately banned the Beatles' music. Although the Catholic Church made no official statement at the time, years later in November 2008 (on the fortieth anniversary of the release of the Beatles' *White Album*), the Vatican, whether inexplicably nostalgic or hoping to attract more followers by appearing "liberal," suddenly felt compelled to forgive John his "trespasses." A public statement published in their daily newspaper, *L'Osservatore Romano*, declared: "The remark by John Lennon, which triggered deep indignation mainly in the United States, after many years sounds only like a 'boast' by a young working-class Englishman faced with unexpected success after growing up with the legend of Elvis and rock 'n' roll."

Determined to set things straight as quickly as possible, Brian Epstein arranged for a press conference in Chicago. Bolstered by his bandmates, Lennon made a judicious effort to placate the offended: "It was wrong," he apologized. Not because he meant it, but because he had to. God, as Lennon reasoned, was not just "an old man in the sky" but "something in all of us."

Released in September 1970, Andrew Lloyd Weber and Tim Rice's rock opera *Jesus Christ Superstar* was immediately banned by the BBC as sacrilegious. The play's producers couldn't have bought that kind of publicity.

Rice and Weber had allegedly invited John to appear in the leading role as Christ in their controversial production. Lennon agreed only upon one condition: that the role of Mary Magdalene would go to Yoko. Not surprisingly, Weber and Rice declined.

Following Lennon's denouncement of "God," Ian Anderson boldly questioned the motives of the Supreme Being (along with his Son and the "bloody Church of England") on Jethro Tull's masterpiece album *Aqualung*. Over the years, Anderson has repeatedly claimed that *Aqualung* "was never [meant to be] a concept album [but rather] just a bunch of songs." Yet the record's second side opens with "My God," as Anderson begs his fellow human beings to take a good, hard look at the foibles of Christianity.

"He is the God of nothing, if that's all that you can see," Tull's Faganesque front man snarled. "So, lean upon Him gently, and don't call on Him to save you." Yet on the following song, "Hymn 43," we find the album's protagonist doing just that . . . desperately asking Jesus to "smile down upon" him from heaven, despite having soiled his soul with earthly concerns from "money games" to "women and his gun." (Hadn't he heard Jim Morrison shriek, "You cannot petition the Lord with prayer!" on the opening evocation to the Doors' 1969's album *Soft Parade*?)

For "Wind Up," the album's finale, Anderson pleads for redemption once more as he boldly demands an answer from God, to which the heavenly Father firmly replies (one of the album's most memorable lines): "I'm not the kind you wind up on Sundays." Having heard it directly from the Lord's lips, the agitated truth seeker then storms back to his "old headmaster" to inform him, "you had the whole damn thing all wrong!" despite certain excommunication for such heresy and insolence.

While critics pronounced *Aqualung* everything from "boring and pretentious" to "extremely profound," Anderson's opus to the "poor old [homeless] sod" remains one of rock's classic "themed" (but not concept!) albums.

While Billy Preston's "That's the Way God Planned It," was one of the highlights of George Harrison's *Concert for Bangladesh* on August 1, 1971, the original version of the song, released on Preston's 1969 album of the same name, was an absolute powerhouse.

In order to sign Billy to Apple, Harrison would purchase Preston's contract from Capitol Records and book him into the studio with an all-star crew to cut a single of his gospel rocker, "That's the Way God Planned It."

The supergroup backing Billy included members of the Beatles, Rolling Stones, and Cream. Billy played soulful gospel organ licks as Harrison and Clapton's guitars intertwined, all supported by a killer rhythm section comprised of Keith Richards pumping a syncopated bass line over Ginger Baker's muscular drums. Preston's yearning vocals were reinforced by the dynamic duo of Madeline Bell and Doris ("That's All It Took") Troy.

"Billy Preston's approach was almost always from a Black gospel viewpoint musically," said 1960s' most valuable session man, Al Kooper. "It always sounded like Black church on Sunday in Harlem or Watts."

"Billy Preston . . . what a lovely man," Bobby Whitlock recalled. "I first met him when he came to play with us [Delaney and Bonnie and Friends]. We were crossing the English Channel on a boat to Amsterdam or Sweden . . . I can't remember all these years later. . . . It was night and we had all these people and equipment. And we just sat out on the deck and talked. It was the coolest thing. We both came from a gospel and R&B background. . . . I was the first white guy signed to Stax records [the classic Memphis-based R&B label]," Bobby said proudly. "Billy had just come from playing with the Beatles up on the rooftop in London. George brought him in. He gave them a much-needed touch of reality, adding that soulful thing."

"Billy was the man, in any given situation," Whitlock explained. "He was the man to call. What he did on John's album was . . . perfect! No one else could have done that. You can't learn that kind of playing from a book. If you ain't got it, you can't play it. And Billy Preston laid it on the line!"

Whether it was destiny, convenience, or Lennon's skewed sense of humor that led him to invite Preston to "church up" "God" with a smattering of gospel piano flourishes, we'll never know. Either way, it seems a bit perverse to feature Preston (whose career was built on playing gospel music) on a song in which John renounced all faith in the Lord that Preston so wholeheartedly worshipped.

In 1971, Marc Bolan of T. Rex would employ a similar musical motif to Lennon's "God" as he implored the Almighty "high in [his heavenly] fields" to "come and be real for us" in "Girl," from his glam-rock opus *Electric Warrior*.

The blunt satire of Randy Newman's "God's Song (That's Why I Love Mankind)" from his 1972 album *Sail Away* was delivered over a mournful, minor-keyed piano tune reminiscent of the New Orleans classic "St. James Infirmary Blues." Newman's grim sarcasm borders on mean-spirited as he reveals the folly of humanity's trust in the supreme being's good intentions, impassively singing:

"Man means nothing, he means less to me
Than the lowliest cactus flower
Or the humblest Yucca tree"

When Randy performed "God's Song" live, he'd often lead the tune off with a caustic quip: "I consider it a great honor to be God's spokesman. I'll try to sit up straighter when I sing his part." But the bleakness of Newman's vision of God as ambivalent to and amused by human suffering far exceeds any offense his wicked humor may have inflicted.

Five years later, Johnny Rotten raised a few hackles when the Sex Pistols released "God Save the Queen" on May 27, 1977. Although sung with a holy fervor, the United Kingdom's unofficial national anthem by the same name (yes, it is still sung in the Commonwealth—including Canada, Australia, and New Zealand) contained a few dark sentiments within its hallowed lyrics, which sounded like their citizenry were enthusiastically casting a hex upon their many "latent foes":

"Oh Lord our God arise,
Scatter our enemies,
And make them fall
Confound their politics
Frustrate their knavish tricks,
On Thee our hopes we fix
Oh save us all"

Although the composer is unknown, England's jubilant praise song was first adopted in September 1745, during the reign of the purportedly temperamental and scandalous George II (1727–1760).

While Johnny Rotten's vindictive valentine to the monarch bore the same title, the Sex Pistols' "God Save the Queen" was an altogether different affair. As homelessness and hopelessness began to reach endemic proportions during what London punks dubbed the "Summer of Hate," "the fascist regime" (as Rotten spat) willfully turned a blind eye to overwhelming societal problems and spent a fortune on parades and parties to celebrate the Queen's Silver Jubilee.

On June 7, 1977, the Sex Pistols, with the help of Virgin Records and their Machiavellian manager Malcolm McLaren, conspired to hire a boat to

cruise down the River Thames as the band repeatedly bashed out their irrev-
erent anthem while passing Westminster Abbey and Parliament. They never
made it that far. Pulled over and docked by a flock of bobbies, the band,
McLaren, and mother of punk fashion Vivienne Westwood were all arrested
for disturbing the peace. To add to the chaos, "God Save the Queen" was
allegedly blocked from the No. 1 spot on the UK Singles Chart by the British
Phonographic Institute, which kept Rod Stewart's ironically titled "I Don't
Want to Talk About It" in the top position, despite McLaren's claim that the
Pistols were currently outselling "Rod the Mod" at the rate of 2 to 1.

In 1986, Andy Partridge had been inspired to compose XTC's controversial single "Dear God" by "a rather tacky book of children's letters to God" of
the same title. The tune's lyrics challenged the basic notion of the supreme
power's existence with the taunting question, "Did you make mankind after
we made you?"

The suits at Virgin Records, who, just a few years earlier helped fuel the
storm over the Sex Pistols' scurrilous slag of God, queen, and country, were
now suddenly troubled by Andy's atheistic tirade. "I just tried to wrestle with
the paradox of god and the last dying doubts of belief that had hung, bat-like,
in the dark corners of my head since childhood," Partridge explained.

Fanning the flames of controversy, the record's producer, Todd Rundgren,
employed an innocent eight-year-old lass named Jasmine Veillette to sing the
taboo tune's opening verse and closing line, "I can't believe in you, dear God."

In constant conflict with Rundgren throughout the making of XTC's brilliant 1986 song cycle *Skylarking*, Partridge considered the finished track
flawed and had no qualms about cutting it from the album's playlist. Rather
than being included on the album, "Dear God" wound up as the B-side to
Colin Moulding's sunny summer anthem "Grass." Then oddly, college radio
stations in the States began to regularly spin "Dear God." Orders poured in at
Geffen Records (the band's American label) for a tune that wasn't on the LP
and of which they were only vaguely aware. Geffen wasted no time, immediately squeezing "Dear God" onto the next pressing of *Skylarking*.

Todd Rundgren considered the axing of "Dear God" to be "a mistake"
and allegedly branded Partridge as "a pussy" for fearing a backlash from his
agnostic verse and allowing businessmen to bury it. But it turned out Andy's
concern was well founded after a bomb threat was called into a Florida radio

station, and in another instance, a student held a member of his school faculty hostage at knife point until the tune was played over the PA.

"Mail started to arrive," Partridge recollected. "And it was 50 percent 'This is fantastic, you've voiced what I've been thinking for years' and 50 percent 'You're going to roast in hell.' It really pissed off some people, but I'm glad it did."

The controversy over "Dear God" had been great for sales. By the time it was finally released as an A-side (the following June 1987), the fracas was over and the song stalled at No. 99 on the charts. In the end, Partridge considered "Dear God" "a petulant failure," unworthy of all the fuss that people made over it.

With her curly golden hair and nose ring, Joan Osborne, like a smart-aleck angel, coyly begged the intriguing question "What if God was one of us? Just a slob like one of us? Just a stranger on a bus, trying to make his way home?" The grungy guitar anthem written by the Hooters' Eric Bazillian topped the charts in March 1995, making her album *Relish* one of the year's best sellers. The song maintains a sweet reverence as Osborne coos, "Yeah, God is great, God is good," while casually tossing out the prospect that God is probably just another no-account slacker riding public transportation through the desolate American night.

Over a crush groove and funky poppin' bass line, Me'shell Ndegeocello's "GOD.FEAR.MONEY." from her 2002 album *Cookie: The Anthropological Mixtape* delivers the sad truth of the derailed American experiment, plain and simple:

> "If Jesus was alive today
> He'd be incarcerated
> With the rest of the brothers"

As the song fades, it is punctuated by two harrowing pistol shots. Other tracks on the album include spoken-word samples by activists Dick Gregory, Angela Davis, and Gil Scott-Heron.

Recorded live at the Roxy in November 2001, Me'Shell and her band, the Conscientious Objectors, delivered "GOD.FEAR.MONEY." with the kind of style and commitment that John and Yoko would have loved—soulful, sensual, and serious as your life.

16

MY MUMMY'S DEAD

John considered *Plastic Ono Band* a masterwork and often referred to it as his
"*Sergeant Lennon.*" While most people didn't immediately recognize *Plastic Ono Band*
as a "concept album"—a term usually reserved for such musical milestones as Sinatra's
In the Wee Small Hours, Sergeant Pepper, Tommy, Dark Side of the Moon, and *Ziggy
Stardust and the Spiders from Mars*—Lennon's "Primal Scream album" wove a number of recurring themes through its forty-minute song cycle. Beginning and ending
with a pair of morbid tunes about his mother, Julia, the album was a psychoanalyst's
picnic.

"We all want our mummies," Lennon told Peter McCabe and Robert Schonfeld
in an interview on September 5, 1971, at the St. Regis Hotel in New York, where
he and Yoko had just moved a few days earlier on August 31. "I don't think there's
any of us that don't. [Paul] lost his mother, so did I. . . . I don't think any of us got
enough of them."

John's half-sister, Julia (Dykins) Baird, claimed their mother's sudden death
"completely, completely rocked" John "as anybody would be," after their "mother
had gone out and never come back." It was just hopeless," she said, recalling how they
both "cried and cried and cried."

"I lost my mother twice," John Lennon lamented. "Once as a child of five [when
she abandoned him] and again at seventeen. It made me very, very bitter inside. I had
just begun to establish a relationship with her when she was killed."

"The loss of a mother, or any close family member, impacts one's soul no matter
who you are. This was an artist in pain, growing up in public," Marvin Etzioni pointed out. "I was growing up too and realized life was not going to be an easy road. It
was clear that the most successful songwriter in the world wasn't the happiest person
in the world; perhaps he was the saddest, if not the angriest. Lennon was looking for
God, love, and wanted mommy and daddy to come home. He was human, expressing it in an art form he knew best, songwriting and record making."

Sung to the gloomy melody of the nursery rhyme "Three Blind Mice," "My
Mummy's Dead" seemed like a dark joke at first. First published by Thomas

Ravenscroft in 1609, "Three Blind Mice" is said to represent the Oxford Martyrs, who in 1555 were put on trial for heresy and burned at the stake during the Catholic/ Protestant conflicts throughout the rule of Queen Mary I. A little over four centuries later, "Three Blind Mice" would be used as the Three Stooges' theme song, while Paul McCartney would quote the macabre children's song in the Beatles' 1968 hit "Lady Madonna," singing "See how they run!"

Unlike Paul's brief "Her Majesty," which closed *Abbey Road*, this was no cute little postscript. However brief and trivial it may seem, "My Mummy's Dead" was the rusty nail in the coffin to *Plastic Ono Band*, the bookend to the album's opening track, "Mother," in which John struggled to lay the lingering trauma of his mother's death to rest, once and for all.

There were two takes of "My Mummy's Dead" originally recorded on a portable cassette player while John was in therapy with Arthur Janov during the summer of 1970. The released track on *Plastic Ono Band* was just a few seconds shorter than the version later included on the 2004 compilation album *Acoustic*, which revealed John had played a simple fingerpicked intro/outro that he ultimately discarded.

The Beatles often revealed their very "Northern" dry sense of humor upon hearing the shocking news of the death of a relative, bandmate, or friend. Distraught over Julia's fatal accident, John sequestered himself in his room at Mendips. While the sudden trauma brought a surge of tears, John's devastating pain was said to inexplicably turn into a fit of mad laughter. John also reportedly laughed when first hearing Stu Sutcliffe had died of a brain tumor and when his friend Tara Browne tragically "blew his mind out in a car" after failing "to notice that the light had changed."

When journalists pressed his former partner for a meaningful word following John's assassination, an ashen-faced Paul McCartney flippantly murmured, "Drag, isn't it?" as if he'd just been informed that some careless motorist had just dented the bumper of his prized Aston Martin. After being questioned about why he hadn't attended his former bandleader Rory Storm's funeral (Storm and his mother would die together in a double suicide, chasing copious amounts of barbiturate with a whisky cocktail), Ringo dryly replied, "I wasn't at his birth either, was I?" But George Harrison supplied the most macabre zinger of them all after he'd been informed of his one-time hero and fellow Wilbury Roy Orbison's passing, when he audaciously quipped to Tom Petty, "Aren't you glad it wasn't you?"

17

LONG LOST JOHN

Whether nostalgic for the old days playing skiffle with the Quarrymen or as a sly commentary about how people perceived him at the time, John Lennon led the band through a rag-tag version of "Long Lost John" during the *Plastic Ono Band* sessions. Not to be confused with the Everly Brothers' "Lost John," who, with the help of plenty of banjo twang and blaring slide trombone and Don and Phil's two-part, close harmonies, "boogied his way to Mexico," Lennon's outtake was a traditional folk song once covered and released as a single by Lonnie Donegan in February 1956. As Donegan explained in the song's intro, the lyric recounted the escapades of an escaped convict known as "Long Gone Lost John" who was on the lam, running for his life. The descending riff over which Donegan sang "Long, long gone," sounded like it inspired Bob Dylan to sing "everybody must get stoned" on his 1966 hit "Rainy Day Women #12 & 35." Lennon lightly strummed an acoustic guitar, while Ringo and Klaus provided a pumping country-rock rhythm, similar to the Beatles' 1965 cover of the "Bakersfield Cowboy" Buck Owens's "Act Naturally."

Whether employing "Long Lost John" as a warm-up number while setting the recording levels or deciding to mine its similar chord changes and rhythmic feel for "Oh Yoko," a cheerful ditty that shed light on John and Yoko's love and life together and appeared on *Imagine* (1971), John dropped the tune after a couple verses, not bothering with it again. Lennon, who claimed to hate folk music, suddenly broke into a herky-jerky Elvis-style vocal, giving the track a rock 'n' roll flare just before it collapsed.

"Hello, Richard?" he called to recording engineer Richard Lush, "I'm defunct."

This rough version of "Long Lost John" later appeared on the 1998 box-set collection *The John Lennon Anthology*. Whatever his intent—whether playing the song to loosen up with the band or with the idea of including it on *Plastic Ono Band*—John (as the Beatles did throughout the *Let It Be* sessions) delved into his vast repertoire, pulling out a few surprising forgotten oldies. During the making of *Imagine*, Lennon would sing Jesse "Lone Cat" Fuller's 1955 classic "San Francisco

Bay Blues," a blue mood interpreted by everyone from the Jim Kweskin Jug Band to Richie Havens to Janis Joplin. Lennon, as we tend to forget, had an ear for American roots music, playing lap steel guitar on George's "For You Blue" (inspiring George to cheer "Go, Johnny, go!") and later slashing a bluesy slide guitar on the home demo of both "I Found Out" and "John Sinclair."

18

OF MADNESS AND GRAPEFRUIT

Although Yoko described her mother, Isoko, as "very beautiful," she claimed she lacked the genuine concern or ability needed to nurture her children. Isoko, in Yoko's estimation, was like "having a film star in the house," who would "show you a film of food" rather than cook for her hungry family. Despite all the trappings that came with being a member of a wealthy family, Yoko claimed she never felt "really fulfilled." Unable to relate to her mother, she was also "scared of the maids," whom she claimed often vented their feelings of personal frustration and anger on her and her siblings. Not only did Yoko's parents expect their daughter to follow strict customary Japanese protocol, but Yoko found her nannies and personal tutors "very tough" as well.

A "sensitive child," Yoko always sensed her father Eisuke's profound disappointment in her. While in therapy sessions with Arthur Janov years later, Yoko exclaimed that "lies are coming out and I'm starting to find out what a phony person I am." Ono claimed to "hate" herself for "always trying to please them" and for feeling weak and being "afraid of losing them." But as she'd instinctively known, her family could never love and understand her and eventually "they'd go anyway."

In 1940, the Onos moved (briefly) from Tokyo to Long Island, where Yoko attended public school. A year later, in the spring of 1941, the family returned to Japan with the world on the verge of war. Eisuke, a financier, was soon sent to work in Hanoi. That December, the bombing of Pearl Harbor changed everything. As a wealthy family, the Onos were not immediately impacted by the war. Meanwhile, Yoko's classmates began taunting her, calling her "an American spy" for having lived in the States. They teased her for dressing like an American girl, wearing her hair in Shirley Temple–style ringlets. Estranged at home and at school, Yoko began feeling like an outsider wherever she went. As the daughter of a Buddhist and a Christian, she also differed from most of her friends, although this cultural mix would later inform her art, which routinely combined elements of Eastern and Western culture.

Turning increasingly inward, Yoko found comfort in solitude, writing poetry, drawing, playing piano, and composing songs. Even as an eight year old, her creativity had become a coping mechanism. "Art allowed me to communicate in a way that didn't require so much courage," she later explained. In her youth, Yoko had a natural tendency to stutter unless focusing clearly what on what she was about to say.

Ono's innate shyness led her to invent "Bagism," a concept that involved climbing into a large sack to hide while peering out through a pair of tiny holes at the chaotic world outside. Initially the idea was to create a safety zone for herself or anyone else in need of sanctuary. Once a person was inside the bag, no one could ascertain their sex, ethnicity, or beauty (or lack thereof).

The original "Bag Piece" was first performed by Yoko and Tony Cox in 1964 at the Sogetsu Art Center in Tokyo, and then again in New York as part of the Perpetual Fluxfest at Cinematheque on June 27, 1965. As another example of her "Social Art," Ono invited spectators to climb into a large, black bag—whether alone or with a partner of their choosing, either someone they knew or a complete stranger. Once inside, they were to remove their clothes and "do a little dance or whatever they will, then get dressed and exit the sack."

On December 18, 1968, John and Yoko put "Bagism" (and the public's patience) to the test at a fundraiser for Arts Lab at London's Royal Albert Hall. Warmly received, Lennon/Ono appeared briefly onstage before climbing inside a large white bag. But their claim of achieving "total communication" with the audience immediately backfired. Even before their performance piece, dubbed the "Alchemical Wedding," began, it was upstaged when a young, blonde woman from Texas named Elizabeth Marsh stood up in the third row and spontaneously stripped as the house band's drummer broke into a frenetic solo. Despite the efforts of the Royal Hall's ushers, Marsh refused to put her dress back on, and soon the police arrived. But the bobbies were met by a human shield formed by the crowd, who, in solidarity with Marsh, also began to disrobe. Eventually the Third Ear Band, a free-form improvisational group (whose members included cellist Paul Buckmaster, later famous for his string arrangements on albums by Elton John, David Bowie, and the Rolling Stones) began to play, helping to calm down the crowd for a moment.

Poet Neil Oram recalled that John and Yoko "got their bag out and got inside it. People were booing." Meanwhile the Third Ear Band began riding white bicycles in circles around Lennon/Ono, who remained inside their bag as Oram improvised on the flute. "They were inside this fucking bag, they then got out to people booing them. . . . John Lennon was really pissed off," Neil claimed. Oram considered their performance "a boring stunt at such a fantastic event." Contrary to his recollection, news reports the following day claimed Lennon/Ono "laid down and stayed there twenty-five minutes, moving occasionally. . . . On emerging, the audience applauded wildly."

As John later remarked, "We didn't know what people were doing outside the bag. We just heard all this thumping and never knew what was going on until we saw a shaky old video of it. It was a beautiful thing, but very nerve wracking. I mean I was scared shitless going into a bag we couldn't see out of. It was worse than singing, going onstage and doing that."

What Lennon didn't initially see during the performance was a demonstrator who'd climbed onto the stage, holding a banner objecting to Britain's involvement in Nigeria while screaming, "Do you care, John Lennon? Do you care?"

In 2002 when the Museum of Modern Art launched a retrospective titled *Yoko Ono One Woman Show, 1960–1971,* her "Bag Piece" performances remained as bold and enigmatic as ever.

* * *

In April 1944, ominous squadrons of American B-29 long-range bombers suddenly darkened the sky above Tokyo, reducing the city to rubble and ash. In the aftermath of the nightmare, food and clean water became scarce. From that point on, Yoko claimed her family was "always hungry." There was a shortage of "everything . . . even toilet paper," she said. The Onos held out for as long as they could, but once Isoko found an unexploded bomb in her garden, she packed up her children with whatever belongings they could carry and fled by train to the little farming village of Karuizawa. East of Tokyo, the small town of Karuizawa, which lay at the foot of snow-peaked Mount Asama, seemed like an idyllic sanctuary. Yoko recalled how her mother often romanticized about moving to the countryside where the "beautiful, honest farmers" lived and worked. But Isoko's fanciful notions were soon shattered after the food shortage triggered an atmosphere of mounting distrust. Rather than welcoming and helping fleeing refugees, the locals despised the intruding wealthy city folk. "Our money couldn't buy food," Yoko explained. Whether or not the family ate, she said, "depended on the farmer's whims." Desperate for a bowl of rice and cabbage, Isoko traded heirloom jewelry for something her children could eat. It wasn't long before, as Yoko recalled, she'd turned into nothing but "skin and bones." With the family servants gone, Isoko was forced to do chores a woman of her social stature never imagined. Yoko and her siblings would spend their days searching for food, taunted by the local children for "smelling like butter." The remark was meant as an insult, as butter, although common in America, implied wealth, as it was never part of a traditional Japanese diet. Beyond the problems they encountered in Karuizawa, the family had also lost all contact with Eisuke, uncertain if he was dead or alive. Eventually they got the news he'd wound up in a POW camp in Hanoi.

Horrific descriptions of the bombing of Hiroshima soon arrived, followed by the unthinkable tragedy of Nagasaki. But without a radio, no one was sure exactly what had happened or if the war was finally over. Returning to Tokyo on the back of a truck, Yoko, now thirteen, with her mother and two siblings, witnessed the brutal and shameful defeat of her country. It was at that point the young girl came to understand two major principles of Buddhism. First and foremost, all life is suffering. And secondly, everything is impermanent. "You don't want to possess anything [because] you might lose it," Yoko explained, claiming she'd temporarily lost interest in anything material or in maintaining relationships, as they were certain to disappear with time. "I just didn't care and was proud that I just didn't care," she said. (This austere attitude would drastically change years later after John retreated from the music business to become a househusband and raise their son Sean, while Ono dedicated herself to business and increasing her family's wealth by making wise investments.)

Following the war, Yoko returned to the safety and privilege of an affluent life. Ono attended Gakushuin, a prestigious school whose student body included Emperor Hirohito's two sons—Akihito (who in 1989 became the 125th Emperor of Japan) and Yoshi (the younger brother, a poet who allegedly had a crush on Yoko).

While Isoko had inadvertently given Yoko hope, encouraging her daughter to "write about [the war] when it's over," Ono would describe her father, Eisuke, as an emotionally stunted man incapable of complimenting his daughter's creativity. He often took out his personal frustration on Yoko after abandoning his own dream of becoming a concert pianist to satisfy his father's dying wish that he pursue a career in finance to properly provide for his family. Eisuke traumatized Yoko, measuring her fingers and bluntly informing her that she should abandon all hope of pursuing a professional musical career as they were too small to properly play the piano. When Yoko explained that her dream was to become a composer, Eisuke stonewalled her again, replying it was impossible for a woman in Japanese society to achieve such a goal, and perhaps she might consider becoming a singer. To her surprise, he offered to pay for vocal lessons. Years later, Yoko expressed her gratitude, pointing out her father was more progressive than most Japanese men.

At nineteen Yoko returned to America once more, moving with her family to the affluent suburb of Scarsdale, New York. She soon enrolled at the prestigious all-women's college Sarah Lawrence. But as an art student, Yoko became frustrated and dropped out during her third year, finding all traditional forms of expression limiting and dissatisfying—from painting, to writing, to poetry and music. "I was like a misfit in every medium," she confessed years later.

Yoko's commitment to art went far beyond neophyte dabbling or fulfilling requirements to receive a degree. Instead, it became an obsessive search for what she called, "an additional act" to keep from "going mad." Feeling like she was literally hanging by a thread, Yoko's salvation came after visualizing herself grasping tightly to a kite string. "The kite," she explained, "was me."

Shy and "very inhibited," Yoko remained a virgin until she was twenty-four, when she eloped with the experimental pianist/composer Toshi Ichiyanagi in 1956. While her husband became well regarded among his peers at Julliard and the New School (where he studied with John Cage), Yoko soldiered on, unrecognized. "I was always writing . . . sending things to the *New Yorker*," who offered nothing but "a polite refusal," she recalled. Frustrated and ignored, Yoko began seeking fulfillment in having affairs with various men, but wound up "always having abortions," because, as she claimed, she was "too neurotic to take precautions." Overwhelmed with guilt, Ono eventually confessed her transgressions to her husband, convincing Toshi, whom she described as "very kind," to save face by leaving her and returning to Japan, as she had been such a dreadful wife.

Back in Tokyo, Ichiyanagi helped organize John Cage's first tour of Japan in 1961, in which Yoko would sing Cage's "Aria" and lay across the strings of the piano while he played a piece titled "Water Walk."

Returning to New York, she rented a dingy cold-water loft at 112 Chambers Street (for $50.50 a month), where she organized what became the first downtown loft concerts in December 1960. While providing a platform that gave "far-out people a chance," Yoko now had her own space, where she could develop and perform her latest works at pass-the-hat parties attended by downtown artists like LaMonte Young and Henry Flynt, as well as art-world luminaries from John Cage and Max Ernst to Peggy Guggenheim. Years later Flynt, the composer/electric violinist credited with having coined the term "concept art," recalled the scene as "informal" with "no standards," yet at the same time "viciously competitive." At his first performance at Yoko's loft in February 1961, Flynt, determined to apply the radical concepts of free jazz saxophonist Ornette Coleman to piano, found his fellow artists "so square, [he] couldn't make anything plausible happen." Hoping not "to be discourteous to Yoko," Henry climbed atop the piano bench (rather than the piano itself) and played a mix of bird calls, squeals, and screeches by biting the mouthpiece of a clarinet. His performance abruptly concluded after he employed a pair of toothpicks and a rubber band as musical instruments. Flynt claimed he was appalled by "the ordeal of the avant-garde," which he sadly deemed no more than "a competition to be the most preposterous, most senseless, [and] the most incomprehensible."

"If you wanted to do head games, there was no reason for them to be in a concert of music," he said (a sentiment similar to those leveled at Lennon/Ono by scores of critics for their radical collaborations in 1969, whether in Cambridge or Toronto). Flynt reportedly returned to Ono's loft the following day to perform "a more conventional concert," proving his credibility to any scoffers by employing traditional music charts. Disillusioned with the avant-garde, Flynt spent the next decade developing a new genre he dubbed "New American Ethnic Music," which bravely blended everything from hillbilly to garage rock to minimalism and Indian ragas.

Living and working in such a tense atmosphere only helped exacerbate Yoko's feelings of instability. While grappling with reoccurring thoughts of suicide, Ono began writing the series of instructions/poems that would become her first book, *Grapefruit*, which she considered "a collection of paintings in printed form." Ono found writing very therapeutic—"a cure for myself without knowing it," she told journalist Charles McCarry.

Not surprisingly, she couldn't find anyone interested in handling the book. Eventually Yoko self-published it in an edition of five hundred copies under the imprint of Wunternaum Press. During the summer of 1964, among the hubbub and spectacle of the Olympics, she tried selling her cardboard-bound book of mysterious instructions to visitors crowding the streets of Tokyo.

Grapefruit would later reach a wider audience after it was published in America by Simon and Schuster in 1971. The poems, or "pieces" as Yoko termed them, were a series of evocative commands and metaphorical recipes that, like Zen, have a powerful way of making readers think outside the box of their minds. "Line Piece" playfully instructed readers to "Draw a line with yourself. Go on drawing until you disappear." Although an impossible surrealist act, this radical concept was nothing new. There have been plenty of artists over the years, such as the eccentric New York painter/jeweler Axel (a.k.a. the "Bloody Genius"), who, whether deliberately confronting societal taboos or hoping to attract attention to themselves, have produced intensely personal artwork by using their own blood without facing lethal consequences.

Enigmatic and provocative, Yoko invited her readers to "Burn [*Grapefruit*] after you read it." "This is the greatest book I've ever burned," John later exclaimed in the jacket notes for the small, square-shaped yellow book. They were both well aware of the controversy over burning books, from ancient China through the Third Reich. Lennon himself had recently experienced an ugly backlash in the American South when gangs of irate fans swarmed down to local church parking lots to ignite their "Beatle trash" in bonfires after his "Bigger than Jesus" comment in March 1966.

As with so many of Ono's concepts, her motivation was to spur the viewer/reader/listener to reconsider their understanding and acceptance of the world around them. "Her book *Grapefruit* speaks for itself," John wrote to radio show host Joe Franklin. "It is now in its fourth edition—paperback. Yoko calls them instructions to help you through life rather than poetry."

Lennon dubbed *Grapefruit* "beautiful and profound," believing its inscrutable Zen-like kōans "could help [people] to live." In John's not-so-humble (if somewhat naïve) opinion, his wife was "one of the world's most important artists."

Presented by the eccentric impresario Norman Seaman, Yoko's concert at Carnegie Recital Hall on Friday, November 24, 1961, showcased her original "pieces"—"A Grapefruit in the World of Park," "A Piece for Strawberries and Violin," and "AOS—dedicated to David Tudor." Ono hand-lettered the life-size poster herself in big, bold India ink on a quilt of newspapers, stuck together with cellophane tape.

* * *

Following the concert, Ono returned to Japan, where much to her surprise she suddenly found herself in demand—albeit briefly. Yoko showed her art and gave poetry readings until an American reporter wrote a scathing review claiming she'd stolen the bulk of her ideas from John Cage. According to Ono the charge was absurd, as Cage, she claimed, disliked her work, considering it "too sexy or erotic." "The whole trend [in vogue at the time] in New York was for homosexual cool art," she explained.

It seemed the disgruntled journalist had confused Toshi with Yoko when it came to the impact of Cage's influence. According to Mark Swed's May 2015 article in the *Los Angeles Times*: "Throughout the '60s [Ichiyanagi had] adapted Cage's ideas to his own voluminous interests, [which] reached a kind of climax with his kitchen-sink *Tadanori Yokoo* opera."

Meanwhile Ono claimed she "went through hell," as no one in the Japanese press came to her defense over the fraudulent accusations. To compound her problems, her mother felt that publicly defending herself would be distasteful and humiliating, and she must maintain her dignity by remaining silent and stoic. Feeling "unloved," Yoko attempted suicide and was immediately committed to a mental hospital, where she was sedated and put under observation.

Toshi visited his ex-wife while she was convalescing. He brought with him an aspiring American artist named Tony Cox, who'd seen some of Yoko's pieces in an avant-garde art anthology and had flown to Japan in hopes of meeting her. Initially Ono refused to see Cox, claiming she was in no condition to receive visitors, but Toshi insisted and Yoko eventually acquiesced.

As she'd previously begged friends and family years before when desperately grasping at the kite string of her life, "Please accept me, I am mad," she confided to Cox. Finding Ono in an asylum seemed to spark a romantic if not heroic urge in Tony. "I helped get her out of the hospital," Cox told *People* magazine in 1986. Yoko and Tony were soon married, in November 1962. Their daughter (and only child) Kyoko was born the following August. "Yoko felt very strongly that if she had kids, the husband should help take care of them. I agreed to it before the marriage," Cox explained. But Yoko, he revealed, quickly "got sick and tired" of being "too close to somebody."

"I just had a baby and didn't want it," Ono confessed to *Esquire* in 1970. Yoko felt as if she'd been coerced into giving birth by both her ex-husband and the man she'd recently married. Believing her nervous breakdown had been triggered by her numerous abortions, Toshi warned Yoko, "It's lousing you up," while Cox vehemently opposed terminating the pregnancy. Yoko initially felt that having Kyoko was "a mistake." "I love my child, but I never loved her when I had her," the brutally honest Ono admitted. Leaving Cox, Yoko returned to New York, where her husband, with Kyoko in tow, quickly tracked her down. Feeling trapped again, she soon fled to London.

Fiercely independent, Ono would remain married to her art before another human being—that is, until she met John Lennon. Lennon/Ono's relationship was constantly in flux, while Tony Cox was, at best, welcome to tag along for the ride as an occasional collaborator. But Yoko mostly viewed his role in the scheme of her life as a necessary househusband.

After the organizers of a Belgian film festival refused to show Ono's new *Film No. 4* on December 26, 1967, Yoko, Tony, and the French poet/political activist Jean-Jacques Lebel protested by publicly dancing in the nude. They were immediately arrested and fled the country after being released on bail. Their trial called for a mandatory sentence of three months behind bars if they ever dared set foot in Belgium again.

After Ono returned to London, saxophonist Evan Parker recalled:

a chance meeting with Yoko at Olympic Studios where the Spontaneous Music Ensemble was recording their album *Karyobin* in February 1968. She heard some playbacks of what we were doing and talked to John Stevens and myself about working together. We had a further meeting/rehearsal, which included [guitarist] Derek Bailey at their apartment on Baker Street, and then did one performance as a quartet at the Arts Laboratory on Drury Lane. The date would have been probably in early March. I think this was recorded, but in the process of their acrimonious separation, Tony Cox took the tapes.

Around this time Yoko would meet and perform with the iconoclastic free jazz saxophonist Ornette Coleman at Royal Albert Hall (see chapter on AOS).

While Tony was off in France with Kyoko, Yoko Ono moved in with John Lennon. Years later she confessed to becoming "a nervous wreck" who "despised herself" but not for the reasons one might assume—like being wrought with guilt over leaving her husband and child or being branded as a "homewrecker" in the press for stealing John away from Cynthia and Julian. Instead her gloomy emotional state was triggered by the unexpected success her work currently enjoyed in London. "My name became bigger," Yoko explained. "But it was a high price to pay."

Only 250 copies of *Grapefruit* remained in print at the time, but not due to a sudden flurry of interest and sales. It seems that an unhinged "friend" entrusted to store Yoko's books had finally read the book and faithfully followed the author's instructions in its provocative introduction, setting the entire batch ablaze.

While such whimsical concepts as "the sound of people perspiring" struck most folks as utter nonsense, Yoko's boundless imagination spoke directly to John, first aggravating him and eventually seducing him. Bewitched by this strange, diminutive Japanese artist, Lennon wrestled with her baffling messages. "Why is this woman telling me to do such mad things?" he mused. Judging from her writing and artwork, John's initial impression of Yoko was of a "fantastic, pushy, aggressive, woman's liberation type." But Lennon soon concluded that that was only a mask, an attitude she projected, while at her core she "was a coward." Although Yoko often described herself as "very shy," John soon realized he'd underestimated her remarkable tenacity.

Lennon claimed he originally planned to record Yoko as a solo artist for Apple and had no intention of collaborating with her, let alone "falling in love and getting married." "The only way to show her was to show her pure . . . nude," John explained. "It was going to be her—not me. All her gallery shows were always white, and it was just going to be her, just in this whiteness."

Designed by British painter and collage artist Richard Hamilton, the stark white cover for *The Beatles* double album (released November 22, 1968) bore the unmistakable influence and aesthetic of Lennon's Japanese concept-artist girlfriend. Both visually and musically, the *White Album* was a deliberate departure from the psychedelic excess of the Beatles' *Sgt. Pepper's Lonely Hearts Club Band* and their more recent *Magical Mystery Tour*.

Overnight a new minimalism had come into vogue. John and Yoko began dressing in matching monochromatic outfits (all white or black, depending on their mood). At the same time, Lennon stripped his music down to its core, exposing his tormented emotional state in songs like "I'm So Tired" and "Happiness Is a Warm Gun," while revealing a remarkable tenderness with "Julia."

The tape John and Yoko assembled upstairs in Lennon's Weybridge home studio during their first night together would soon become an album in need of a cover. "It's a very strange feeling seeing yourself naked. There's a little chill," John confessed, regarding the couple's nude selfie.

At Apple, Lennon/Ono were taken aback after they were met with "the most ridiculous Catholic onslaught. . . . They really gave us hell," Lennon said of his bandmates. "They were saying, 'Why . . . why?'"

"Yoko used to tell me about the in-laws she married," Lennon quipped, comparing Paul and George's judgmental attitudes to those of unbearable family members. But for the "Two Virgins," appearing naked together on their album cover was no big deal. "We forgot the shame," Yoko remarked. "We didn't do it for pornography," Lennon insisted, although he offered no further explanation or "meaning" behind what many considered an outrageous publicity stunt.

***

"Yes is the answer," John Lennon later sang in his autobiographical anthem "Mind Games," evoking the couple's momentous meeting at the Indica Gallery in November 1966, when he climbed atop a white-painted ladder to peer through a looking glass at the tiny letters of encouragement Yoko printed on the ceiling. Throughout her career, Ono complained, she had been constantly perceived as "a very rich girl who was just playing avant-garde." There is little doubt that the help her wealthy family provided (despite the shame they felt her eccentric behavior brought them), as well as the benefit of a Beatle's patronage, allowed her to operate outside the mainstream, in the lofty realm of conceptual art. Yet Ono's work continues to endure, well beyond the fleeting impact of many of her contemporaries like Chris Burden, whose master's thesis for the University of California, Irvine, was based on enduring life crammed into a locker for five days. In 1971, Burden staged the happening "Shoot," in which he allowed himself to be shot in the arm with a .22 rifle before a gallery of stunned and repulsed onlookers. Three years later, on April 23, 1974, still pushing people's buttons in the name of performance art, Burden had himself crucified on the hood of a Volkswagen Beetle. Unlike the Savior, Burden did not expire, but the whole affair, as George Harrison coined the word in *A Hard Day's Night*, was "grotty"—short for "grotesque."

Although she relished the media's attention, Ono's events rarely matched such levels of unbridled narcissism. Yoko regularly invited the audience's participation in completing her "unfinished" works, such as "Cut Piece" (first performed at the Yamaichi Concert Hall in Kyoto, Japan, in 1964 and subsequently at Carnegie Hall in 1965), where members of the crowd were encouraged to approach the stage, one at a time, with a pair of scissors and snip off a piece of Ono's long-sleeved black dress as she knelt, staring silently into space. While seemingly absurd, the ritual soon exposed her vulnerable, naked body laying beneath the thin armor of apparel. "Cut Piece" made a powerful statement on issues of gender and identity. The participants were also encouraged to take scraps of Ono's clothing with them, which some kept, whether as a souvenir or talisman.

Yoko continued to blur all boundaries between the audience and the artist when viewers of her "Smoke Painting" were requested to light a match to smudge and streak a blank white canvas, leaving behind a residue of carbon. In "Painting to Be Stepped On," Ono employed the Dadaist concepts of Marcel Duchamp. The revolutionary French provocateur challenged the "preciousness" of art hanging on gallery and museum walls when he created what he called "Readymades" by substituting everyday objects such as urinals and wine bottle racks in place of treasured paintings and sculptures. The notion of "stepping" on a canvas and wiping one's feet to create a work of art boldly defied the very notion of the piece having any value.

People generally take conceptual art too seriously, often missing the inherent humor of the work. In one of Ono's instructional poems titled "Chess Piece" (a.k.a. "Play It by Trust"), two people are requested to play a game of chess, except all the pieces on both sides are white. A seemingly simple, if whimsical, idea, "Chess Piece" cleverly removes all strategy and motivation to win the game, while befuddling and hopefully amusing everyone involved. Ultimately the piece proposes the question of "how to proceed when the opponent is indistinguishable from oneself?"

One of Yoko's greatest intellectual pranks took place in December 1971, after a series of ads in New York's alternative paper, *The Village Voice,* announced the opening of a solo exhibition titled "Yoko Ono—One Woman Show—Museum of Modern [F]art." The culturally curious soon flocked to the famed 57th Street galleries between December 1 and 15 to experience Ono's inscrutable art and perhaps partake in a celebrity sighting. But upon their arrival at MoMA, Yoko's work was nowhere to be seen. Instead, the management had posted Yoko's mischievous advertisement in the box office window along with a notice tersely stating, "THIS IS *NOT* HERE" (which coincidentally happened to be the title of her one-woman show at the Everson Museum a few weeks earlier in Syracuse, New York).

Ono's lark, played at the public's expense, was her way of taking on the powers that be who refused to exhibit her art. And besides, shouldn't people have suspected something funny about an ad promoting an exhibit at the "Museum of Modern [F]art?"

Very few grasped that Yoko's art *was* the announcement itself, and even fewer got the joke when polltakers (hired by Ono) approached them to ask their opinion of Yoko's show.

No matter how ambiguous or whimsical the concept, Lennon/Ono earnestly begged public participation in completing many of their works. Their first two albums, *Two Virgins, Life with the Lions* (which bore the subtitle "Unfinished Music") and *Wedding Album,* invited listeners to complete the recordings in whatever ways their imagination deemed fit, from simply singing along or playing an instrument to employing mechanical sounds made by household appliances or even power tools. "We made a point that it's an 'Unfinished Music' and you can put something of yourself over a track," Yoko explained. Lennon/Ono hoped that if listeners took part in some way, these albums might become a more personal experience for them.

19

YOKO ONO PLASTIC ONO BAND

I had to go over the top because they were playing electric guitars
and they were very ruthless about it.

—Yoko Ono

Released simultaneously with John's album on December 11, 1970, *Yoko Ono Plastic Ono Band* (Apple SW3373) was produced by Lennon/Ono. While the album reached No. 82 on the charts, some complained that they'd bought it by accident, as both records bore the same name and similar album art. Both cover images had been shot by Dan Richter, just moments apart, while the record's back sleeves featured vintage black-and-white photos (respectively) of John and Yoko as children (which became a popular motif ten years later when many '80s bands began using childhood snapshots on their album covers).

"John wanted to do that so that people would be confused and maybe buy my record as well," Yoko told WNYC's David Garland with a laugh. "It was a trick," Sean Lennon concurred. "It sort of didn't help [Yoko's] album. Ultimately, I find that people think there's only one *Plastic Ono Band* record . . . [and] that it's dad's."

Ono's album would also feature the same rhythm section of Klaus and Ringo with John on guitar. While the musicians were identical, Yoko's *Plastic Ono Band* was a very different kind of album than her husband's. Both records functioned as vehicles for the artist's emotional release, although in contrasting ways. While John strongly relied on his well-crafted but minimal lyrics to convey his anger and disappointment, Yoko's approach was more spontaneous and "pure," employing a vocabulary of visceral shrieks, wails, and grunts.

"While John Lennon's album was an articulation of his primal scream therapy with Arthur Janov, Yoko Ono's was the scream itself," John Diliberto wrote in *(((echoes)))*. "We were both involved in [Janov's primal scream therapy]. John more heavily," Yoko explained. "I was just going along with it, but it was a very important experience for us. It was so funny because somebody sent us the book called *Primal*

Scream and John said, 'Somebody's doing you.' Because I was screaming before that, right?"

As Bill McAllister observed for *The Record Mirror*: "If you like melody and what we recognize as logical form, [Yoko's album] is much harder to take. Most people will write it off as just weird [and] not worth listening to. But it has its value. Yoko takes music beyond its extremes into the realms of non-music you might say."

Struggling to describe Ono's enigmatic approach, McAllister concluded that she creates "human electronic music" that "breaks through more barriers with one scream than most musicians do in a lifetime."

In his column in *The Spectator*, Duncan Fallowell deemed Yoko's *Plastic Ono Band* "a whole new territory of sound. . . . Unless her voice has been fed through electronic modulators, she has quite remarkable tonsils. But I doubt whether this album will receive the attention it deserves. Such is the antipathy to Yoko Ono that she can do no right."

"It wasn't until later that I heard Yoko's *Plastic Ono Band*, even though my brother Alex and I were certainly interested in and sympathetic to Yoko and her work," Nels Cline explained. "We only had so much allowance money, all of which we spent on records, so Yoko had to wait. Yoko was certainly ubiquitous then. *Grapefruit* was everywhere we bought alternative newspapers and books, and we had admired her song on the B-side of 'Instant Karma,' 'Don't Worry Kyoko (Mummy's Only Looking For A Hand In The Snow)'—especially Alex, who was always more avant-garde than I."

While John's *Plastic Ono Band* was recorded over the period of a month, Yoko "was left with . . . one afternoon," Sean pointed out. "'Why' and the whole record . . . was recorded and mixed that day."

As Ono explained: "We were up against everything at the time. In the sense that nobody really wanted to record my songs . . . there was a kind of intermission where everybody was just kind of relaxing a bit. So, I just went to the mike and started doing it and he was very happy about that. That's why you hear John say [to the engineer at the end of 'Why'], 'Did you get that?'"

"In those days when I would start to sing all the engineers would just go to the bathroom and nothing was recorded," Yoko laughed. "So [John] was really concerned that this was recorded.

"This was [her] first true album," Sean pointed out. "It kind of hits you over the head."

20

WHY

There's a scream inside every one of us at every moment.
And every one of us has had the experience of listening
to a record and feeling that scream take over.
Release. Abandon. Let it all out . . .

—Paul Williams

The opening track to Yoko's *Plastic Ono Band*, "Why" is just over five and a half minutes of skull-searing punk rock, recorded six years before anyone had a clue what punk was. Spurred on by John's grungiest guitar work since "Cold Turkey," Yoko's terrifying screeches and screams conjure the haunted, disembodied spirits unleashed by the bombing of Tokyo. Ono ceaselessly repeats the nagging question "Why?" like a child throwing a fit, unable to be placated no matter what answer the adult struggles to provide. Eventually "Why" transforms into a terrifying mantra that embodies the cruelty and absurdity of human existence.

Journalist/author Duncan Fallowell considered "Why" to be "the most ferocious and frantic piece of rock [he'd] heard in a long time."

"John Lennon was always able to make his guitar talk," said guitarist Gary Lucas, formerly of Captain Beefheart's Magic Band. "He was one of the most visceral, from-the-gut rock guitarists of all time. But never more so than on 'Why,' where his guitar spits lovely, processed shards of metal to inspire Yoko Ono's uninhibited caterwauling. This is some of the most radical rock guitar soloing of the era, rivaling Lou Reed's 'I Heard Her Call My Name,' Syd Barrett's 'Interstellar Overdrive,' and [King Crimson's] Robert Fripp on 'Cat Food' for sheer sonic bravado."

"[John] was very proud of that," Ono pointed out. "He said, 'Nobody recognized my guitar playing!' Of course, he was brilliant, totally avant-garde . . . very unique and original."

"It's obvious he wouldn't have played that way if he hadn't met [Yoko]," Sean added. "It was a pretty radical move. If you look at the careers of other artists who were comparatively successful to those guys, for him to make those records with [Yoko] . . . after the Beatles had finished . . . it's a pretty shocking move."

"More than the Stooges' '1969,' 'Why' invented punk rock," Peter Case proclaimed. "I still play that record in my pad, loud, on a regular basis. It's so focused and unhinged. The band rocks so completely! 'Why' just says everything about 'why' I love rock 'n' roll . . . the first thirty seconds, with John's shouts and sliding guitar chaos, and Yoko's sometimes cutting, sometimes sustaining screams . . . there's horror and humor in it too."

Following in the wake of the Beatles' lush melodies and harmonies, Yoko Ono's music might have seemed more extreme and disturbing to someone who'd discovered it on its own. While "Mrs. Lennon" benefited from the publicity of having "bagged a Beatle," the slings and arrows of the Fab Four's furious fans, in need of a scapegoat for their recent acrimonious breakup, were more than most mortals could endure. As Robert Palmer pointed out in his liner notes to *Onobox* (a six-CD compilation box set of Yoko's music released by Rykodisc in 1992): "It is quite likely that having John Lennon fall in love with her was the worst possible thing that could have happened to Yoko Ono's career as an artist."

One must wonder what the experience of hearing Yoko's music for the first time might have been like without the looming presence of her famous husband. It is almost impossible to judge the originality and intensity of this sonic onslaught fairly without the story of their love affair swaying it. Despite John's complete obsession with Yoko and deep appreciation of her art, as well as her powerful, raw vocals, she remains, to a vast majority of the public, a kook and an interloper who cast a dark spell over the Beatles' leader.

New York–based singer/songwriter Larkin Grimm believed that:

[Yoko's] legacy as an artist was harmed by her association with John Lennon more than it was helped. Partnering with John undermined her unique ideas and pushed her in front of an audience that wasn't ready to meet her. She was ahead of her time [by] maybe twenty years . . . and that always hurts. The love of John Lennon made her the most loathed woman in the universe, because she was so powerful and so brilliant that our biggest rock star sacrificed the pop glamour of the Beatles' lifestyle in order to love her and learn from her. The world could not accept a woman with that much power. Who would she have been without all that hatred and grief marking her life? I certainly prefer her solo records to the ones she recorded with

John Lennon, but it is nice to see that the world has changed enough to reissue these first records that Yoko and John made together. When life gets me down, I think of Yoko and find strength in her bravery. She is a feminist icon. Her work is always getting me to see the limitations of my own sight, forcing me to look from different angles or think in spaces I had never considered exploring before.

"I couldn't stand the suffering that came from seeing the way people were treating Yoko," John told author Robert Hilburn. "People say Yoko split the Beatles. In truth it was the Beatles that split John and Yoko. . . . She was more buried by the Beatles in a way. It just took a long time because part of us is very tough. But all the shit from those days finally accumulated until what burst was the two of us." Lennon and Ono parted in the summer of 1973, which led to John's relationship with their young Chinese assistant, May Pang, as well as binge drinking with pals Harry Nilsson, Ringo, and Keith Moon during his notoriously wild "Lost Weekend" in L.A. After returning to New York in June 1975, Lennon abandoned Pang and moved back in with Yoko at the Dakota, after coming to realize that "Without her, I'd probably be dead." For Yoko, their love was a "karmic relationship. . . . To John, I'm his reality and he's my reality," she later explained.

"Yoko was a powerful influence," Peter Case said.

But John didn't know how to hold his own in that relationship as time went on. He didn't know how to be himself in a family unless he dominated them, like in the Beatles. He didn't have any examples in his background of an equal relationship, and he couldn't do that with her. But from the *White Album* into "Cold Turkey" and the *Plastic Ono Band* records, when they were still in the first flush of love . . . they could walk through walls. In time John lost his ability to navigate the world; he was lost. I think he felt he had to disown his rock 'n' roll, especially after the so-called "Lost Weekend," or year, or whatever it was. . . . His freedom became destructive, and he couldn't bear it.

"When I was growing up in West Virginia, all you ever heard was that she was this evil dragon witch lady who broke up the Beatles," explained Ann Magnuson, actor and singer with the '90s outrageous indie band Bongwater. The word *ugly* was used a lot too. The more hated she became, the more I thought, 'Hmm, this woman must be on to something.'"

Magnuson didn't really hear Yoko's music until moving to New York and falling into the downtown punk scene. "It wasn't exactly easy listening, but it stopped everyone in their tracks," she said. Ann recalled seeing Ono on the cover of the *Soho Weekly News* just days before Lennon was shot, and the subhead was a quote of hers that said something along the lines of "Those hate vibes can be as strong as love vibes."

"I was inspired by that; that she used the horrific and usually male antagonism towards her to not only soldier on but to fortify her. People joked that her voice could shatter glass, but it was her spirit that shattered many an artistic glass ceiling."

"A lot of those people were idiots who gave her grief through all the years," Steve Shelley concurred. "Either you open your mind or not. *Grapefruit* is still relevant today and her tweets are really good! As a Beatles fan I've always had my differences with her, but as a philosopher, she's always opening minds."

"The hate vibes, they're like love vibes, they are very strong. It kept me going. . . . Hate was feeding me," Yoko told *Soho News* in December 1980.

"The minute I got together with John many hate letters came in from Japan," Ono recalled. "In Japan they put all the Yoko albums in a garbage can. By then I learned my lesson, that you can't even trust Japs!" she said incredulously.

The songs (for lack of a better term) on Yoko's *Plastic Ono Band* tended to be more focused and possessed a clearer concept and sense of composition than the randomness and inherent egoism that informed much of the couple's earlier experimental work.

With 1969's third installment, *Wedding Album*, it seemed like John and Yoko were purposely testing the frayed patience of even their most devoted fans. There is an inherent awkwardness when artists of different disciplines (John in pop music and Yoko primarily a visually based concept artist with a strong poetic streak) suddenly and eagerly embrace new forms of expression. While Ono had received musical training as a child in both traditional Japanese and Western music, she was an unseasoned if fearless performer, while Lennon's improvisational skills were arguably sharper when cracking witty comments at press conferences than expressing himself with spontaneous bursts of free-form guitar. Having raised the pop song to the level of art, literature, and cinema, John initially sounded lost in the uncharted realms of avant-garde improvisation.

While something of a savant in the studio, Lennon's bag of sonic tricks was initially limited to old Chuck Berry riffs and whatever shrieking feedback he managed to wrangle from his guitar when accompanying his wife's hair-raising performances. Years later, Yoko admitted she hadn't been too impressed with John's contribution to their first collaboration, *Unfinished Music No. 1: Two Virgins*. Ono complained that Lennon was "not being abstract enough. . . . It was more like vaudeville I thought." But John would soon find his confidence in the music, weaving jagged shards of raw sound in and around Ono's abrasive caterwaul.

With the release of *Live Peace in Toronto*, Yoko, as Lester Bangs wrote in *Rolling Stone*, "began to show some signs that she was learning to control and direct her vocal spasms, and John finally evidenced a nascent understanding of the Velvet Underground–type feedback discipline that would best underscore her histrionics."

Bangs deemed *Live Peace* "listenable, even exciting." All these years later, Yoko's *Plastic Ono Band* stands as the most successful avant-garde collaboration she made with John, if not in her entire career. "This one will grow on you," Bangs assured his readers. "This is the first J&Y album that doesn't insult the intelligence; in fact, in its dark confounding way, it's nearly as beautiful as John's album."

When Lennon/Ono turned their worlds upside down for each other overnight, divorcing their spouses (with whom they'd both grown increasingly dissatisfied) and suddenly abandoning their children (as they both had been in their youth) it was not just out of blind impulse. It went deeper than that, revealing a continuation of a pattern that ran in both of their families. Madly in love, Yoko's mother (Isoko Yasuda) and father (Eisuke Ono) followed their passion rather than their family's desires, and married not for wealth or social position but for love. Eisuke had been an aspiring classical pianist who specialized in playing works by Bach, Beethoven, and Brahms, until his father, on his deathbed, earnestly begged him to abandon such lofty ambitions and follow his footsteps into the world of finance.

Well respected in Japan, the Yasuda family was enormously rich. Attended to by a crew of kimono-clad nannies, tutors, and chauffeurs, their privileged daughter would never want for anything—until the advent of World War II. There was also the matter of religion: While Eisuke's family had adopted Christianity, Isoko was Buddhist. Ironically, it was his banking career, not the dubious lifestyle of an itinerant musician, that led Eisuke away from home to California for the first two and a half years of Yoko's infancy, a crucial time in any child's development. Upon her father's return, Yoko began to fear the presence of this strict-tempered stranger and later evoked visions of Eisuke with "a huge desk in front of him."

With war looming and anti-Nipponese attitudes steadily on the rise in America, the Onos returned again to their homeland before winding up in an internment camp. Yoko, now four, attended Jiyu Gakuen in Tokyo, an elite private school where she studied piano and wrote her first compositions inspired by bird songs and various sounds of the city. By the following year, Yoko's class-conscious mother transferred her to the elitist Gakushūin academy (originally established to educate the children of Japan's aristocracy), where she composed her first haiku (the traditional seventeen-syllable poem) and created illustrations to accompany her original songs.

Yoko described her mother as "a good painter" but found her competitive and "intimidating." Having spent many of her formative years in America (she and Isoko and her brother Keisuke returned once more, taking a train across the country from California to New York in 1940), Yoko was far more independent than traditionally subservient Japanese females. Different from her classmates, she spoke English, openly questioned elders, and formed her own opinions.

Being different forced Yoko into a "terribly lonely" childhood, eating most of her meals in silence with the hired help. In response to his parents' negligence, John crowed, "They didn't want me, so they made me a star" in his song "I Found Out." But he might just as well have been addressing Yoko's feelings of childhood abandonment.

Following John's murder on the night of December 8, 1980, a shocked and bewildered crowd spontaneously gathered outside of the Dakota. A bereaved woman held a one-word sign reading "Why." Suddenly, Yoko's 1970 recording seemed like a harrowing harbinger of the future.

While there have been many songs over the years that help soothe our weary souls in the face of the world's hatred, violence, and madness, "Why" is plainly not one of them. Yet none is more capable of capturing the sheer chaos and tragedy of such moments. This piece of sonic mayhem symbolizes man's inhumanity to man, as Yoko repeatedly asks, demands, and shrieks "Why? Why? Why?" over John's scorching guitar.

The sonic conversation between Yoko and John on "Why" is one of their most successful collaborations. Years later Yoko explained their creative process to author Paul Zollo: "We'd talk about it. Like I would say, 'I'm going to go like this, you go like this.' I don't mean 'go like this' in terms of notes, but just the mood of it. . . . On 'Cambridge' [Lennon and Ono's first public musical performance], he wanted to know how to do it, so I kind of explained it to him before we went to Cambridge. With 'Why,' I was talking about the kind of dialogue we could do in terms of my voice and his guitar. But it's not like telling him what note to play."

"'Why' is so wild," Bill Frisell enthused. "They are so hooked up—in tune with each other . . . on the same wavelength. They're not messing around!"

"As for John's slide freak-outs on 'Why,' the incendiary opening track from Yoko's *Plastic Ono Band*, it is the perfect expressive and sonic foil to Yoko's blood-curdling shrieks," Nels Cline stressed.

> As two people deeply in love and beginning a long and tumultuous journey of discovery together, it does not surprise me that John Lennon was able to be so free on guitar, so perfectly intense, such a perfect sonic companion to his beloved's wailing voice. He may even have heard [avant-jazz guitarist] Sonny Sharrock by this time, who knows? Even as a thirteen-year-old I found a lot of psycho-expressive power in a bottleneck slide played way above the fingerboard on an electric guitar. It just seems natural. . . . John Lennon's guitar stabs into the track, grabs one by the throat, and all the while serves the song by making it instantly memorable.

"They were definitely into the New York free-jazz scene," Elliott Sharp imparted. "It wouldn't surprise me if John and Yoko hung out at Slug's." A little hole-in-the-wall on New York's Lower East Side, Slugs was home to radical improvisational music from the mid-'60s until closing in 1972, after trumpeter Lee Morgan was shot over a domestic dispute and bled to death on a snowy February night, waiting for an ambulance to arrive.

"John and Yoko were supposedly listening to a lot of Sonny and Linda Sharrock," Sharp said. "The influence is obvious on [the Sharrock's collaborative albums, 1969's] *Black Woman* and *Monkey Pockie Boo* [1970], where Linda was going full-force."

Sonny Sharrock's distorted, Coltrane-inspired guitar riffs enhanced albums and live shows by Herbie Mann, Pharoah Sanders, Miles Davis, and, later in his career, producer/bassist Bill Laswell. In 1966 Sharrock married the avant/gospel singer Linda Chambers. Together they recorded and performed some of the era's most hauntingly innovative music (without the fame or financial security that Lennon and Ono enjoyed).

* * *

"Eleven years after the twin release of *Plastic Ono Band*, John Lennon added his slashing, emotional fretwork to Yoko's [1981 single] 'Walking On Thin Ice.' And then he was gone," Nels Cline said. "Strangely, about forty years later, after meeting my now-wife Yuka C. Honda and her friend Sean Lennon, I ended up playing songs such as 'Why' and 'Walking on Thin Ice' with YOKO ONO PLASTIC ONO BAND [Yoko, as Nels pointed out, prefers that the band's name appear in all-capital letters without punctuation] when it was under the musical direction of Sean and Yuka."

To his amazement, Cline has performed with Yoko on numerous occasions over the last ten years, in New York, London, and Japan: "I must admit I knew more than a little about how to manifest catharsis on an electric guitar and had no inhibitions about sounding 'raw' or 'undisciplined.' Guitarists like John Lennon had already pointed the way!"

Yet when asked to play on "Why," Cline was initially hesitant: "Could I really get to *that place?*" he asked rhetorically. "But as has happened so many times in my musical life, I agreed to do it, so I did it . . . I went for it. With much respect to the powerful, direct, and emotional guitarist John Lennon, I went for it."

Like Ono, Cline threw himself into the music with everything he had. Yoko employed her voice in a way similar to Jimi Hendrix's use of the guitar on "The Star-Spangled Banner." Perhaps if Yoko had played saxophone like free-jazz improvisors Albert Ayler and Archie Shepp or piano like Cecil Taylor, musicians who are still celebrated for their contribution to the avant-garde, she might have received the respect due her adventurous music.

"There's some people who believe that music is like a fashion show," Yoko explained in a 1992 interview with *(((echoes)))* magazine. "You look thin and beautiful and no blemish on your face. Some people believe that it's actually sort of showing your guts, bringing your guts out. I'm one of those people who believe that you should really expose your heart, expose your emotion. So, in that sense sometimes my sound is not pretty."

"Whenever people ask me about Yoko, they usually seem open-minded, but haven't listened to the music and are wondering if it's just 'noise.' I always put on 'Why.' That's the touchstone song for Yoko, to let people hear the aggressiveness, the wildness, but it's also catchy as hell. It totally inspired Sonic Youth," Steve Shelley said enthusiastically.

I did a trio with Yoko and [Steve's bandmate, guitarist] Thurston [Moore] at Café Oto in London, 2014. That was a blast. We did versions of "Why" and "Greenfield Morning." It was all very loose. At the soundcheck she did a little vocalizing and screaming. The energy coming out of this small person was incredible. She's so tiny and strong! For a lot of the set I played quietly with mallets and softly on the cymbals. I remember Yoko turned around and looked at me with the biggest smile on her face. She was duetting with the cymbals. Later on, someone told me she really likes it when the drummer doesn't wail the whole time.

The 2017 reissue of *Yoko Ono/Plastic Ono Band* included an 8:41-minute extended version of "Why" that begins with John tuning up and a couple of random thwacks from Ringo's drums. Lennon's maniacal slide guitar is utterly sinister as shards of spiky notes stab at your ears, while Yoko's nerve-rattling yodeling is simply frightening, short-circuiting our nervous systems. Ringo and Klaus guard the beat, laying down a solid, driving gangster groove as Lennon shreds on guitar. This is truly radical music, but no matter how demanding it gets to listen to, no matter how challenging, the experience is worthwhile, not just as an historical document but for the pure, unrestrained energy, as edgy as any punk rock that followed.

As Ween bassist Dave Dreiwitz observed, "Klaus Voormann's bass playing on 'Why' was some serious punk-rock trailblazing. I guess he had some good bass training from his friends in the Beatles."

John's grinding guitar evokes Creedence Clearwater Revival's "Born on the Bayou." He slashes the strings as the band falls in and Yoko enters, shrieking like a giant, radioactive insect from a 1950s horror movie. A give and take between John's howling guitar and Yoko's screaming ensues, creating one of the most radical listening experiences in the history of rock. The overall effect is otherworldly.

"Listening to a piece like 'Why' as her voice flutters and howls and splits into multi-phonics, you can hear the stunning control Yoko had over her voice," Diliberto wrote in *(((echoes)))*. "The state she obtained was more like a trance, where the body becomes a pathway for something beyond. 'When I do an improvisation, I free myself totally and just allow sounds to come out of me,' she said. 'So those are the sounds that came out of me.'"

Albert Ayler

In his liner notes to the 1992 six-CD collection *Onobox, New York Times* music critic Robert Palmer pointed out that Yoko's music was not mere "willful provocation . . . [but] part of a musical revolution already sweeping both classical music and jazz" that bridged elements of modern music pioneer Karlheinz Stockhausen's fragmented compositions with the yearning cries of spiritual free-jazz saxophonist Albert Alyer.

Born in 1936, Ayler, who died mysteriously in November 1970, just days before the dual release of *Plastic Ono Band*, was perhaps the only artist to inspire both the Beatles and Yoko Ono (before she met John Lennon). In the documentary *Magical Mystery Tour Revisited*, aired on the PBS program *Great Performances*, Paul McCartney recalled being in Paris in the mid-'60s, filming various street scenes with a Super 8 camera. Experimenting with the new technology, Paul double-exposed the film, creating a surreal scene in which ghost cars appeared to drive through a gendarme as he directed traffic. The soundtrack Paul employed for his short film was Albert Ayler's deeply emotional, off-kilter version of "La Marseillaise."

"It was quite funny," McCartney told Barry Miles. "It was a great little movie, but I don't know what happened to it." There is little doubt where the Beatles got the idea to use the French national anthem as the opening to their 1967 Summer of Love hit single "All You Need Is Love."

"Don't forget, McCartney was into the avant-garde. He gave Ian Somerville a studio, and helped support William Burroughs when he was in London," Hal Willner pointed out. (Sommerville was a brilliant jack-of-various-media who mostly worked behind the scenes, building the celebrated, trance-inducing "Dream-Machine" with writer/painter Brion Gysin while producing spoken-word/audio/cut-up tapes with beat novelist William S. Burroughs, as well as building a small home studio for Paul to record at Ringo's Montagu Square pad.)

As Paul explained in the Beatles' *Anthology* documentary: "People were starting to lose their pure-pop mentality and mingle with artists. . . . A kind of cross-fertilization was starting to happen."

Singer/producer Peter Asher (brother of McCartney's girlfriend Jane and half of the pop duo Peter and Gordon) opened a new world of possibility to

Paul, introducing him to the work of avant-garde artists Karlheinz Stockhausen, John Cage, and Luciano Berio. Paul soon began assembling his own sound collages and tape loops, which the Beatles employed to create an otherworldly atmosphere for their first psychedelic opus, "Tomorrow Never Knows."

"There was a time when I was the avant-garde one in the Beatles," McCartney said. Although commonly perceived as the "straight" member of the band, as Lennon branded him in "How Do You Sleep?" Paul claimed he'd been "trying to get everyone in the group to be sort of farther out and do this far-out album [*Sgt. Pepper's*]."

"It was a very free, formless time for me," Paul told Barry Miles. "So I would sit around all day, creating little tapes," which he enjoyed playing for people at far-out London parties. "It was really a kind of stoned thing," he confessed. "You knew you'd be 'round someone's house later that evening and if you had an interesting piece of music, it would be quite a blast, whether it be Ravi Shankar or Beethoven or Albert Ayler."

Like Louis Armstrong, Charlie Parker, and Ornette Coleman before him, Ayler was on a mission to raze jazz to the ground and reinvent the music on his own terms. Demanding complete artistic freedom, Albert expressed himself with a wide range of sounds and colors, and a breadth of emotion that few musicians (then or now) have been capable of. Breaking down conventions of tonality, Ayler's riotous "energy music" once inspired *Down Beat* magazine to describe his sound as "a Salvation Army band on LSD."

By refusing to swing or blow over traditional chord changes, Albert managed to alienate himself not only from most jazz fans but from most of his fellow musicians as well. Ayler quickly abandoned the innovations of bebop, which he felt had already become antiquated. From his perspective, the music of Charlie Parker and Dizzy Gillespie was too simple, like "humming along with [cheery musical TV host] Mitch Miller."

"It's a new truth now," Ayler proclaimed. "And there have to be new ways of expressing that truth." Like his hero/mentor John Coltrane, Albert believed music could be used to open people's minds and end ignorance and war. And like Yoko Ono, Ayler's dream was to bring peace to the world through his much-maligned music. "Our music should be able to remove frustration, to enable people to act more freely, to think more freely," he declared.

While known around the clubs of his hometown of Cleveland by the derogatory nickname "Bicycle Horn" for his unorthodox tone, John Coltrane embraced Ayler's philosophy and artistry, claiming he'd moved "the music into even higher frequencies." "Trane" eventually became Albert's champion, helping him financially and using his enormous influence to squeeze him onto concert bills and land him a record deal with the prestigious Impulse Records.

Raised in the Baptist church, Ayler eventually developed his own personal belief system, no longer viewing himself as simply a musician but as a shaman with a saxophone on a mission to heal the world with music. But shamanism is tricky stuff. It's usually an act best caught live and doesn't necessarily make great records. As cutting-edge guitarist Marc Ribot told me: "The main thing I got from listening to Albert Ayler's records is that his records, and I suspect his concerts—since I never heard him live—were not primarily aesthetic commodities. What you get from an Albert Ayler record isn't a polished aesthetic gem where everything is perfect. What you get is an artifact of a ritual experience."

The sheer apocalyptic intensity and outrageousness of Ayler's sound blew the door of modern jazz off its hinges. Yet at the same time Albert's call for "spiritual unity," wailing prayers to the infinite in a hand-tailored green leather suit, was another glittering link in the fourteen-carat-gold chain of audacious Black performers that stretched back to Josephine Baker, Little Richard, and James Brown and continued with Jimi Hendrix and Prince.

Ayler's producer, Bob Thiele, believed in the saxophonist's potential to reach a larger audience and saw him as a crossover R&B singer whose wild fashion sense and cosmic message (with the help of his girlfriend and muse Mary Maria Parks's lyrics) would make him a star. In a surprising move—not unlike Yoko's foray into pop music—Ayler suddenly abandoned the avant-garde and cut an album of populist-message songs that you could twist to. To bring a new, harder-funk edge to his music, Albert teamed up with guitarist Henry Vestine of the high-voltage boogie band Canned Heat and the legendary session drummer Bernard Purdie to lay down a crisp 4/4 beat.

"It was an obvious attempt by Impulse to make Albert Ayler's music a commodity," Marc Ribot assessed. "The music clearly wasn't jazz, and as far as rock 'n' roll records go, they are some of the oddest to be found. It may not be any accident that they were also Ayler's last two records."

Albert had found his muse in the poet Mary Maria Parks. Inspired by poems Albert discovered in her notebooks while "rambling through" her stuff, Ayler set Mary Maria's lyrics to music. "I wrote 'Message from Albert,'" Mary Maria claimed. But resenting her overwhelming influence on Albert, Thiele (according to Mary Maria) denied her credit on the album. "I thought Albert would die if he didn't record 'Music is the Healing Force of the Universe!'" she laughed. "I did the original vocals on the record, but they were replaced by Vivian [Bostic]." Parks also claimed to have produced Albert's stunning Love Cry sessions, yet when the album was released, the credit read "Bob Thiele." Mary Maria Parks had found herself persona non grata in the boy's club of the jazz world.

One of Parks's fondest memories (that no one can dispute) was of making music together with Albert on tenor and herself on soprano saxophone, which she had picked up at Ayler's suggestion. "I played soprano until my knees shook!"

Like a crazy saint or a wandering prophet, Albert's short visit on Earth was fraught with scorn and degradation. Twenty years after his death, a plethora of malicious metaphors continued in print. In 1992 one cranky critic in the pages of Stereo Review likened the re-release of Ayler's Love Cry to the musical equivalent of "New Year's Eve in Times Square." Author Eric Nisenson also slammed Ayler, calling his music an "intense cacophony the likes of which the human ear has not heard outside of medieval insane asylums."

Whether blowing with joyful abandon or wailing an eerie, disquieting howl filled with anguish and despair, Ayler's scope of emotion, like Yoko Ono's, was truly astounding.

21

WHY NOT

As the song's title suggests, "Why Not" is a mirror, or perhaps a bookend, to the album's astonishing opening track. Ringo kicks off the piece with a steady floppy-foot shuffle, while John slips and slides the length of his guitar's fretboard, working out a loose, bluesy groove that stretches the boundaries of boogie, creating a more suitable abstract framework for Yoko's improvisations. When she opens her mouth, a thousand locusts seem to sing, high, shrill, and haunting. At times she whimpers like a hurt animal with true tenderness and deep sorrow in her voice. Klaus Voormann's bass throbs a steady heartbeat while suddenly Lennon unleashes a kinetic shower of splintering, sparkling notes, as Yoko beckons his name . . . calling "Jahhhhannnn! Jahhhhannnn!" as if despairingly searching for her lover in a dark primeval forest or calling to him across the eternal valley of time.

Lennon's guitar starts to feed back as Yoko sounds as if she's falling backwards through a black hole in the universe. Ringo suddenly breaks out of a shuffle and picks up the rhythm, pushing the piece faster and faster toward oblivion, as the sound of a rushing train hauls everything into silence.

22

GREENFIELD MORNING
I PUSHED AN EMPTY BABY CARRIAGE
ALL OVER THE CITY

Written in the spring of 1961, "City Piece," which first appeared in Yoko's book *Grapefruit*, is an instruction/poem directing the reader to "Walk all over the city with an empty baby carriage." Whether originally conceived as a way of processing her anguish following a series of miscarriages while married to Toshi Ichiyanagi (from 1956 to 1962), with whom she had no children, or inspired by the inconceivable grief in the wake of the Hiroshima and Nagasaki bombings that shaped her youth, "Greenfield Morning" evokes the image of a woman in deep distress, unable to accept or process her feelings of overwhelming loss.

In keeping with her "life as art" philosophy, it was not unusual for Yoko to have conceived of and created a self-healing ritual by steering an empty pram through the streets of London as a way of dealing with her trauma and sorrow in the wake of her recent miscarriage in November 1968. (Yoko also experienced a series of difficult pregnancies while married to John, miscarrying three times until eventually giving birth to Sean Ono Lennon on John's birthday, October 9, 1975.)

Rather than trying to ignore and erase the more difficult aspects of life, Ono openly embraced pain and constantly encouraged others to do so, in hopes of better understanding the experience and fully healing from emotions that linger after such disturbing events. In some ways, "Greenfield Morning I Pushed an Empty Baby Carriage All Over the City" works as a bookend to John's bitter "I Found Out" on Lennon's *Plastic Ono Band* release. While Ono's piece is gentler and more atmospheric, Lennon spells out his message bluntly, instructing fans to "feel [their] own pain."

"Yoko radically experimented with her voice in sound as well as in message," Thollem McDonas pointed out. "She expressed deeply personal experiences, like 'Greenfield Morning,' after her miscarriage. It is an incredibly personal statement that is both somehow transcendental and existential, a mourning song for all women in the world. Yoko juxtaposes the cycles of life with the image of an empty baby carriage being pushed down the sidewalk. Bringing in bird songs at the end of the piece was so simple yet transformative, making a connection not only with humankind but with all kind."

Built off the (uncredited) drone of George Harrison's mesmerizing sitar and the persistent thwack of Ringo's drums, "Greenfield Morning I Pushed an Empty Baby Carriage All Over the City" seems as if it might have inspired Harry Nilsson's reverb-drenched, nightmarish jam "Jump into the Fire." Nilsson, who recorded his song the following year with Klaus Voormann (who also played bass on Yoko's track) providing rhythm guitar, may have been moved by Ono's "Greenfield Morning." The hard-rocking "Jump into the Fire" was a departure for Nilsson, best known for his achingly beautiful ballads; it peaked at No. 27 on the *Billboard* charts.

Overdubbed layers of Ono's ethereal voice weave like phantoms through the air until suddenly dissolving into the sound of singing birds as the track fades. This unexpected juxtaposition creates a stirring moment of peace and beauty.

"The lyric is so beautiful," Sean Lennon said. "[It's] a very poignant image . . . very original. The beat is super funky."

"Give it a try," Lester Bangs coaxed skeptical readers in his review of Yoko's *Plastic Ono Band*, suggesting they brave "at least a handful of listenings before [casting a] verdict. There's something happening here."

23

AOS

It's far out, but don't let that frighten you.

—John Lennon

Ornette Coleman was courting trouble again. Like Yoko Ono, the free-jazz saxophonist had a knack for stirring up controversy wherever he went. Even the most devoted jazz fans often found themselves shaking their heads in bewilderment and heading for the exit before his concerts ended. Some complained that (like Ono) Ornette was out of tune, or that his music was "crazy," as it cut directly to their core, challenging their basic understanding of logic, aesthetics, and life itself. Coleman's "free jazz" or "Harmolodics," as he later termed his revolutionary music (as audiences attending his concerts often expected them to be "free") was purely democratic in the truest sense. Every instrument from Coleman's perspective was considered equal. There was no sonic hierarchy or caste system within his musical philosophy. No one was designated to play repetitive forms in support of a soloist.

In 1959 Ornette turned the jazz world upside down when he first performed at the Five Spot in New York City. Everyone from Miles Davis to bassist/composer Charles Mingus and bebop drummer Max Roach (who once stood outside Coleman's apartment threatening to punch him in the mouth) took offense at Ornette's unconventional yet spirited approach to playing the music. Wild as the music seemed, the roots of Coleman's free jazz could be found in early New Orleans group improvisational ensembles with wailing clarinets and cornets and tailgating trombones.

But the rhythm section of bass and drums (unless featured as a solo) was no longer designated to serve the "lead instruments." In Coleman's case his alto saxophone, trumpet, and violin were free to respond to the melody how and whenever they felt—or not at all. But the intensity of emotion with which Ornette played was often too much for people. Coleman's music, as Jethro Tull's Ian Anderson complained, was "a bit brisk."

"I was always trying to find the idea, not the melody," Ornette told me in a November 2006 interview with *Wax Poetics*. "I never believed that the idea was the melody. I believed the idea was only the idea. I still think that way."

According to Yoko Ono, she had been "doing a concert in Paris of my own work . . . and after the concert was over, somebody said that Ornette was in the audience and introduced me to him. And he immediately said, 'I like what you are doing.'" Coleman then surprised Ono when he spontaneously invited her to perform with his quartet on Leap Day, February 29, 1968, at London's Royal Albert Hall. But the concert was at risk of being cancelled. Ornette had already run into trouble with both the British musician's union and Labour Ministry, which refused to allow him to perform as he was primarily known as "a jazz musician." They also rejected his previous classical works, *Dedication* (1961), *Forms and Sounds* (1965), and *Inventions of Symphonic Poems* as evidence of his compositional abilities. Having received a prestigious grant from the Guggenheim Museum didn't seem to matter very much to the powers that were.

According to jazz journalist/author Barry McRae, who witnessed the February 29th performance, Ono had more artistic clout than Coleman in the classical world, having previously worked with John Cage and composed two operas, *Grapefruit in the World of Park* and *Strawberries and Violin*, which premiered at Carnegie Recital Hall on November 24, 1961.

It was through Ono that Ornette was able to finally secure the concert date. McRae ironically pointed out that "in order to get a work permit, [Coleman] had spent many hours convincing the authorities that he wasn't a jazz musician. In Albert Hall, he spent little more than two proving he was one of the greatest."

One of the few critics to review the concert, McRae observed how Yoko's vocals "dovetailed beautifully with Coleman's trumpet and Blackwell's economical and static drum figures and fully justified the title of the work." The performance concluded with "Three Wise Men and a Sage," written for a string trio featuring Ornette, who played (left-handed) violin in his unconventional skittery style, along with tandem bassists Charlie Haden and David Izenzon. As McRae described the scene: "Coleman's folkish fury sounded crude, but it had an ineluctable vitality."

"You can't translate the more complex sounds into traditional notation," Yoko once told journalist Robert Palmer. "The minute you do notate it, and someone plays what you've written, the sound becomes totally different. I wanted to capture the sounds I'd heard of birds singing in the woods, things like that."

What most people failed to understand about Yoko (particularly fans who still ludicrously blame her for the Beatles' breakup) was the key role she played in the downtown New York avant-garde scene of the early 1960s. After dropping out of Sarah Lawrence College, having studied composition, Yoko rented a cheap, soot-stained loft on Chambers Street, where she presented a series of informal house concerts, much like the rent parties once integral to the Harlem jazz community. The first soiree took place on a freezing cold December night. It was a rather rustic affair, with a tangle of long, black, snake-like extension cords used to syphon off electricity from a hall socket, while an old iron wood-burning stove provided warmth for a small crowd of approximately twenty-five people who sat on orange crates in lieu of chairs. Among the audience were musical refugees from the uptown classical scene, including John Cage, minimalist La Monte Young, and violinist/composer Henry Flynt. The multifarious Flynt was credited with coining the term "concept art," after composing a manifesto entitled *Concept Art* in 1961, which resolutely stated that "ideas or concept is the most important aspect of [any] work."

"All of [the group of uptown musicians who attended her soirees] had this dissatisfaction about just writing musical notes," Yoko pointed out.

Dedicated to David Tudor (the avant-garde composer/pianist best known for his collaborations with John Cage and who'd favorably reviewed Yoko's first exhibition in New York City), the original version of "AOS" was presented in 1961 at Carnegie Recital Hall as part of Ono's concert *A Grapefruit in the World of Park*. Performed in total darkness and silence, whatever sound occurred during the piece was by happenstance. Lining up two performers back to back, Yoko tethered an assortment of empty bottles and cans to their bodies and then wrapped them in gauze before instructing the pair to walk across the stage as quietly as possible. Ono's intent was, as always, to provoke the audience to think and listen beyond whatever prejudicial thoughts and attitudes they clung to.

Recorded during a rehearsal earlier on February 29, 1968, Yoko's "AOS" was performed as part of Ornette's larger work "Emotion Modulation." It was essentially a seven-minute improvisation that featured Ono's keening vocals in the context of Coleman's current quartet, consisting of Ornette on trumpet (in lieu of his usual alto saxophone), double bassists Charlie Haden and David Izenzon, and the polyrhythmic drummer Ed Blackwell.

Coleman had arrived in New York in 1959 after leaving his home of Fort Worth, Texas, and migrating to L.A., where the breezy style of West Coast jazz (Chet Baker,

Gerry Mulligan) dominated the scene at the time. Reflecting the Civil Rights struggle for freedom, Ornette's unwavering democratic attitude helped liberate the jazz rhythm section from its assigned roles of time keeping and supporting the lead instruments. Coleman single-handedly shattered the caste system of modern music. Suddenly everyone was equal—the bass and drums were encouraged to solo whenever the spirit struck. Whether you found his music exhilarating or exasperating, Coleman was one of the most important abstract thinkers of his day. His "free" approach deeply resonated with Yoko Ono, who believed, as Coleman once said, that "the idea is to give creativity a run for its money!"

"The Plastic Ono Band was, and has continued to be, a concept, no matter who is on the team," percussionist Michael Blair said.

> In recent years it has featured Sean [Lennon] and Yuka Honda [Cibo Matta's multi-instrumentalist], or anyone who happened to be in the room at the time with Yoko and John, or whoever they asked to accompany them, improvise with them, record with them. And on this track, masterful jazz players are acting, reacting, and supporting Yoko's vocal expression. In my world, the "best" jazz musicians can enter a sound design world whether they are playing [Jerome Kern's standard] "All the Things You Are" or making believe they are throwing themselves down a flight of stairs. Ed Blackwell has that moment where he enters on Yoko's distorted screaming and he responds in kind.

"It's all about expression, whether abstract or completely structured," Blair emphasized. "The intention is what matters."

According to Coleman, the track that later appeared on *Plastic Ono Band* had been released without his knowledge or consent. There was also the issue of authorship, over which Ornette remained miffed forty years later when he complained that he'd never received any royalties as a composer or performer. This was not the first time Yoko or John had been blamed for artistic appropriation. Lennon had previously wound up in trouble with the music publisher/mobster Morris Levy over nicking the opening line to Chuck Berry's "You Can't Catch Me" for the Beatles' hit "Come Together." And their jam with the Mothers of Invention at the Fillmore East on June 6, 1971, would cause a long-standing rift with Frank Zappa after John and Yoko released the recordings the following year on their double album *Some Time in New*

York City. Without bothering to consult Frank, Lennon and Ono gave the jams new titles while taking full songwriting credit.

Ono would eventually abandon the avant-garde in hopes of reaching a wider audience. As she told *(((echoes)))*: "It was a pity that I couldn't have done more of that. . . . In a way I think the world shut me up. There's a certain point when an artist gets totally discouraged. In the beginning I wasn't listening to [negative criticism]. I was just going on with my thing. But there was a point when I realized that I couldn't record another song like ["AOS"] and put it out, because nobody's going to buy it."

Despite the squabble over releasing "AOS," Ornette harbored no ill will toward Yoko and invited her to perform at the Meltdown Festival (which he curated) in London in June 2009. In Ono's defense, it should be noted that she'd previously specified that "AOS" was to be "her piece—not the musicians'." While foregoing traditional musical notation, the score included a series of directions indicating how and what she wanted the musicians to play. Ono encouraged Ornette and his band to: "Think of the days when you had to suffer in silence for ten days of eternity before you could give, and yet you were afraid of giving because what you were giving was so true and so total, you knew that you would suffer a death after that. . . . Think of the days when you allowed silences in your life for dreaming. . . . This is no shit. No mood or whatever you call it. It's real." She also implored them to: "Forget about what you've learnt or heard in the music academy world." This last direction was redundant, as Coleman and his crew of improvisors had little or nothing to do with the attitudes and methods of "the music academy world."

In a 1980 interview with *Soho Weekly News*, Ornette would regale Yoko as "an advance punk," recalling how Albert Hall refused to print her concert program, "'cause she said [the words] *pussy, cunt,* and *penis.*"

The version of "AOS" that appears on Yoko's *Plastic Ono Band* features Ornette squeaking and blaring on trumpet (in lieu of his usual alto sax) while Ono weaves a sonic spell, heaving and sighing until a primal scream (years before Dr. Arthur Janov popularized the term) burst from her lungs, triggering a violent explosion from the band.

In a 2017 interview Yoko recalled the inspiration behind "AOS":

When I performed at Carnegie Recital Hall in 1961, and performed subsequently in Sogetsu Kaikan in Tokyo in 1962, I took and morphed my vocalization, consciously, from Kabuki and Noh [traditional Japanese vocal techniques]. It was a very early avant-garde musical attempt made only by me at the time, and I was conscious of presenting something that had a familiar reference to it, to be understood more clearly. Otherwise, I usually fly away from all references. Therefore, I am not aware of what I am doing with my voice in terms of where it stems from.

Although one theory circulated that the acronym "AOS" stood for the LSD guru Augustus Owsley Stanley III, the title "AOS" has its origins in the Japanese word *ao*, meaning blue (or perhaps, in this case, the blues) while *aos* are the three last letters of the English *chaos*. It seems unlikely that the title, which has also been interpreted as "Blue Chaos," was inspired by Miles Davis's classic 1959 album *Kind of Blue*, as journalist Madeline Bocaro previously suggested.

AOS is also the name of a nine-minute animated film made by Yoji Kuri in 1964, the soundtrack of which featured a variety of vocalizations by Yoko Ono that include rhythmic, sexual moans, groans, and whispers, along with what sounds like "backwards" singing at times. The film begins with Yoko cawing like a mad crow as the head of a disgruntled ogre repeatedly lunges at the viewer like a nightmarish jack-in-the-box. Ono sighs and slurps as a pair of disembodied lips inside a matchbox part to reveal a long tongue that slithers, snake-like, aimlessly about. Surrealist images abound. A man with a finger for a head runs from a building as dozens of fingers begin to poke through the ceiling. In many ways *AOS* appears to be a forerunner to the Beatles' 1968 animated feature, *Yellow Submarine*.

"Kuri's films have bite," said Chris Robinson, the artistic director of the Ottawa International Animation Festival. "He helped lift Japanese animation out of decades of cozy narrative cartoons into a new era of graphic and conceptual experimentation." Robinson sees Kuri's quirky cartoon as a powerful statement about alienation in modern Japan, populated by "frustrated and repressed men and women who exist in cramped, isolated trappings," who remain "desperate [and] unable to connect."

Ono's vocal segment in Ornette's "Emotion Modulation" encompassed a wide range of human feelings, from fear to ecstasy. Years later, in 1973, Pink Floyd's *Dark Side of the Moon* featured Richard Wright's instrumental "Great Gig in the Sky," a wordless improvisation of volcanic emotion that poured from vocalist Clare Torry (for which she'd initially been paid a mere one-time fee of thirty pounds for weekend studio work). Torry eventually sued Pink Floyd and settled out of court in 2004, as her contribution to Wright's piece went far beyond the role of a backup singer to becoming essential to its enormous popularity and success. In 2013, Yoko would perform her own interpretation of "Great Gig in the Sky" for a small crowd during her retrospective at the Museum of Modern Art in New York. The performance was said to have inspired a possible collaboration with Lou Reed to remake the entire *Dark Side of the Moon* album with the working title of *The Dark Side of Yoko Ono*, but Lou passed away in October 2013 after a battle with liver cancer, leaving Yoko, in the words of her publicist Bethany Millbright, "devastated."

"In a way, the track with Coleman is the weakest," Lester Bangs ruminated in his *Rolling Stone* review of [Yoko's] *Plastic Ono Band*. "Yoko is into her 'Ohh, John!' riff, and Ornette's band is laying down the kind of rhythmic noodling that seldom finds them at their peaks. It was a rehearsal tape anyway." Yet "AOS" reveals Ono's diversity as an innovative singer, whose unorthodox vocal style can work in any setting—from free jazz to the electric exorcism of "Why."

"It was a great experience," Yoko recalled in a 1997 interview. "Ornette's band of musicians were very, very kind to me."

Lennon famously had little regard for jazz, once disparaging it as "just a lot of old blokes drinking beer at the bar, smoking pipes and not listening to the music." Since his early days with the Quarrymen, John found himself at odds over trad jazz to the point of allegedly coming to fisticuffs. While trad jazz enthusiasts were willing to stomach the Quarrymen's amateur skiffle music (as skiffle, often played on banjo and propelled by a washboard, had its roots in blues and early jazz), the conflict over modern jazz, as Chuck Berry sang in "Rock 'n' Roll Music," arose when the musicians "try to play it too darn fast, and change the beauty of the melody, until they sound just like a symphony." And a cacophonous one at that.

John was not beyond contradiction, particularly when it came to his wife's cause. In a letter addressed to New York TV chat show host Joe Franklin dated December 13, 1971, Lennon, hoping to secure a spot for Yoko on Franklin's popular late-night program, wrote:

> Dear Joe, I know you're a musician at heart and especially I know you dig jazz—Well . . . Yoko's music ain't quite jazz. But . . . to help you get off on it, or understand it, please listen to a track on *Yoko Ono/Plastic Ono Band* called "AOS," which was recorded in 1968 with Ornette Coleman at Albert Hall, London. You could call it "Free Form." Anyway, Yoko sits in the middle of avant-garde classic[al], jazz and now through me and my music, rock 'n' roll.

The letter went on to explain that Ono "was a trained classical musician" and had been a composition major at Sarah Lawrence College.

"It's far out, but don't let that frighten you," John cajoled.

Whether or not Ono's music and art terrified Franklin, we'll never know. Not only did Joe decline to have Yoko on as a guest, he sold Lennon's handwritten letter years later. It was put up for auction in 2014 and offered to the highest bidder for approximately $20,000.

"The sense of freedom and possibility that permeated the counterculture back then was really quite innocent," Nels Cline said.

> It had its share of guile and greed, and it all mushroomed out of control, leaving so many idealists scratching their heads and wondering where it all went wrong. The twin *Plastic Ono Band* records not only addressed this specifically in John's lyrics but also musically—but particularly on Yoko's record, wherein she improvises with Ornette Coleman's quartet while ignoring virtually every musical boundary. It is in these self-aware, bitter, naked, and exhilaratingly free and candid works that the way into the future—to some of the most adventurous new music that was to come in the 1970s—is foreshadowed.

24

TOUCH ME

"'Touch Me' is a desperate plea for connectivity," Thollem McDonas observed. "John's guitar seems to ascend, going on infinitely, while Ringo plays the drums like orchestral timpani. The pause at 3:25 is so pregnant. It makes you wonder, where is the piece going? It's like the beginning of the end. . . . Sweet anticipation that is ultimately unfulfilled, before dissolving into the sound of joyful, or wrathful, creatures."

"These are pretty much noise/texture-oriented tracks," Michael Blair explained. "So Ringo could focus on the toms to keep the energy moving, without the expectation of any traditional rock guitar/bass/drums configuration."

"Both [John's and Yoko's] *Plastic Ono Band*, along with the *White Album*, are my favorite Ringo records," Steve Shelley said enthusiastically. "It's amazing how open Ringo was when playing on Yoko's stuff. I hadn't heard him play drums like that. It was so pre-punk, aggressive and formless at times. A lot of the music on those *Plastic Ono Band* albums predated a lot of things Sonic Youth wound up doing."

25

PAPER SHOES

The album's closing track begins with a minute-and-a-half recording of train wheels whooshing down the track. The rhythm is as steady as a giant metronome. While detrimental to the environment, the Industrial Revolution inadvertently introduced a palate of surprisingly new harsh sounds. Generally viewed as noise pollution, the incessant clanging and pounding of factories and various machinery has inspired some great music over the years, from the driving Delta blues of Muddy Waters' "Rollin' and Tumblin'" to the bluegrass standard "The Orange Blossom Special" (which glorified the first "all-electric" train that ran direct from New York to West Palm Beach, Florida, in a mere thirty-five hours) to Elvis Presley's rockabilly rave-up "Mystery Train" that inexplicably pulled "into the station in the middle of the night," only to disappear moments later into the foggy night with the bewildered protagonist's girlfriend on board. By the mid-1970s, Genesis P-Orridge's innovative "noise" band Throbbing Gristle helped create a new musical genre that simply became known as "industrial."

"In many ways you could count [Ono] as a forebearer of industrial music and krautrock and even emo," Thollem McDonas said. "'Paper Shoes' is a transcendent song for traveling around your psyche! As an artist and a human, Yoko's been consistently outspoken about feminism, social justice, antiwar causes, and ecology, tearing back the fabric of illusion that hides the oppressive mechanisms of modern society. Her approach to music and life has always been a cathartic wake-up call. Harnessing the original raw spirit of rock 'n' roll, devastating blues, and the wildest explorations of the avant-garde, creating a sonic socio-political revolution that you can look at, listen to, think about and *feel!*"

"I really like the groove of 'Paper Shoes,'" D. J. Bonebrake said. "Ringo's rhythm comes from a literal train beat, from [the recording of] a real train! *Musique concrète* with rock jams. You can't beat it!"

John hammers out a choppy, syncopated rhythm on his guitar as Yoko releases a whirlwind of "oohs," conjuring visions of banshees wailing around a midnight fire.

"I noticed a lot of kind of Japanese Kabuki kind of thing comes out of me," Yoko told (((*echoes*))). "I'm thinking, ohhh . . . probably that's something that I got from my childhood or something like that."

But beyond any traditional or classical influence, Yoko believes that rock 'n' roll was the greatest influence on her. "I think it has to do with the rock beat, that my voice came out that way," Yoko told WNYC's David Garland. "I was doing that sort of thing, voice modulation, using my voice as an instrument even before that in the avant-garde and then I did it with Ornette Coleman and jazz and all that. But it was quite different. The beat itself helped me to sort of produce this sort of famous Yoko Ono [lets out a shriek], you know, that one."

26

OPEN YOUR BOX

There are a total of seven versions of "Open Your Box," including a censored version, a 2001 remix, a dub mix, and various edits for radio and club play. The original (and the take released on the 2017 reissue of Yoko's *Plastic Ono Band*) was recorded at Trident Studios, featuring John, Ringo, and Klaus working out on a floppy funk groove as Yoko repeatedly taunts the listener to "Open . . . open . . . open your box!" The enigmatic "box" that Yoko throws before us is second only to Pandora's, whether meant to symbolize the psychic armor we all don to guard our emotions, or our limited imaginations, or the small world we inhabit defined by our lifestyles.

Sometimes crying, sometimes gargling, sometimes growling, until letting loose with a feral scream, Yoko demands us to "Open! Open! Open . . . All you have to do. . . ." Suddenly Ono begins to cough, as pure sound erupts, burbling from the depths of her soul. A moment later, John's slashing guitar and Klaus's pumping bass drop out, leaving Ringo to bash the beat. Starr's playing on "Open Your Box" is one of the rare moments in his recorded career where he totally cuts loose, abandoning his preferred role of tastefully serving the song. He hammers the skins with a ferocious intensity, reminiscent of the final moments of "Helter Skelter," before he famously shouts "I've got blisters on me fingers!" Perhaps Ono's cries, which resemble a mad bird in distress, were enough to finally push Ringo over the edge.

The second version of "Open Your Box" was actually the first version of the song to be released, on March 22, 1971, as the B-side to John's "Power to the People." With Jim Gordon (of Delaney and Bonnie's band and later Derek and the Dominoes) playing drums, the song takes on a dark, swampy Talking Heads *Remain in Light*–era groove. While "censored," this take of "Open Your Box" is still some pretty sexy stuff, as Yoko cries: "Open your trousers. . . . Open your thighs. . . . Open your legs. . . ." In the second verse, Ono's message becomes an all-inclusive plea for peace as she wails, "Let's open the cities. . . . Open, open, open the world!" Due to its provocative lyrics, "Open Your Box" was replaced by "Touch Me" as the flip side to the American pressing of John's "Power to the People," while in the UK no one seemed to either notice or mind Ono's sexual innuendos. The second version of "Open Your Box" to be released on Yoko's 1971 album *Fly* was musically the same, but uncensored and renamed "Hirake" (開け or simply "Open"). John sounds as if he's trying to saw his guitar in half, while "Mrs. Lennon" incessantly begs people everywhere to uncross the legs of their minds and openly embrace their sexuality.

Starting with a series of breathy pants and gasps, the 2001 Orange Factory Remix of "Open Your Box" leaves little to the imagination as Ono, the senior citizen sex therapist/cheerleader, shouts a series of commands: "Open your legs! Open your thighs! Open your mouth!" over a writhing sea of synths and sequencers.

27

THE SOUTH WIND

Released as a bonus track on the 2017 edition of Yoko's *Plastic Ono Band*, "The South Wind" is an exhaustive (over sixteen-minute) exploration into sonic possibilities, with John playing a loosely tuned acoustic guitar, randomly plucking and tapping the strings while sometimes employing a swooping slide. The instrument's rumbling tone evokes a mashup sound, from a *koto* (Japanese zither) to a pair of garbage-can timpani. Meanwhile Yoko's sonic vocabulary mixes nerve-rattling shrieks and guttural mad-monkey chatter with frantic bird calls. At times her multiphonic voice (capable of creating more than one tone at a time) captures the raw energy and fear of animals fighting. A duet, the interaction between Lennon/Ono on "The South Wind," was rarely better, as they spark each other on into unknown realms. This track will redefine the term *music* for anyone brave enough to give it a spin.

Provoked by John's slippery slide work, Yoko's gasp transforms into a sexual pant. Fourteen and a half minutes into the piece, Lennon provides a brief respite, playing a familiar-sounding guitar motif while employing open chords and fingerpicking reminiscent of Sandy Bull or John Fahey. But a moment later he begins detuning the bass strings of the guitar as low as they can go, as Ono sighs . . . exhausted.

28

AFTERSHOCK:
LENNON REMEMBERS . . .
AND REGRETS

If you could use propaganda for war,
you could certainly use it for peace.

—Edward Bernays (Sigmund Freud's American nephew)

Annie Liebovitz's iconic portrait of a bearded John Lennon clad in overalls, which graced the cover of *Rolling Stone* on January 21, 1971, was nearly as stunning as the ex-Beatle's bitter interview within its newsprint pages. In her retrospective book, *At Work* (published in 2018), Liebovitz recalled how her first major assignment for America's most popular alternative paper came about. Guaranteeing Jann Wenner that she would do the job "cheaper than anyone else," the rookie photographer agreed to fly student fare and crash with friends in New York City, where Wenner was scheduled to conduct the interview.

During the historic shoot, Yoko made a back-handed remark that Liebovitz wisely let slide. Ono said she and John were "'impressed that Jann let someone like [her] photograph people who were so famous.' They were used to the best photographers in the world and this kid showed up. But John didn't treat me like a kid," Liebovitz imparted. "He put me at ease." She added that Lennon was "honest, straightforward, and cooperative." While Annie measured the availability of light in the room, she suddenly noticed: "John looked up. . . . It was a long look. He seemed to be staring at me, and I clicked the shutter."

It was no secret that Jann Wenner adored John Lennon. Launched on November 9, 1967, the debut issue of *Rolling Stone* featured a bespectacled Lennon on its cover, in his cameo role as Sgt. Gripweed in Richard Lester's latest film, *How I Won the War*. A year later, *Rolling Stone* celebrated their first anniversary with a cover shot of

Lennon and Ono's rear ends, which graced the back of their *Two Virgins*. And now, in a two-part exclusive interview conducted by Wenner himself, *Rolling Stone* would publish the stark manifesto of John's battered soul. As Jann pointed out, it was "the first time that any of the Beatles, let alone the man who had founded the group and was their leader, finally stepped outside of that protected, beloved fairy tale and told the truth."

Lennon brimmed with malice. Despite months of grueling therapy sessions with Arthur Janov, whose brisk philosophy inspired the soul-bearing lyrics and feral vocals that comprised much of *Plastic Ono Band*, nothing could quell Lennon's unrelenting flamethrower of rage. No one except Yoko was immune from John's bullwhip tongue lashings. He wielded insults like a mace, razing everything and everybody in sight. Even Dylan, who'd once inspired him to stretch beyond the simple rhymes of his early girl/boy love songs, became a target of John's anger and disillusionment.

The interview took place on December 8, 1970 (ten years to the day before his shocking assassination), in Allen Klein's wood-paneled office in midtown Manhattan. As far as John was concerned, he was just telling it like it was—direct and brutally honest, with no blubbering walruses or marmalade skies, no matter how much we once adored his poetic imagery.

Without a trace of nostalgia, Lennon stripped away every trace of artifice from his life. The act of standing nude before the camera beside his beloved Yoko as the *Two Virgins* was no longer enough; John was now publicly shedding his skin, ridding himself of every nonessential. Everything else was now merely a distraction from the truth. What remained after the smoke cleared was just "a boy and a little girl trying to change the whole round world," as he sang in "Isolation."

But there was plenty of collateral damage along the way. None suffered more than Paul McCartney—the prime target of John's volcanic vitriol. Lennon's resentment toward his old partner had been brewing since the early days of the band. As he told Peter McCabe and Robert Schonfeld on September 5, 1971:

> Paul always wanted the home life. . . . He liked it with daddy and the broth-
> er [Mike] and [he] obviously missed his mother. . . . He wouldn't go against
> his dad and wear drainpipe trousers. And his dad was always trying to get
> me out of the group behind me back. I found out later. He'd say to George,
> "Why don't you get rid of John, he's just a lot of trouble. Cut your hair nice
> and wear baggy trousers." Like I was the bad influence because I was the

eldest. . . . And I was always saying [to Paul], "Face up to your dad, tell him to fuck off. He can't hit you. You can kill him. He's an old man."

I used to say, "Don't take that shit off him." Because I was always brought up by a woman, so maybe it was different. But I wouldn't let the old man treat me like that. He treated Paul like a child all the time, [telling him to] cut his hair and . . . what to wear, at seventeen, eighteen. But Paul would always give in to his dad. His dad told him to get a job, he fucking dropped [out of] the group and started working on the fucking lorries, saying, "I need a steady career." We couldn't believe it. . . .

He rang up and said he'd got this job and couldn't come to [play with] the group. So I told him on the phone, "Either come or you're out." So he had to make a decision between me and his dad then, and in the end, he chose me.

Although Lennon directly profited from the commercial appeal of McCartney's music, he'd had his fill of Paul's vaudevillian ditties, deeming tunes like "Lady Madonna," "Your Mother Should Know," "Honey Pie," and "Ob-la-di, Ob-la-da" unforgivably square. *Abbey Road*'s "Maxwell's Silver Hammer" was the final straw. Lennon simply refused to play on it.

With his new partner by his side 24/7, who not only inspired him to open the box of his mind but revolutionized his soul, John felt that Paul's corny tunes were beginning to undermine his artistic integrity. He even claimed to have been proud to have had no part in composing McCartney's regretful masterpiece "Yesterday." Yet due to their 50/50 songwriting partnership, Lennon often benefited financially from some of Paul's greatest hits, although he had nothing or little to do with them.

Despite his defiant attitude, Lennon understood pop music as a business and made plenty of compromises to help pave the way for the Beatles' initial success. He stopped swearing and smoking on stage and begrudgingly allowed Brian Epstein to dress his band in cute collarless suits. John wisely chose Paul McCartney not just for his brilliant musicality but also for his sex appeal. But McCartney, the doe-eyed chick magnet, turned out to be a wolf in sheep's clothing. His limitless ambition combined with his outstanding musical chops, which allowed him to play nearly any instrument and write the majority of the Beatles' A-sides, transformed McCartney into an authority figure in his bandmates' eyes. And much to his credit, Paul held the Beatles together for a few more years after Epstein's sudden death in August 1967.

While Paul's eponymously titled debut *McCartney* was largely considered a light-weight affair, the devastatingly stark *John Lennon/Plastic Ono Band* hit Beatle fans like a ton of bricks. Despite McCartney's multi-instrumental mastery, John found little to say about Paul's solo effort beyond being "surprised" the album "was so poor." While allowing that Paul was "capable of great work," John dismissed *McCartney* as a load of "rubbish." Lennon said he'd hoped his record might "scare him into doing something decent" in the future. "Then he'll scare me into doing something doing decent, and I'll scare him," John quipped.

McCartney, not surprisingly, was more diplomatic, even generous, when assessing his former partner's work, claiming to like *Imagine* despite the toxic "How Do You Sleep?" "But there was too much political stuff on the other albums," Paul groused. Without skipping a beat Lennon shot back: "So you think 'Imagine' ain't political? It's 'Working Class Hero' with sugar on it for conservatives, like yourself!" while further taunting him to "Join the Rock Liberation Front before it gets *you*."

Music critics inevitably compared their solo efforts, and John took offense whenever they did. As Michael Watts wrote in *Melody Maker*: "[*Plastic Ono Band*] is not going to convert anyone who does not already like Lennon's musical approach. . . . Melodically there is nothing earth shattering but then, Lennon has never set out to become another Cole Porter." Perhaps Mr. Watts should have given Lennon's lilting "Love" a second spin before passing judgment, as his comments only helped reinforce long-held stereotypes of John as the creative genius/rocker and Paul, the sentimental melodist (a theory set in stone years before by Jann Wenner in *Rolling Stone*). That said, McCartney's lyrics were never his strong suit, while he had an amazing knack for composing tunes throughout his career that stuck in your head like hot glue (whether you liked them or not).

Yet John and Paul's first solo efforts had more in common than either of them would ever care to admit. Both albums had been very private affairs, recorded with a minimal amount of production. While McCartney worked in total solitude, only trusted friends were invited to witness and play on Lennon's sonic therapy sessions.

What ultimately irked John about Paul's album was not the music but the "great hype" of publicity that fueled its release. Once again McCartney had beaten him to the punch, when the front page of the *Daily Mirror's* headlines shouted "Paul Quits Beatles" on the morning of Friday, April 10, 1970. Lennon fumed about how McCartney's surprise announcement (exactly one week before his debut album was released) was perfectly timed in order "to sell a record. . . . I was a fool not to do it," John groused.

In truth, Ringo had been first to quit the Beatles. Feeling "unloved" and insecure about his playing on the *White Album* sessions, Starr walked out of EMI Studios on Thursday, August 22, 1968, followed by Harrison on Friday, January 10, 1969, after he'd had enough of McCartney's harassing him over how to play his instrument. For the last few years, George had wrestled with a growing resentment over Lennon and McCartney ignoring his steadily expanding portfolio of songs (many of which would comprise his brilliant debut album, *All Things Must Pass*) in favor of recording every whim that came into their heads.

When Lennon blurted out on September 20, 1969, that he "wanted a divorce" and was leaving the band, he was quickly persuaded by the unlikely team of McCartney and Allen Klein to keep silent for the time being and not spoil a new publishing deal their blusterous manager had been in the thick of negotiating.

It was not the first time McCartney's media savvy would thrust him into the spotlight. Although John, George, and Ringo had all experimented with LSD months before Paul gathered the courage to take the leap, McCartney was the first to alert the press that the Beatles had dabbled in hallucinogenic drugs—as if their lyrics, music, and clothes weren't enough to tip everyone off. Expecting praise as a groovy trendsetter, Paul, instead, wound up in a nasty crossfire of criticism for leading the youth of the Western world down the primrose path to madness and apathy.

And now a chain-smoking and bitter John Lennon had no qualms about airing the Beatles' dirty laundry, as he unabashedly lashed out at everyone in his life (with the exception of Yoko, of course) from his parents to his bandmates and former heroes—anyone who'd ever caused him pain.

While Ringo and Maureen were "alright," "the other two," John claimed, "really gave it to us." "I'll never forgive them," he said of Paul and George. "I don't care what fucking shit about Hare Krishna and God. . . . I can't forgive 'em for that, really. Although I can't help loving them either."

According to Paul, Lennon's "open hostility . . . was so far out [that I] actually enjoyed it. . . . It didn't hurt me," he assured *Life* magazine.

"The [*Rolling Stone*] interview was full of ridiculous shit like 'Paul wasn't the walrus. I was just saying that to be nice. But I was the walrus,'" Hal Willner said. "Michael O'Donoghue did a great parody of John's interview in *National Lampoon* called 'Magical Misery Tour' [with terrific illustrations by Randall Enos]."

In 1972 the *Lampoon* released an album called *Radio Dinner* featuring the track "Magical Misery Tour" with music by Chris Cerf (*Sesame Street*) and vocals by Tony Hendra (who played the role of the road manager Ian Faith in *This Is Spinal Tap*) imitating John hysterically screaming "Genius is pain!" As "John's" torturous cater-wauling finally dwindles, Melissa Manchester, who played the piano, imitates Yoko in a fake-Japanese accent, proclaiming "The dleam is ovahhh." A brilliant yet painful bit of satire.

For someone who loved to "take the piss" out of everyone from Dylan to McCartney and Mick Jagger for "all his stupid faggot dancing," one hopes that John, if he ever heard it, got the joke.

Responding to Lennon's harsh remarks in an open letter sent to *Melody Maker* that minimized his incalculable creative input to the Beatles' music, George Martin, always the gentleman, brushed off John's insults, politely replying, "That's silly, of course," while adding that he felt "sorry for him." By Martin's estimate, Lennon's behavior appeared "schizophrenic. . . . Either he doesn't mean it, but if he does . . . he can't be in a normal state of mind at the time."

While Lennon granted Jann Wenner the rights to publish the interview in two consecutive issues of *Rolling Stone*, Wenner did not legally own the piece. Quick to seize a business opportunity when he saw it, Jann published John's vicious tirade in 1971 as a paperback titled *Lennon Remembers*, certain it would be a bestseller. Sadly, Wenner's arrogance and greed would damage his relationship with the Lennons for many years, until the release of their 1980 comeback album *Double Fantasy*.

Once again *Rolling Stone* sent Annie Liebovitz to photograph the couple. But following the historic portrait session, an assassin's bullet made certain Lennon and Wenner would never meet again.

Despite his reputation as a serial bridge burner, Wenner found losing Lennon's friendship (and advertising account) to be devastating. While in awe of John's star power, the sycophantic editor greatly admired Lennon's "compulsive humor." Even during the worst of his deportation battles with the Nixon administration and har-rowing drunken benders on Sunset Strip, boozing with Harry Nilsson, Keith Moon, and Ringo with a tampon strapped around his head like the halo of a degenerate saint (a classic rock 'n' roll antic on par with Keith Richards hurling televisions out of hotel windows or Joe Walsh destroying hotel shag carpets with a weed-eater), John managed to maintain a healthy sense of absurdity.

30

1971 AND BEYOND: UNFINISHED ART, UNFINISHED MUSIC, AND AN UNFINISHED LIFE

For Yoko Ono, being "unfinished" is a state of grace.

—Alexandra Munroe, Japan Society Gallery Curator

On June 5, 1971, Howard Smith, the *Village Voice* columnist and disc jockey on WPLJ from 1969 to 1972, was on his way to interview Frank Zappa, whose newly revamped Mothers of Invention (now simply known as the Mothers) were scheduled to play four shows at Bill Graham's Fillmore East—New York's legendary temple of rock. When John Lennon expressed his great admiration for Frank, as an innovative bandleader who was "trying to do something different," Smith immediately invited John along to join him.

Frank and his crew of long-haired weirdo/musical virtuosos had been holed up at One Fifth, a favorite haunt of touring rock stars and itinerant bohemians of the day. According to Barry Miles, Frank was "absolutely deadpan" when he opened the door to his hotel room to find Smith with Lennon and Ono in tow.

If Cal Schenkel's album cover art to *We're Only in It for the Money* (a brutal and hilarious parody of *Sergeant Pepper's*) was any indication of Zappa's feeling toward the Beatles' music and myth, then he clearly had some reservations about the Fab Four. On the other hand, Lennon was quite impressed with Frank. As he said later that day on Smith's radio show: "I expected a sort of grubby maniac with women all over the place, you know—sitting on the toilet."

Frank, it turned out, was relieved as well. Apparently, he feared John and Yoko might be nothing more than "a couple of nude freaks." While Lennon respected Zappa, Ono, a veteran of New York's avant-garde scene, showed only a modicum of

admiration for the mad maestro. In turn, Frank steered clear of Yoko, having almost
no direct interaction with her at all.

Zappa's latest version of the Mothers featured the vocal gymnastics and wacky
stage antics of Flo and Eddie—better known as Howard Kaylan and Mark Vollman,
the former lead singers of the Turtles. In his 2016 memoir *Shell Shocked*, Kaylan
recalled the awkward atmosphere of the informal meeting between two of rock's
most brilliant minds. Sometime around two in the afternoon, John and Yoko arrived at Frank's East Village hotel room, when "Zappa started noodling on an un-
plugged Strat, searching for something that he and John could jam to at the show
later that night." Both Lennon and Ono appeared nervous, while Zappa remained
aloof. When John called for some weed, Howard enthusiastically responded, despite
Zappa's sternly enforced antidrug policy. Kaylan quickly "fetched [his] new hash pipe
and some pot." Frank, true to form, "politely declined." But Howard was euphoric to
get stoned with the former Beatle. "I don't think I've ever been that high in my life.
I was sailing," he recalled.

Lennon had plenty of reasons to be nervous after crossing paths with Kaylan
and Vollmer again, as there had been some ugly history between the Turtles and the
Beatles one night in 1967 at the Speakeasy, a popular club in "swinging" London.
Following the tremendous success of "Happy Together" (and their recent back-to-
back appearances on Johnny Carson's *Tonight Show* and *The Ed Sullivan Show*), the
Turtles' meteoric hit shoved "Penny Lane" out of the *Billboard* No. 1 slot, and it continued to hold steady throughout late March and the first half of April. Nonetheless,
Paul McCartney adored the Turtles' perky number with its sing-along chorus of bah-
bah-bahs, while a drunk and rather snide John Lennon openly resented this crew of
look-alike American upstarts. He quickly zeroed in on the band's most vulnerable
member, rhythm guitarist Jim Tucker. Lennon soon eviscerated poor "Tucko" as he
called him, attacking his ill-fitting suit and imitative hair style until the bewildered
Turtle finally snapped, calling Lennon "a total shit" and openly regretting that he'd
ever met him. Tucker, it turned out, had been so deeply traumatized by his one-time
hero that following the Turtles' English tour, he flew home and abruptly quit the
music business. John never forgot his nasty attack on ol' "Tucko," and upon seeing
Flo and Eddie again, managed a brief but limp apology.

That night, John and Yoko joined Zappa and his band for a loose and somewhat confounding jam. It was nearly 2 a.m. Sunday morning when the Mothers
finished their third encore of the night, and the house lights suddenly went black.

Just moments before taking center stage at the legendary Fillmore East, Lennon/Ono were suddenly overcome with overwhelming anxiety at the thought of facing a live audience again. But thankfully, their crippling case of stage fright was placated by a couple lines of cocaine. When the lights came up again, the crowd went wild upon recognizing Zappa's special guests. Frank stood glowering at everyone like a substitute teacher babysitting a room full of juvenile delinquents.

Dressed completely in white, John approached the microphone and greeted the crowd: "Just like to say hello. It's wonderful to be here," while Yoko smiled, repeatedly thrusting peace signs in the air. Zappa handed Lennon his trusty Gibson SG and helped set the volume and tone controls on the amp for him while the audience screamed and cheered.

"Sit down and cool it for a minute so we can hear what we're gonna do," Frank admonished the crowd, while instructing his band who later admitted they had "no idea what's about to happen." Zappa informed his musicians that the first song would be in the key of A-minor, "and it's not standard blues changes," he added. John was in good voice as he delivered "Well," an old standard by Walter Ward that the Beatles often sang back in their Cavern Club days.

Flo and Eddie added lilting harmonies while Yoko began to cry like a wounded cat, which worked in an abstract sort of way while John pled, "You know I love you, please don't go. . . ." Meanwhile Zappa wrestled a series of intricate riffs from a hollow-body Gibson as he intermittently conducted the band with a wave of his right arm. Wild as the Mothers were, they were disciplined musicians who could play virtually any style of music, from doo-wop to free jazz.

Again, one must consider Ono's unconventional mode of expression. If such startling sounds had been created on violin, saxophone, electric guitar, or any instrument other than the human voice—the most personal instrument of all—would the public have responded to her in such a visceral fashion? After all, Captain Beefheart was venerated for squeaking, squawking, and screeching atonally, whether with his five-octave-range voice or any variety of reed instruments he put in his mouth. Although far from mainstream until the early 1980s, the legendary Don Van Vliet (as he was known at home) tended to be more ignored than reviled.

As Yoko repeatedly growled "Please don't go!" aspects of John Coltrane, Albert Ayler, and Pharoah Sanders' free-jazz extrapolations could be heard in her delivery. Flo and Eddie's swooping vocals evoked a ghostly wind as Yoko chattered like the death rattle of the soul escaping the body, taking the banal breakup plea of "Please

Don't Go" to a completely different level than perhaps even the musicians themselves were aware of.

Conducting the band, Zappa attempted to pull together a tight, crisp ending to their loose, bluesy jam, when John, in jest, began imitating Frank's musical gestures. Suddenly Flo and Eddie's vocals turned primal (something both John and Yoko could relate to), barking and screaming as Lennon gleefully conducted the sonic mayhem. Don Preston conjured a whooshing, swirling sound from his keyboards, as Zappa once more took over conducting duties, but this time employing his middle finger as the voices turned into a mad monkey house of screams and yelps. Suddenly Lennon began to leap in the air, scissor kicking his skinny legs, as Frank led the band into the Mothers' "King Kong" while Don Preston played the song's distinctive descending riff. Chewing gum (as he often did on stage), Lennon appeared somewhat clueless, watching Frank for a cue. Meanwhile his wife, who followed no form of protocol when jamming with rock musicians, unleashed a whirlwind of cryptic vocalese.

Although Yoko received a more rigorous classical musical training in her youth than most of the musicians that she shared a stage with that night, she was first and foremost a performance artist, which meant she was expected to be, at the very least, "unpredictable." Ono defiantly ignored the structure of whatever pop songs and blues tunes she freely improvised over. Refusing to acknowledge such arbitrary boundaries, she was consistently accused by audiences and musicians alike for "ruining" the music.

Listening back nearly fifty years later with fresh (post-punk and post–free jazz) ears, this much-maligned jam now seems more mischievous and playful beyond the sum of its inherent flaws. Frank, as Howard Kaylan recalled, "played some amazing licks that Lennon couldn't keep up with." Kaylan began improvising lyrics off the top of his head, which would earn him a writing credit with John on the track that later became known as "Scumbag" when it was released on *Some Time in New York City*. Zappa facetiously invited the audience to sing along: "Right on, brothers and sisters, let's hear it for the scumbags!" Frank then began chanting "Scumbag," as he thrust both of his middle fingers into the air while Kaylan and Vollman improvised dance steps and the Mothers' brilliant multi-instrumentalist, Ian Underwood, shredded his soprano sax. John joined in the madness, repeatedly crowing "Scumbag baby, Scumbag," as Yoko shrieked and shook her hips with an ammo belt loosely draped around her waist, until finally climbing into a large bag from which she peered out at the audience.

Perhaps the crowd anticipated something more "meaningful" from the meeting of the mad maestro and counterculture's most creative couple than a nonsensical noise jam with a dash of performance art. It's easy to understand why the audience felt disappointed at the time, dismissing John and Yoko's performance as a load of narcissistic bullshit. But within the frantic groove and burbling keyboards and the continuous chant of "Scumbag," you can hear the influence Lennon/Ono had on the wacky new wave band the B-52s.

Years later, the deluge of disparaging comments coming from YouTube's peanut gallery were both humorous and brutal. One writer compared Ono's vocals to "beating a dolphin with a sack of cats," while another claimed, "Yoko returned the bomb [from Japan] back to us." Ironically, Ono might have appreciated such remarks, as both animal sounds and her haunted memories of WWII have remained major inspirations throughout her career.

According to one audience member who was there that night, the performance took on mystical proportions: "When the Mothers were on, it was just another stage. With Lennon on it, the stage became something else. It became like a visitation."

"Goodnight, boys and girls," Zappa said, mocking the half-cheering, half-bewildered crowd as John knelt before his amp and unleashed a hellish barrage of feedback, melting whatever was left of the audience's brains as the band staggered offstage.

Following John and Yoko's release of *Some Time in New York City*, a discrepancy arose over the impromptu jam's songwriting credits. Lennon (or more specifically his lawyers) had taken all rights, renaming Zappa's "King Kong" (which previously appeared on the Mothers of Invention's 1968 double album, *Uncle Meat*) "Scumbag." In the end, Frank's attorneys cut a deal, sharing credits to all compositions. Still irked by John and Yoko's sense of entitlement, Zappa got his revenge twenty years later when he released an album entitled *Playground Psychotics* in 1992, which featured six minutes of feedback and Ono's supernatural shrieking, which he humorously dubbed "A Small Eternity with Yoko Ono."

As with *Live Peace in Toronto*, John and Yoko's jam with Frank Zappa and the Mothers was something of a missed opportunity. Both performances featured two of rock's greatest guitarists, the venerated "God" of the six-string, Eric Clapton (on *Live Peace*) and the virtuosic Frank Zappa. Interesting as these recordings are, they both fail to hold up to repeated listening, as they were comprised of a loosely improvised mix of oldies and blues, peppered with Yoko's primordial/avant shrieks. One must wonder if either Lennon simply didn't care or his hubris was so great that he believed (as was later said about Wall Street) he was just "too big to fail."

From Ono's perspective, there was a total lack of consideration of how to utilize her strange and singular artistic expression. A rock band was not always the best vehicle for her unusual brand of vocalese, particularly when her husband and the musicians jammed over simple blues forms or classic rock 'n' roll rhythms. As brilliant a composer and bandleader as Frank Zappa was, no one could have expected him to whip up a fresh arrangement of a Beatles song and teach it to his band with just a few hours before show time. But Zappa had years of experience in the avant-garde, while John merely dabbled in it as a way of breaking free from the limitations of the kind of pop music he played with the Beatles. One might expect Frank—an ardent fan of the French composer Edgard Varèse's dissonant *Ionizations*, which he claimed to like because it was "mean" —to have been more supportive and creative when jamming with Yoko Ono, a bona fide member of New York's legendary Fluxus Movement.

The fall of 1971 was a busy time for Lennon/Ono Inc. On Wednesday, September 8, John and Yoko made an appearance on the *Dick Cavett Show*. At one point, a nervous, chain-smoking Lennon peered into the camera and quipped, "Didn't work, did it, Arthur?" regarding his compulsive nicotine consumption and the four months he and Yoko spent in therapy. Critics and audience members alike were not charmed, complaining that Lennon/Ono essentially used Cavett's platform to blatantly hawk their new albums and films. John's *Imagine* was released the following day on September 9th.

On September 10, John and Yoko would finish recording and editing the soundtrack to their new film, *Clock*. While the session produced John's new instrumental demo, "Just Give Me Some Rock 'n' Roll" (later retitled and released as "Meat City" on Lennon's 1973 *Mind Games*), they spent the bulk of their time mixing down old outtakes from John's *Plastic Ono Band* album, including "Glad All Over," "Honey Don't," "Maybe Baby," "Not Fade Away," "Peggy Sue," and "Peggy Sue Got Married." *Clock* was shown as part of Yoko's ten-year retrospective exhibit of "unfinished paintings and sculpture" titled *This Is Not Here*, which opened in Syracuse, New York, at the Everson Museum on Saturday, October 9, 1971, John's thirty-first birthday. A television special titled *John and Yoko in Syracuse, New York* was filmed and broadcast the following spring on May 11, 1972. Despite it being John's party, he gave away silver zodiac necklaces to a slew of famous guests said to include Ringo, Andy Warhol, Frank Zappa, Bob Dylan, John Cage, and Phil Spector.

Speaking freely in an interview on October 8, the day before the opening, to promote her exhibit at the Everson, Yoko inadvertently made herself a target for ridicule once more. Whether inspired by Joseph Beuys, the former German Luftwaffe pilot turned conceptual artist who posed the idea that "everyone is an artist," or just making a naïve sentiment, it quickly backfired. "In this show," she stated, "I'd like to prove you don't need talent to be an artist. Artist is just a frame of mind. Anybody can be an artist. Anybody can communicate if they're desperate enough."

Thousands of Ono's detractors had a field day with her statement. Without realizing it, Yoko had reaffirmed every criticism of her art and music when she said, "Anybody can be an artist"— "as long as they were married to a Beatle" was certain to have followed that flippant remark.

While many people hated and ridiculed Yoko, Peter Case found inspiration in her art. "In October 1971, I hitchhiked [from Buffalo] to Syracuse, New York, to see Yoko's 'This Is Not Here' at the Everson Museum. I missed the opening by a day but saw the show. I came out of the museum feeling very refreshed, hopeful, and alive. I bought a copy of *Grapefruit* and from then on followed Yoko's work just about as avidly as I did John's."

In his 1970 *Esquire* article with the sensationalist (read: sexist and racist) title *John Rennon's Excrusive Gloupie*, journalist Charles McCarry claimed it was "John's love for Yoko," not her art, film, or mind-bending vocals, that "has made her famous . . . [and] fame has made them mad."

"Celebrity really did become her medium . . . as it was for Andy Warhol," wrote Michael Kimmelman in the *New York Times* years later for the opening of *Yes—* Ono's one-woman retrospective exhibit at the Japan Society in October 2000. While Kimmelman recognized Yoko as "a wry and gentle concept artist who was ahead of her time," particularly appreciating her films, the critic had no stomach for her often nerve-wracking sonic explorations. "The music is unbearable, and let's leave it at that," he groused.

Two days later, on October 11, 1971, Lennon's new single, "Imagine" was released in America. Embracing the Greenwich Village/bohemian lifestyle, John and Yoko would move into their Bank Street apartment.

"It's the best place to live in the world," John proclaimed. "Everybody cycles around the Village," Lennon said. "Dylan goes on his [bike] all the time. . . . Nobody ever recognizes him. I can't wait to get on mine."

With a recharged sense of optimism, Lennon composed his sing-along anthem "Happy Xmas (War Is Over)." On Tuesday, October 28, with Spector producing, John and a handful of guitarists, including veteran session player Hugh McCracken, who'd recently loaned his chops to Paul's sophomore release, *Ram*; pianist Nicky Hopkins; and drummer Jim Keltner all met in Manhattan at the Record Plant to lay down the song's rhythm tracks. Klaus Voormann, whose flight from Germany had been delayed, would arrive the following day to overdub his bass on John's song and help Yoko record an updated version of her "Listen, the Snow is Falling." An earlier take of the song had provided the shining moment on their self-indulgent *Wedding Album*—which was less about music and more about elaborate packaging (a treasure trove of photos, press clippings, and inky sketches by John, along with a copy of their marriage certificate, a photo of the wedding cake, and a plastic bag with the word *Bagism* printed on it). John's sweet-soul guitar riffs perfectly frame Yoko's heartfelt vocal. Sadly, Ono's soft, breathy delivery that opens and closes the original version was dropped, cutting the song down to 3:11, in the thin hope of garnering "Listen, the Snow Is Falling" some radio play.

Later sung by Naomi Yang, bassist with Boston indie-rockers Galaxie 500, on their 1990 album *This Is Our Music*, Galaxie 500's treatment of "Listen, the Snow Is Falling" evokes the early Velvet Underground with Nico, as the gentle atmosphere of the song explodes into a charging rhythm, driven by the drums and a two-chord repetitive guitar vamp, building into a wailing coda by guitarist Dean Wareham.

Released on December 1, 1971, "Happy Xmas (War Is Over)" glowed with love and hope in the face of a world stricken by war and hunger. Despite having written and sung the feel-good single of the season, Lennon once more skewered his old partner, McCartney, three days later in a *Melody Maker* interview. Their ongoing tit-for-tat rift flared once more after John heard "Too Many People" from *Ram*, in which Paul gently nagged, "You took your lucky break and broke it in two, now what can be done for you?" Lennon immediately fired back with the scurrilous "How Do You Sleep?" which quickly balanced out the loftier sentiments of his utopian hymn, "Imagine."

As a houseguest at Tittenhurst Park during the recording sessions for *Imagine*, Felix Dennis, one of the editors of *Oz* magazine, recalled the creative process of "How Do You Sleep?" While the song was initially funny, Felix felt that John, spurred on by Yoko, had taken the joke too far. Many of the musicians involved began feeling uneasy after hearing the scathing lyrics directed at Paul. As Dennis recalled, "Ringo [who didn't play drums on the track] was getting more and more upset by this," until he finally spoke up, saying, "That's enough John, [there's no need] to be so brutal." Dennis watched uncomfortably as Yoko gleefully scribbled down a flurry of lyrics and raced into the studio "waving a piece of paper [to] show John she had an idea."

A second song on *Imagine* also took aim at Paul, the mocking "Crippled Inside," which contained the stinging lyric: "One thing you can't hide, is when you're crippled inside," sung to an old-timey tune in a similar style to Paul's "Honey Pie" and "Lady Madonna"—songs that John once ridiculed as "Granny music."

"I was just using my resentment towards Paul to write a song," John shrugged. While Lennon played hardball with McCartney (dismissing him as nothing more than "pizza and fairytales"), such biting sarcasm seemed petty, beneath the utopian "dream weaver," as he previously dubbed himself in "God."

"Paul must have been some sort of authority in Lennon's life because you don't take the piss out of somebody that isn't a figure of authority," Dennis reckoned. "They were taking the piss out of the headmaster. . . . [There was] a lot of giggling, a lot of laughter. . . . It was a bit of a shame he ever let it out," Dennis said, believing John would have been better off if he'd left "How Do You Sleep?" "in the vaults for posterity."

"I always find myself wanting to excuse John's behavior just because I loved him," McCartney told Barry Miles. "He's a naughty child. I think he was a sod to hurt me. . . . He knew exactly what he was doing."

After months of reliving his traumatic past in torturous sessions with Arthur Janov, the grueling ordeal of primal scream therapy seemed to have had little or no effect whatsoever on John's emotional well-being. He remained terribly insecure, constantly needing to reaffirm his every accomplishment and innovation. As the former leader of the world's most popular band, John Lennon had nothing to prove to anyone (but himself) and could easily have remained above such self-humiliating public displays of malevolence.

"Do I contradict myself?" the great nineteenth-century bard Walt Whitman once wrote, "Very well, then, I contradict myself; I am large—I contain multitudes." Apparently, John Lennon did as well.

Whether the public considered them revolutionaries or sellouts, Lennon/Ono flew to Ann Arbor on Thursday, December 9, 1971, to loan their cultural clout to a rally aiming to free John Sinclair, a poet and manager of Detroit's radical rock band MC5. Sinclair had been found guilty and faced an extremely harsh ten-year prison sentence for selling two marijuana joints to an undercover agent. Other high-profile luminaries scheduled to appear included beat poet Allen Ginsberg, Black Panther Bobby Seale, and Yippie instigator Jerry Rubin (who convinced John and Yoko to appear at the concert), along with Stevie Wonder, who soon would start addressing the problems faced by Black America on his 1973 masterpiece *Innervisions*. Backstage before the show, John jammed with legendary protest singer Phil Ochs on his "Chords of Fame." This was Lennon's first public acoustic set since playing skiffle with his old mates, the Quarrymen, back in Liverpool. Lennon's brief performance was comprised of new political material—"Attica State," "Luck of the Irish," and the bluesy "John Sinclair," which Lennon had written in honor of the marijuana martyr, while Yoko sang her yearning ode, "Sisters O Sisters." The next day the *Detroit News* ran a headline complaining that "Lennon Let His Followers Down." Following Stevie Wonder with a fifteen-minute acoustic set of four short songs (and none of them old, familiar Beatle hits) undoubtedly inspired the negative review.

Jeff Alder, a young musician in the crowd that night, claimed he "was disappointed by John and Yoko's 'street art' performance . . . [and witnessing] the great Beatle jamming with Jerry Rubin playing bongos or congas or something he had no idea how to play, along with David Peel and the freakin' lousy Lower East Side." Yet, at the same time, Adler was deeply "impressed that John came to support our guy. . . . Regardless of any critiques . . . it *worked*."

"There weren't too many people in prison with marijuana charges at the time," John Sinclair imparted. "So, what was the big deal? It was all right for Thomas Jefferson to grow marijuana in Virginia. Sadly, dope is a product. When they realized how popular it was, it turned into this big fight over who was going to control the sales. Either they will put you in jail for it, or they will make you buy it."

"[But] some good things came out of that terrible mess," Sinclair reckoned, referring to his entrapment. "They held that big rally and John Lennon got me out of prison. I liked the Beatles a lot before I got to know him, but I mean, that was heaven-sent!"

Sadly, the film entitled *Ten for Two*, documenting the event, was not released until seventeen years later in 1989. Lennon, who had broken a string during his set, was apparently unhappy with his flawed performance.

* * *

On Christmas day, 1971, Radio Luxembourg voted Lennon's *Imagine* the "Album of the Year." Two years earlier (almost to the day) a full-page advertisement had appeared in the Sunday *New York Times* on December 27, 1969, announcing "War is Over if You Want It." Looking for a simple and direct way to explain the motivation behind their peace campaign, John surprisingly cited Henry Ford as his inspiration, claiming the controversial automotive tycoon "knew how to sell cars by advertising." "Yoko and I are just one big advertising campaign," he told Jann Wenner. "It may make people laugh, but it may make them think too. Really, we're just Mr. and Mrs. Peace."

Perhaps George Harrison's explanation for the contradiction in the Beatles' behavior was a bit more to the point: "We're all talking about peace and love, but really, we're not feeling peaceful at all."

By September 1972, Lennon/Ono's crusade to save the world bordered on parody when they appeared on the annual *Jerry Lewis Labor Day Telethon* for muscular dystrophy. In a totally deadpan introduction, Lewis introduced Lennon/Ono as "two of the most unusual people in all the world, and I don't mean just in the world of entertainment. They fit no patterns, meet no standards, except the standards of excellence." (Some might claim the madcap host was being gratuitous regarding Yoko's limited ability as a pop singer.) While Ono's performance was both sincere and enthusiastic, it was clearly amateurish when compared to John's "Imagine."

As a concept/performance artist, Yoko lacked the basic vocal skills and timing expected of any pop singer. This is not to say she didn't produce some stunning musical moments throughout her career, but the more she relied on traditional Western music forms, the less daring her music became. While Ono's message of peace and equality in "Now or Never" was clear, her shaky vocal delivery ultimately caused the song to fall upon deaf ears.

Next up was Lennon's "Give Peace a Chance." Dispensing with the various controversial lyrics within the song's free-associative proto-rap verses, Elephant's Memory repeated the song's chorus *ad nauseam* as John sang, "All we are saying is give peace a chance!" peppered with shouts of "Send your money, money, money, money," in time to the band's rhythm. "C'mon, sing!" John yelled at the audience, while he and Yoko chanted a litany of slogans from "No more war!" to "Save the children" to "Peace for everybody!" to "Vote! Vote! Vote!" Adding to the surrealism of the moment, Jerry Lewis leapt into the fray, fingering an inaudible pocket trumpet (similar to the instrument jazz trumpeter Don Cherry played with the Ornette Coleman Quartet).

While still the same song (and employed for a righteous purpose), this was ultimately a toothless version of "Give Peace a Chance." It was many years and miles from the Montreal hotel room where Lennon/Ono once led a gaggle of counterculture revolutionaries, from Allen Ginsberg and Timothy Leary to television's hilarious bad boys, the Smothers Brothers, in a sing-along that despite its ragged "lefty" aesthetic rose to No. 14 on the *Billboard* charts.

Perhaps Ono felt she stood a better chance of getting her message of feminism and world peace across by diluting the intensity of her delivery, which usually shocked and alienated anyone who came within earshot. But the deck had been stacked against her from the beginning as the meddling witch responsible for breaking up both Lennon's band and marriage. Sadly, few of John's fans ever seem to consider his role in their fateful union.

In sharing and doing everything together, Lennon/Ono presented their relationship to the world as one of the great loves (or mergers, as the title "Lennon/Ono" to Betty Rollin's *Look* magazine article implied) of the Twentieth Century. Lennon often seemed puzzled, adversarial, and bitter when the press and public failed to celebrate their unique union as anything short of magnificent. But in insisting that Yoko remain beside him 24/7 throughout the recording of the final Beatle albums, whether at home, onstage, or in the studio, one must wonder if Lennon's unquenchable need for love wasn't born out of desperate codependence brought on by childhood trauma more than an eternal spring of unbridled joy and affection.

"John was not with his mother very much when he was a child," Yoko explained to Barbara Graustark in *Rolling Stone* in the months following Lennon's shocking murder. "He was with me twenty-four hours a day, so maybe I resolved his need for that kind of closeness." On the other hand, John "was a very independent guy," Yoko added. "He *chose* to be with me," she said, illuminating the dynamic behind their relationship. "And that goes with me, too. I did not need him, but I *chose* to be with him."

* * *

A truth seeker, albeit with little patience and a short attention span at times, John Lennon repeatedly and whole-heartedly embraced nearly every form of self-improvement available, from meditation and diet to whatever drugs were in vogue, in hopes of attaining a higher perspective. But once he got the message, he inevitably rejected the teacher, doctor, or guru who delivered it, as they quickly came to represent authority figures to him. Whether taking acid, meditating, chanting Hare Krishna, taking heroin, following a macrobiotic diet, submitting to the grueling routine of primal scream therapy, or spouting feminist and revolutionary views after emigrating to New York City, John and Yoko briefly tried them all on for size. But their most lasting and significant effort, which still endures to this day, is their resolute attitude toward waging peace, no matter how flawed or foolish they may have appeared.

On December 8, 2018, the thirty-eighth anniversary of Lennon's assassination, his widow took to Twitter with yet another simple but inspirational message: "Everything you think and do affects our society," Yoko said. "So, think peace. Start with that."

BIBLIOGRAPHY

Books

Badman, Keith—The Beatles: Off the Record—Outrageous Opinions & Unrehearsed Interviews—Omnibus Press, London, UK, 2000

Baird, Julia—Imagine This—Hodder Stoughton, London, UK, 2007

Bangs, Lester—Psychotic Reactions & Carburetor Dung—Vintage Books, New York, NY, 1988

Beram, Nell, Boriss—Krimsky, Carolyn—Yoko Ono: Collector of Skies—Amulet Books, New York, NY, 2013

Blake, Mark, Mojo, the Editors of—Dylan: Visions, Portraits & Back Pages—DK, London, UK, 2005

Boyd, Pattie—Wonderful Tonight: George Harrison, Eric Clapton and Me—Three Rivers Press, New York, NY, 2007

Brown, Mick—Tearing Down the Wall of Sound: The Rise and Fall of Phil Spector—Alfred A. Knopf, New York, NY, 2007

Carlin, Peter Ames—Paul McCartney: A Life—Touchstone Books, New York, NY, 2009

Cott, Jonathan, Doudna, Christine—The Ballad of John and Yoko—Doubleday/Dolphin, Garden City, NY, 1982

Cott, Jonathan—Days That I'll Remember: Spending Time with John Lennon and Yoko Ono—Doubleday, New York, NY, 2013

Cott, Jonathan—Dylan—Doubleday/Rolling Stone Press, Garden City, NY, 1984

Courrier, Kevin—Randy Newman's American Dreams—ECW Press, Toronto, Ontario, Canada, 2005

DeCurtis, Anthony—Rocking My Life Away—Duke University, Durham, NC, 1998

Doggett, Peter—You Never Give Me Your Money: The Beatles After the Breakup—Harper Paperbacks, New York, NY, 2009

Goldman, Albert—The Many Lives of John Lennon—William Morrow and Company Inc., New York, NY, 1988

Goswami, Satsvarupa Dasa—Prabhupada—The Bhaktivedanta Book Trust, Los Angeles, California, 1983

Harrison, Olivia—George Harrison: Living in the Material World—Abrams, New York, NY, 2011

Herzogenrath, Wulf & Hansen, Dorothy (editors)– The Art of John Lennon: Drawings, Performances, Films—Cantz Verlag, Ostfildern, Germany, 1995

Hilburn, Robert—Cornflakes with John Lennon and Other Tales from a Rock 'n' Roll Life—Rodale Books, New York, NY, 2009

Janov PhD, Arthur—The Primal Scream—Perigee Books, New York, NY, 1980

Kaukonen, Jorma—Been So Long: My Life and Music—St. Martin's Press, New York, NY, 2018

Kaylan, Howard, Tamarkin, Jeff—Shell Shocked: My Life with the Turtles—Backbeat Books, Montclair, New Jersey, 2013

Kostelanetz, Richard—A Dictionary of the Avant Gardes—a cappella books, Pennington, NJ, 1993

Liebovitz, Annie—At Work—Random House, New York, 2008

Leitch, Donovan—The Autobiography of Donovan: The Hurdy Gurdy Man—St. Martin's Press, New York, NY, 2005

Litweiler, John—Ornette Coleman: A Harmolodic Life—William Morrow & Co., New York, NY, 1992

MacDonald, Bruno—Pink Floyd: Through the Eyes of the Band, its Fans, Friends and Foes—Da Capo Press, New York, NY, 1997

MacDonald, Ian—Revolution in the Head: The Beatles' Records and the Sixties—Chicago Review Press, Chicago, Illinois, 2007

McRae, Barry—Ornette Coleman—Apollo Press Ltd., London, UK, 1988

Miles, Barry—Paul McCartney: Many Years Ago—Henry Holt, New York, NY, 1997

Miles, Barry—Zappa: A Biography—Grove Press, New York, NY, 2004

Palmer, Robert—Blues & Chaos: The Music Writings of Robert Palmer—Scribner, New York, NY, 2009

Partridge, Elizabeth—John Lennon: All I Want Is the Truth—Viking, New York, NY, 2005

Rivelli, Pauline & Levin, Robert—The Rock Giants—The World Publishing Company, New York, NY, and Cleveland, OH, 1970

Schaffner, Nicholas—The Beatles Forever—MJF Books, New York, NY, 1978

Schaffner, Nicholas—The British Invasion—McGraw-Hill Books, New York, NY, 1983

Sheff, David—All We Are Saying: The Last Major Interview with John Lennon and
    Yoko Ono—St. Martin's Griffin, New York, 2010

Spizer, Bruce—The Beatles: Solo on Apple Records—498 Productions, New
    Orleans, LA, 2005

Thompson, Dave—Phil Spector: Wall of Pain—Omnibus Press, London, UK,
    2010

Thomson, Graeme—George Harrison: Behind the Locked Door—Omnibus Press,
    London, UK, 2013

Toop, David—Into the Maelstrom: Music, Improvisation and the Dream of
    Freedom: Before 1970—Bloomsbury, New York, NY, 2016

Turner, Steve—The Beatles: A Hard Day's Write—The Stories Behind Every
    Song—Carlton Books Limited, 1994

Wenner, Jann—Lennon Remembers: The Rolling Stone Interviews—Fawcett
    Popular Library, New York, NY, 1972

Wenner, Jann—Phil Spector—The Rolling Stone Interviews Vol. 1—Straight
    Arrow Publishing/Warner Paperback Library, New York, NY, 1969

Articles

Calio, Jim—People magazine: Yoko Ono's Ex-Husband, Tony Cox, Reveals His
    Strange Life Since Fleeing with Their Daughter 14 Years Ago—February 03,
    1986 12:00 p.m: https://people.com/archive/yoko-onos-ex-husband-
    tony-cox-reveals-his-strange-life-since-fleeing-with-their-daughter-14-
    years-ago-vol-25-no-5/

Evans, Max—Express: John Lennon made desperate bid to boost Yoko Ono's music
    career, new letter reveals—Mon, Oct 13, 2014,—16:15 p.m.

Glenn, Allen—The Ann Arbor Chronicle: The Day a Beatle Came to Town

John Lennon at the John Sinclair Freedom Rally in Ann Arbor https://
    annarborchronicle.com/2009/12/27/the-day-a-beatle-came-to-town/index.
    html

Gotthardt, Alexxa—Yoko Ono's 5 Most Iconic Works https://www.artsy.net/article/
    artsy-editorial-yoko-onos-5-iconic-works?fbclid=IwAR2WbjNbGN-T3ehICrE
    paaRPmGx0EQQIVFckJ5bMQZoQF1lpXML576E1GKg

Hopkins, Jerry—Rolling Stone: "The Primal Doctor" Arthur Janov treats neurosis
    with screams and counts John Lennon among his fans—February 18, 1971
    https://www.rollingstone.com/culture/culture-news/the-primal-doctor-82117/

McCarry, Charles—Esquire magazine: John Rennon's Excrusive Gloupie—
December 1, 1970 https://classic.esquire.com/article/1970/12/1/
john-rennons-excrusive-gloupie

Meth, Clifford, The Aquarian: Alan White interview—June 5, 2019 https://
www.theaquarian.com/2019/06/05/interview-with-alan-white-
of-yes/?fbclid=IwAR2oAoFhW7qFn3RazGZYBgpzmTFHxuow
2K_waqNQ90HImRsiU65vBMgGjZY

Palmer, Robert—The New York Times: The Real Way to Remember John
Lennon—December 9, 1981

Sommer, Tim—Sag Harbor Express: Historical Society Exhibit Captures Spirit of
the 60s Aug 5, 2015 https://sagharborexpress.com/east-hampton-historical-
society-exhibit-captures-lennon-ono-the-spirit-of-the-60s__trashed/

Swed, Mark—A dean of Japanese music talks boundaries, John Cage and life with
Yoko Ono, Los Angeles Times, May 15, 2015—https://www.latimes.com/
entertainment/arts/la-ca-cm-toshi-ichiyanagi-profile-20150517-column.html

Sites

beatlesbible.com—https://www.beatlesbible.com/people/john-lennon/songs/
instant-karma/

https://archive.vn/20130504223932/http://www.cambridge-news.co.uk/
News/How-John-Lennon-turned-to-Cambridge-for-life-after-The-Beatles.
htm#selection-1268.0-1419.62

dangerousminds.net—John Lennon's School Detention Sheets
Go Up For Sale-https://dangerousminds.net/comments/
john_lennons_school_detention_sheets_up_for_sale

feelnumb.com—http://www.feelnumb.com/2010/01/24/adolf-hitler-did-not-make-
the-cut-on-the-beatles-sgt-pepper-album-cover/#lightbox/0/

hhhhappy.com—Richard Lush interview: https://hhhhappy.com/what-was-it-
like-to-record-with-lennon-and-mccartney-a-conversation-with-sgt-pepper-
sound-engineer-richard-lush/?fbclid=IwAR19NE-_1fuokYG7pymvJsAQTs4_
F982ybfF10P6qSDkgDC-LHtPUZoRGVs

soundcloud.com—Yoko Ono Lennon & Sean Lennon on WNYC 93.9FM—
'Spinning On Air' with David Garland. Mother's Day 13 May 2012 https://
soundcloud.com/yokoono/wnyc-spinning-on-air-yoko-sean-mothers-day

tittenhurstblogspot.com—Interview with Peter McCabe and Robert Schonfeld on September 5, 1971 at the St. Regis Hotel http://tittenhurstlennon.blogspot.com/2009/08/john-lennon-st-regis-hotel-room.html

Youtube

Henry Flynt in New York—https://vimeo.com/benjaminpiekut

John Lennon talks about the Beatles *Abbey Road* album track by track—https://www.youtube.com/watch?v=aLfZTBJylEY

Brian May—"God"—https://www.youtube.com/watch?v=0SKoMniFuAc

John Sinclair—Ten for Two—https://www.indiewire.com/2011/12/why-ten-for-two-is-the-john-lennon-yoko-ono-music-doc-you-havent-seen-50735/

ACKNOWLEDGMENTS

A big warm thank you to everyone I interviewed for *Hold On World* (whether in person, on the phone, or by email). They include:

Ian Anderson (Vocalist, flautist—Jethro Tull)

Michael Blair (Percussionist—Tom Waits, Elvis Costello)

DJ Bonebrake (Drummer, mallet percussionist—X)

Peter Case (Singer/songwriter, guitarist)

Nels Cline (Guitarist—Wilco, Plastic Ono Band)

Ornette Coleman (Free-jazz saxophonist, cosmic philosopher)

Dave Dreiwitz (Bassist—Ween)

Marvin Etzioni (Songwriter/producer/founding member—Lone Justice)

Bill Frisell (Guitarist, devoted interpreter of Lennon and Beatles' music)

Louise Harrison (Sister of George Harrison)

Jorma Kaukonen (Guitarist, singer, and founding member—Jefferson Airplane)

Al Kooper (Keyboardist/producer, founder of Blood, Sweat and Tears)

Gary Lucas (Guitarist—Captain Beefheart, Jeff Buckley)

Thollem McDonas (Pianist/composer)

Evan Parker (Saxophonist)

Mary Maria Parks (Saxophonist/wife of Albert Ayler)

Barry Reynolds (Guitarist—Marianne Faithful)

Marc Ribot (Guitarist—Tom Waits, Elvis Costello)

Brian Ritchie (Bassist—Violent Femmes)

Elliott Sharp (Guitarist, multi-instrumentalist, composer)

Steve Shelley (Drummer—Sonic Youth, Plastic Ono Band)

John Sinclair (Poet, manager of the MC5)

Benmont Tench (Keyboardist—Tom Petty and the Heartbreakers)

Bobby Whitlock (Keyboardist, guitarist—Derek and the Dominoes, Delaney and Bonnie)

Hal Willner (Producer—Lou Reed, Marianne Faithful, Lucinda Williams . . .)

And sparkling oceans of gratitude to my beautiful more-than-wife, Marilyn Cvitanic, and our funky puggle, Kooper, and massive tabby, Little Tail State Park, who listened and listened and compassionately sat through the worst of it.

Big thanks to: Betsy Israel, Jeff Hamilton, Pat Thomas, Paul Zollo, Oliver Trager, Willie Aron, Marvin Etzioni, Donald Rubenstein, Thollem McDonas, Bruce Hollihan, John S. Hall, and John Cerullo for holding on.

INDEX

Bramwell, Tony, 84, 134
Brautigan, Richard, 24–25
"Bring It on Home to Me," 107
Broken English, 98
Brower, John, 35
Brown, James, 38
Browne, Tara, 97, 150
Bruce, Lenny, 24–25, 31
Buddha, 134–35
Buddhism, 156
Burden, Chris, 163
Burroughs, William S., 66, 176
the Byrds, 11

Cage, John, 176–77; Ono, Y., and, 8, 32, 157, 159,
    186–87
Ćaleta, Tomo, 75
Camardese, Vittorio, 33
"Cambridge 1969," 26–30, 33, 172–73
Cambridge Evening News, 26
Candlestick Park, Beatles farewell concert at, 6, 36
Capitol Records, 40
Captain Beefheart, 209
Carnegie Recital Hall, 159, 187, 189–90
"Carolina in My Mind," 14
Cartier-Bresson, Henri, 68
Case, Peter, 19, 25, 61, 82–83; on Dylan and
    Lennon, John, 92–93; on "I Found Out," 87; on
    "Lost Weekend" of Lennon, John, 169; on *Plastic
    Ono Band*, 76, 102; on "Remember," 108; on *This
    is Not Here* exhibit, 213; on "Why," 168
Cavern Club, 36, 79, 209
Cavett, Dick, 9, 212
"Celluloid Heroes," 107
Cerf, Chris, 205–6
"Changing of the Guard," 130
Charles, Tommy, 143
"Chess Piece" (Ono, Y.), 164
the Chiffons, 13–14
"Chords of Fame," 216
"City Piece" (Ono, Y.), 183
Clapton, Eric, 16, 30, 144–45, 211; in Plastic Ono
    Band, 35–39, 41, 43–44
Clarkson, Lana, 16
the Clash, 10
Classic Albums: John Lennon/Plastic Ono Band, 68
Cleave, Maureen, 6, 135, 142
Clifford, Doug, 108
Cline, Nels, 37, 62, 115, 166, 173–74, 192
Clock, 212
Cobain, Kurt, 81
Cocker, Joe, 104
"Cold Turkey," 37, 39–41, 43, 61, 66, 68, 87
Cold War Kids, 117
Coleman, Ornette, 21, 157–58, 161; Ono, Y., and,
    185–92, 196
Collage, 140
Collins, Judy, 82
Coltrane, John, 21, 27, 177–78
"Come Together," 48, 65–66, 188
"Congratulations," 109
"The Continuing Story of Bungalow Bill," 1–2

Cooke, Sam, 107
Cookie, 148
Coolidge, Rita, 13–14
Cooper, Michael, 133
Costello, Elvis, 88–89
Cott, Jonathan, 21, 40, 101
country music, 11–12
Cox, Tony, 1, 5, 41–42, 44–45, 160–61
Coyne, Wayne, 26–27
Creedence Clearwater Revival, 87, 108, 175
"Crippled Inside," 215
Crowley, Alistair, 127–28
"Crying," 64
the Cure, 114
Curtis, Anthony, 115
"Cut Piece," 163

Daily Mirror, 56, 204
"Dancing with Mr. D," 127–28
Dark Horse label, 76
Dark Side of the Moon, 190–91
Daruni, Rocky, 117
Datebook, 143
The David Frost Show, 77
Davies, Hunter, 105
Davies, Ray, 107
Davis, Angela, 49, 82, 148
Davis, Miles, 21, 31, 185, 190
"A Day in the Life," 19–20, 97
"Dear God," 147–48
"Dear Prudence," 33, 119–20
Democratic Convention in Chicago, 1968, 9
Dennis, Felix, 214–15
Denver, Nigel, 142
Derek and the Dominoes, 15
The Dick Cavett Show, 25, 212
Diddley, Bo, 38
Diliberto, John, 165, 175
Dirty Mac, 30
Disc + Music Echo, 31
"Dizzy Miss Lizzy," 3, 39
Dolenz, Mickey, 34
Donegan, Lonnie, 151
Donovan, 119–20
"Don't Be Cruel," 79
"Don't Let Me Down," 79–80
Don't Look Back, 103
"Don't Pass Me By," 11
"Don't Think Twice It's Alright," 64
"Don't Worry Kyoko (Mummy's Only Looking for a
    Hand in the Snow)," 38, 41–44, 166
the Doors, 67, 144
Double Fantasy, 49, 132, 206
Douglas, Al, 31
Down Beat, 177
Drake, Pete, 11
Dreiwitz, Dave, 115, 175
Duchamp, Marcel, 163–64
Dulčić, Pave, 75
Dunbar, John, 1, 128
Dylan, Bob, 16, 19, 21, 97, 124–25, 151; the Beatles
    and, 64, 91–92, 137–39; the Bible and, 130;

Hare Krishna: mantra and chant, 14, 46–47, 78, 85–86, 135, 218; movement and philosophy, 17, 84–86, 132
Hare Krishna Maha Mantra, 135
"Hare Krishna Mantra," 86
Harrison, George, 5, 7, 9, 12, 36; on the Beatles, 17, 126–27, 139, 217; *Benefit Concert for Bangladesh* by, 84, 144; childhood of, 97–98; Dark Horse label of, 76; Dylan and, 92; on "Greenfield Morning," 184; Hare Krishna and, 84–86, 132, 135; *I Ching* and, 130; at "Instant Karma!" recording session, 45, 50; on Lead Belly, 93; Lennon, John, and, 14–16, 24, 42–43, 46, 69, 78, 84, 86–87, 96–97, 109, 132, 135, 140, 152, 205; on Lennon, John, and McCartney, 42, 86–87, 205; on Lennon, John, and Ono, Y., 42; on Lord Krishna, 13–14, 17, 85–86; on Ono, Y., 84; on Orbison, 150; in Plastic Ono Band, 35, 43–44, 140; Preston, B., and, 144–45; Shankar on, 43; Shyamsundar and, 85; Spector and, 46–47, 51; Starr and, 12; transcendental meditation and, 13, 85; *White Album* sessions, 130, 205. *See also All Things Must Pass*
Hart, Bobby, 34
"Have a Marijuana," 77
Havens, Richie, 99, 102
"Have You Seen Your Mother Baby, Standing in the Shadows," 67
"Heartbreak Hotel," 123
heavy metal music, 66
Hell's Angels, 73
Help! (film), 2–3
"Help" (song), 64
"Helter Skelter," 10, 19, 66, 197
Hendra, Tony, 205–6
Hendrix, Jimi, 30, 33, 174
"Her Majesty," 136
"He's So Fine," 13–14
"Highway 61 Revisited," 38
Hilburn, Robert, 46, 69, 169
Hinduism, 13
Hirohito (emperor), 156
Hiroshima bombing, 156, 183
Hitler, Adolf, 63, 133
Hoffman, Abbie, 73
"Hold On," 78–80
Honda, Yuka C., 174
"Honey Don't," 79
Hooker, John Lee, 38
Hopkins, Jerry, 56–57, 76
Hopkins, Nicky, 35, 47
"Hound Dog," 79
Howard, Harlan, 70
"How Do You Sleep?," 86, 177, 204, 214–15
How I Won the War, 201
Hoyland, John, 96
Hunter, Meredith, Jr., 73
"Hymn 43," 144

"I Am the Walrus," 32, 61, 65, 74
I Ching, 129–30, 132
Ichiyanagi, Toshi, 5, 157, 159–60

"I'd Have You Anytime," 16
"I Don't Wanna Be a Soldier," 98
"I Don't Want to Talk About It," 147
"I Feel Fine," 29–30
"If Not for You," 16
"I Found Out," 81–84, 86–89, 115, 152, 172, 183
"I'll Cry Instead," 2
"I'll Get You in the End," 2
Imaginary Landscape No. 4 for Twelve Radios, 32
Imagine (album), 49, 75–76, 98, 139–40, 151–52, 204, 215–16
"Imagine" (song), 21–22, 82, 139, 204, 212–13, 217
"I'm a Loser," 92
"I'm Only Sleeping," 6, 24
"I'm So Tired," 19, 88, 119, 162
"I'm the Greatest," 12
Indica Gallery, 1–2, 128, 163
Industrial music, 195
In His Own Write (Lennon, John), 2–3, 91
"In My Life," 65
Innervisions, 216
"Instant Karma!," 44–45, 49–51, 61, 68, 81–82
Ionizations, 212
Isle of Wight Festival, 1969, 16
"Isn't It a Pity," 15–16
"Isolation," 77, 101–4, 202
"It Don't Come Easy," 12
"It's Johnny's Birthday," 109
"I Want to Hold your Hand," 102
"I Want You (She's So Heavy)," 107

Jackson, Al, Jr., 69
Jagger, Mick, 9–10, 73, 116, 127–28, 138
James Taylor, 14
Janov, Arthur, 27, 46, 106, 124; Lennon, John, and, 53–59, 61, 105, 135–36, 150, 165, 202, 212, 215; Lennon, John, Ono, Y., and, 54–59, 212; Ono, Y., and, 153, 165, 189; *The Primal Scream* by, 53–54, 56–57, 165–66
Janov, Vivian, 54–57
Jazz & Pop, 33
"Jealous Guy," 57
Jefferson Airplane, 10, 73, 76
Jenkins, Gordon, 48
Jerry Lewis Labor Day Telethon, 217
Jesus Christ, 123–24, 133–34, 136, 142–44, 159
Jesus Christ Superstar, 143
Jethro Tull, 144
JFK. *See* Kennedy, John F.
"John, John (Let's Hope for Peace)," 24, 39
John and Yoko in Syracuse, New York, 212
John Lennon Anthology, 104, 108, 151
John Lennon's Jukebox, 47
"Johnny B. Goode," 36
"John Sinclair," 152
Johnson, Robert, 38, 87
Johnson and Jonson, 80
John Wesley Harding, 124–25, 130
Jolson, Al, 63, 67
Jones, Brian, 10, 128
Jones, Davy, 34
Jones, Pauline, 105

"Julia," 19, 65, 113, 119–20, 162
"Jump into the Fire," 184
"Just Gimme Some Truth," 98

Kaiserkeller, 3
Kantner, Paul, 10
Kaukonen, Jorma, 10
Kaylan, Howard, 208–10
Kelly, Walt, 95
Keltner, Jim, 35, 76
Kennedy, Bobby, 9
Kennedy, John F. (JFK), 134
Kent State, 9
Keys, Bobby, 74
Kiedis, Anthony, 88
Kimmelman, Michael, 213
Kind of Blue, 190
King, Martin Luther, Jr., 9
King, Tony, 125
"King Kong," 210–11
"King of Fuh," 43
Kircherr, Astrid, 3–4
Kirshner, Don, 34
Klein, Allen, 12, 45, 50, 58, 84, 135–36; Beatles
   breakup and, 40–41, 205
Klein, Joe, 141
Klein, Yves, 21
Kooper, Al, 124–25, 138, 145
Krause, Bernie, 15
Krishna (lord), Harrison on, 13–14, 17, 85–86
Kunstler, William, 82
Kuri, Yoji, 190

LaBelle, Patti, 48
"Lady Madonna," 150
"Lay Lady Lay," 11
Layton, Doug, 143
Lead Belly, 93
Leary, Timothy, 73, 134–35
Lebel, Jean-Jacques, 161
Leckie, John, 69
Led Zeppelin, 127–28
Leiber, Jerry, 47
Lennon, Alf, 63–64, 83, 105–6, 135
Lennon, Cynthia, 1, 5–6, 20, 23, 26, 41, 56, 161
Lennon, Jack, 93
Lennon, John: on *All Things Must Pass*, 15, 47, 57;
   arrest for cannabis possession, 30–31, 50, 73–74;
   assassination of, 132–34, 172, 202, 218–19; Aunt
   Mimi and, 2, 6, 97, 123; on *Beaucoups of Blues*,
   12; birth, 63; on "Cambridge 1969," 27, 29;
   chart-topping hits by, 21–22; childhood traumas
   of, 51, 53–54, 57, 64, 74, 83, 135, 150, 172,
   215; death of mother, 2, 149; Dylan and, 42,
   64–65, 82, 91–93, 127, 131–32, 137–39, 202;
   Epstein and, 6–7, 91, 95–96, 135–36, 142–43,
   203; folk music and, 93–94; on God, 123–24; on
   Grapefruit, 159; as guitarist on "Why," 167–68,
   172–75; in *A Hard Day's Night*, 34; Harrison and,
   14–16, 24, 42–43, 46, 69, 78, 84, 86–87, 96–97,
   109, 132, 135, 140, 152, 205; *In His Own Write*
   by, 2–3, 91; Janov, A., primal scream therapy

and, 53–59, 61, 105, 135–36, 150, 165, 202,
   212, 215; on jazz, 191; on Jesus Christ, 123–24,
   133–34, 136, 142–43, 159; jukebox of, 47–49;
   on Kircherr and Sutcliffe, 3–4; Lennon, C., and,
   1, 5–6; Liebovitz *Rolling Stone* cover photo of,
   201; "Lost Weekend" of, 169; on MBE, 66; on
   McCartney, 204; McCartney and, 8, 11, 40–42,
   54–56, 68, 70–71, 74, 86–87, 92, 119, 136, 202–
   6, 214–15; middle-class upbringing of, 97–98;
   on "My Sweet Lord" success, 14; on Presley, 123;
   "pure sound" elements in songs of, 29–30; rock
   'n' roll and, 3, 45, 47–48; *Rolling Stone* interviews,
   65, 69, 77, 82–83, 97, 124, 126, 131, 137–38,
   201–2, 205–6, 217; *Skywriting by Word of Mouth*
   by, 75; Spector and, 48–51; on the Turtles, 208;
   visual art of, 2, 24; *White Album* songs by, 19; on
   women, in early songs, 2; on Zappa, 207–8. *See
   also specific albums and songs*
Lennon, John, and Ono, Y.,: at Apple Records, 162;
   avant-garde music of, 28–29, 31, 61; "Bag Piece"
   performance, 154–55; Bag Productions of, 102;
   the Beatles and, 4–5, 8–9, 20; Bed-Ins for Peace,
   42, 53, 77; *Benefit Concert for Bangladesh* and,
   84; breakup, 1973, 57, 169; "Cambridge 1969"
   live recording, 26–30, 33, 172–73; Cox and, 42;
   family histories and patterns of, 171–72; final
   concert, 116; Franklin and, 191–92; Grimm
   on, 168–69; Hare Krishna movement and, 86;
   Harrison on, 42; Janov, A., and, 54–59, 212;
   Lennon, C., and, 161; Liebovitz photos of, 98,
   201, 206; on love, 113; Malik and, 82; marriage
   and wedding, 23; Martin on music of, 30;
   McCartney on, 5, 8; media on, 74; meeting, 1–2,
   4, 160; minimalism of, 162; *musique concrète*
   and, 31–32; in New York City, 76–78, 213; *New
   York Times* advertisements, 129, 216–17; peace
   campaigns, 23–24, 42–44, 53, 77, 81, 124,
   217–19; postcards, 7; relationship as "destructive,"
   57; sexuality of, 116; Sharrocks and, 173; Spector
   on, 49–52; Starr and, 5, 74; at Tittenhurst Park,
   24, 54–55, 58, 74, 214; "Unfinished Music"
   series, 28–29, 32, 165; *Yoko Plus Me: Half-a-
   Wind* exhibition and, 8; Zappa and, 67, 188–89,
   207–12. *See also* Plastic Ono Band; *specific albums
   and songs*
Lennon, Julia, 65, 93–94, 123; death of, 2, 149;
   Lennon, A., and, 63–64, 83, 105
Lennon, Julian, 1, 6, 56, 83
Lennon, Sean, 49, 83, 165–66, 174, 183–84
Lennon Remembers (Wenner), 206
"Leopard Skin Pillbox Hat," 38
Lester, Richard, 103, 201
Let It Be (album), 13, 45–46, 58, 84, 125–26
Let It Be (film), 8, 10, 58, 126
"Let It Be" (song), 127
Let It Be . . . Naked, 46
"Let It Bleed," 116
Levy, Morris, 48, 188
Lewis, Jerry, 217
Lewis, Jerry Lee, 37–38
Liebovitz, Annie, 98, 201, 206
Lightnin' Hopkins, 38